Common Law Liberalism

Common Law Liberalism

A New Theory of the Libertarian Society

JOHN HASNAS

OXFORD
UNIVERSITY PRESS

OXFORD
UNIVERSITY PRESS

Oxford University Press is a department of the University of Oxford. It furthers the University's objective of excellence in research, scholarship, and education by publishing worldwide. Oxford is a registered trade mark of Oxford University Press in the UK and in certain other countries.

Published in the United States of America by Oxford University Press
198 Madison Avenue, New York, NY 10016, United States of America.

Library of Congress Cataloging-in-Publication Data
Names: Hasnas, John, author.
Title: Common law liberalism : a new theory of the libertarian society / John Hasnas.
Description: New York : Oxford University Press, [2024] |
Includes bibliographical references and index.
Identifiers: LCCN 2024013873 | ISBN 9780197784600 (hardback) |
ISBN 9780197784624 (epub)
Subjects: LCSH: Common law. | Liberalism.
Classification: LCC K588 .H37 2024 | DDC 340.5/7—dc23/eng/20240505
LC record available at https://lccn.loc.gov/2024013873

DOI: 10.1093/9780197784631.001.0001

Printed by Integrated Books International, United States of America

MIX
Paper
FSC
FSC® C183721

To Irving and Doris, who made me, and Ann, Annette, and Ava, who sustain me

Contents

Preface

Because this book represents a compilation of work that was done over more than a quarter-century, it is impossible to thank all those who aided in its creation. As a result, I will not even try. I must, however, thank Professor Ralph Slaght of Lafayette College and Professor Martin Golding of Duke University for inspiring me to pursue a career in philosophy. Special thanks are owed to Steven Wall, Mihailis Diamantis, Peter Leeson, Ilya Somin, Ryan Davis, Peter Jaworski, and Joshua Stein and two anonymous reviewers for their helpful comments on earlier drafts of this book, and Creigh Greensmith for his invaluable research help and his aid in assembling the manuscript. Finally, I owe thanks to the John M. Olin Foundation, the Cato Institute, and the Institute for Humane Studies, each of which provided funding at various times that aided in the production of several chapters.

Chapter 1 is abstracted from "The Problem of Punishment," originally published in *Rethinking Punishment in the Era of Mass Incarceration*, edited by Chris Surprenant (London: Routledge, 2017), pp. 15–33. Chapter 2 was originally published in the *Georgetown Journal of Law and Public Policy* 19 (2021): 813–840. Chapter 3 was originally published in *Social Philosophy and Policy* 26 (2009): 95–120. Chapter 4 was originally published in *Social Philosophy and Policy* 22 (2005): 111–147. Chapter 5 was originally published in the *Georgetown Journal of Law and Public Policy* 21 (2023): 541–558. Portions of Chapter 6 originally appeared in *New York University Journal of Law & Liberty* 1 (2005): 79–110 and *Theoretical Inquiries in Law* 9 (2008): 529–552. Chapter 7 was originally published in *Social Philosophy and Policy* 30 (2013): 450–479.

Finally, Chapter 8 is reprinted by permission of the Publishers from "The Obviousness of Anarchy" in *Anarchism/Minarchism*, edited by Roderick T. Long and Tibor (Machan: Ashgate, 2008), pp. 111–131. In each case, changes have been made for this publication.

John Hasnas

October 2023

Introduction

I.

Since early in my career, I have been a skeptic of the conventional approach to political philosophy, which focuses exclusively on the actions of government. Invariably, this approach traces back to the thinking of Hobbes and Locke, who view government as the necessary cure for the ills of the state of nature. This approach views the world as one in which human conduct is regulated by the conscious actions of those invested with government power or is not regulated at all. Since my first year of law school in which I encountered the impressive edifice of the common law—law that evolved without conscious human direction—I have regarded this model of the world and its corresponding conception of political philosophy as deeply flawed.

Accordingly, over the course of many years, I explored the extent to which a wide array of government functions can be supplied—and better supplied—by the common law than by centralized politically directed action. This exploration eventually suggested that all of them could be, and led me to the conclusion that people would be better off without government.

II.

This book is written with two ends in mind, which, although logically consistent, are in tension with each other. The first is to establish the fairly moderate proposition that good public policy requires a comparative assessment of the effectiveness of common

Common Law Liberalism. John Hasnas, Oxford University Press. © Oxford University Press 2024.
DOI: 10.1093/9780197784631.003.0001

law and legislation as regulatory mechanisms. The second is to establish the more radical proposal that a peaceful and prosperous society can exist without legislation, and ultimately without any essential services being supplied on a monopolistic basis by a government. The second can be expressed more concisely by saying that a good society does not require the existence of a state.

My aspiration is to persuade my readers of both propositions, but I will be happy if I persuade them only of the first. In fact, I will be happy if all I accomplish is to cause people to question the underlying assumptions of the social contract approach to the justification of government.

The tension between the arguments exists because in making the argument for the first proposition, I assume that a government exists and supplies the necessary law enforcement and adjudication services. In essence, I am temporarily relying on propositions I later intend to challenge. One may think of this first argument as an exploration of the extent to which the legislative function of government may be reduced while maintaining the executive and judicial functions.

The argument for the second proposition dispenses with this assumption. It seeks to show that the same nonpolitical forces that produce law can also produce effective mechanisms for adjudication and law enforcement. In this argument, I seek to move from the claim that human beings do not need a state to make law to the claim that human beings do not need a state at all.

III.

The book is divided into three parts. Parts I and II pursue the more modest objective of establishing that good public policy requires a comparative assessment of the efficacy of common law and legislation—the law consciously created by the state. Part III pursues the more radical proposition that a peaceful and prosperous society can be grounded exclusively on the common law—without legislation—and, in fact, without any essential services being supplied by a state monopoly. Hence, Part III presents an argument for anarchy.

Part I is called Questioning Assumptions. In this part of the book, I show that much of contemporary public policy analysis is based on the assumption that political regulation—regulation of human conduct by the state—is the only alternative to a completely unregulated environment. I then question this assumption. I argue that the common law provides an alternative mechanism for regulating human conduct that does not require conscious action by those invested with political power. Specifically, I question the assumptions that the state must supply the rules of law necessary for people to live cooperatively in society without violence—that it must supply the criminal law (Chapter 1), and that the state is necessary to provide economic regulation of the market (Chapter 2) and to protect the environment (Chapter 3). In each case, I argue that whether the state is necessary cannot be determined *a priori*, but requires a comparative assessment of the relative effectiveness of common law and state-created legislation.

Part II is called Applications. In this part of the book, I show how an understanding of the nature and functioning of the common law can shed light on long-standing philosophical and jurisprudential issues—how the common law can be applied to provide new answers to old questions. Specifically, I show how the common law can provide the missing theoretical grounding for a coherent theory of natural rights (Chapter 4) and can resolve the conundrum of how to protect freedom of speech in a liberal society (Chapter 5).

Part III is called Anarchy. In this part of the book, I argue that not only is the state not necessary for the production of the rules needed to sustain a prosperous liberal society, but that the state is not necessary at all. In this part of the book, I amplify the historical account of the evolution of common law provided in Part II to show how the common law can provide all the rules needed for a successful liberal society (Chapter 6). I then show that there can be a moral duty to obey the law in a common law legal system, and hence that there can be a meaningful concept of the rule of law (Chapter 7). And finally, I show how all of the functions currently provided by the state can be provided, and in fact better provided, in the absence of a state monopoly (Chapter 8).

IV.

I intend for each chapter to be able to stand on its own and contain a complete argument for its particular conclusion while simultaneously working together with the other chapters to establish the book's larger theses. In this way, I hope to allow those who are not persuaded to follow me all the way to my ultimate conclusion to nevertheless be able to make part of the journey with me.

V.

This book employs legal terms of art that may not be familiar to those without a legal education. In addition, the meaning of some of these terms varies with context, and thus may cause confusion. To address these concerns, I include a guide to legal terminology in the Appendix.

PART I

QUESTIONING ASSUMPTIONS

It is commonly assumed that the state must provide the law necessary to maintain a peaceful and orderly society, to regulate the market, and to protect the environment. In this part of the book, I argue that these assumptions derive from a false dilemma—from the belief that the only options are legal regulation by the state and no regulation. This overlooks a third option: the regulation of human behavior by binding rules that emerge from human interaction—most importantly, by common law civil liability.

I argue that the recognition of this third possibility implies that a proper analysis requires a comparative assessment of the effectiveness of state-created law and emergent law.

Chapter 1 offers such an assessment of the criminal law and tort law as mechanisms for reducing violence sufficiently to allow human cooperation and prosperity. Chapter 2 offers a comparative assessment of legislation and common law as mechanisms for ensuring that market exchanges do not impose costly, unconsented-to harm on third parties. And Chapter 3 offers a similar assessment of legislation and common law as mechanisms for preventing environmental degradation.

1

Whither Criminal Law?

Most people assume without question that a system of criminal law is necessary to preserve order in society. This is because most people also assume that there is no other option. When they think about a world without criminal law, they imagine a world with no mechanism for discouraging violent, harmful, and dishonest actions. And because such a world calls to mind the chaos of Hobbes's war of all against all, such a world is instantly dismissed.

But this is not the proper comparison. The choice is not between a system of criminal law and nothing. It is between a system of criminal law and alternative mechanisms for creating and maintaining an orderly society. A proper comparison suggests not only that criminal law is not necessary to preserve a peaceful, orderly society, but also that it is a significant impediment to maintaining such a society.

This may seem surprising, but it should not be because criminal law is not and was never designed to maintain order in society. Criminal law is designed to punish people who violate the state's rules, *which is not the same thing.*

I. An Initial Distinction

Our legal system is composed of public and private law. Public law is the law that regulates the relationship between the state and individuals. Private law is the law that regulates relationships among the individual members of society.

Common Law Liberalism. John Hasnas, Oxford University Press. © Oxford University Press 2024.
DOI: 10.1093/9780197784631.003.0002

Criminal law is public law. It is the law that determines when the state is permitted to punish—to coercively impose harm on—those subject to its jurisdiction. Criminal law is not designed to compose interpersonal disputes or provide compensation to wrongfully injured parties. It is designed to *punish* those who break the law. Criminal liability is liability to be punished by the state.

Tort law is private law. It is the law that determines when one who has caused harm to another is required to compensate that person for the injury he or she has suffered. When one member of society wrongfully harms another, he or she owes the injured party restitution. Tort law is designed to vindicate this interest. When one negligently harms another, tort law requires the wrongdoer to restore the harmed party to the position he or she would have been in had the negligent conduct not occurred. Indeed, when one acts in a way that creates an inordinate risk of harm—when one engages in abnormally dangerous activity—and another suffers harm as a result, tort law requires the risk taker to restore the harmed party even though the risk taker has exercised all due care.[1] And when one intentionally or recklessly harms another, tort law can require the wrongdoer not only to restore the harmed party, but also to pay additional exemplary or "punitive" damages to the harmed party. Tort law gives rise to civil liability.

Criminal liability is wholly distinct from civil liability. Criminal law authorizes the state to impose a harm on individuals who violate the law that is independent of any finding of civil liability. Criminal punishment is an additional penalty imposed by the state beyond any compensatory and exemplary damage payments that one may be required to make to an injured party.

This means that the question of whether criminal law is necessary to preserve a peaceful, orderly society is equivalent to the question of whether an additional penalty imposed by the state

[1] This is the doctrine of strict liability in tort. See Restatement (Third) of Torts: Phys. and Emot. Harm § 20 (2010).

beyond any compensatory and exemplary damage payments required by civil liability is necessary to preserve a peaceful, orderly society. There are good historical, psychological, and philosophical reasons to believe that the answer to this question is no.

II. History

Philosophers love to speculate about how human beings move from a state of nature to an ordered society. English history provides empirical evidence of how this occurs in the real world.

Early in the fifth century, the Romans, who had ruled Britain for three and half centuries, suddenly left the island, taking their civil government with them. As the literate Romans left, so did their law, and as the legions departed, so did its enforcement. This left the inhabitants living in kinship and tribal groupings exposed to outside aggression and with no authoritatively established mechanisms for dealing with internal disputes—a good approximation of the state of nature. What happened?

Telescoping a thousand years of legal history into a few words: tort law evolved. In the absence of any centralized authority, some mechanism was needed for resolving conflicts and discouraging violence. The earliest such mechanism consisted of efforts to compose disputes through negotiations. Rather than fight, parties would bargain with each other to redress injuries, with the members of the relevant kinship groups or communities serving as mediators to aid the process.[2] Through repetition over time, such compositions gave rise to "extraordinarily detailed schedules of tariffs . . . for various injuries,"[3] with the result that "[t]he institution of fixed monetary sanctions payable by the kin of wrongdoer to the

[2] *See* Julius Goebel, Jr., Felony and Misdemeanor: A Study in the History of English Criminal Procedure 25–44 (1937).

[3] Harold Berman, Law and Revolution 54 (1983).

kin of the victim was a prominent feature of the law of all the peoples of Europe prior to the twelfth century."[4] This nascent system of tort law was,

> in many respects, a very sensible system. The threat of heavy financial burdens upon the wrongdoer and his kin is probably a more effective deterrent of crime than the threat of capital punishment or corporal mutilation, . . . and at least equally as effective as the modern sanction of imprisonment; and it is surely less expensive for society. Moreover, in terms of retributive justice, not only is the wrongdoer made to suffer, but in addition—in contrast to today's more "civilized" penology—the victim is thereby made whole.[5]

What we might today recognize as criminal law did not come into being until the twelfth century.[6] Moreover, the newly recognized offenses against the community that could be punished by the lord or king did not replace the underlying tort system, but existed side by side with it.[7] This early criminal law was introduced, not because it was necessary to maintain an orderly society, but to gratify a taste for vengeance.

> The distinction between crime and tort was not a difference between two kinds of wrongful acts. In most instances, the same wrong could be prosecuted either as a crime or as a tort. Nor was the distinction a difference between the kinds of persons who

[4] *Id.* at 55.
[5] *Id.*
[6] *See* Trisha Olson, *The Medieval Blood Sanction and the Divine Beneficence of Pain: 1100–1450*, 22 J. L. & Religion 63, 68 ("Whereas in the central Middle Ages crimes such as homicide, arson, and theft were private wrongs that entitled the victim or his kin to demand compensation or to engage in a blood feud, beginning in the twelfth century, serious wrongdoing came to be seen as against the entire community and subject to punishment by the lord or king who acted on the community's behalf").
[7] *Id.* at 69.

could initiate the actions. Victims could initiate actions of both kinds. According to the lawyers, victims who preferred vengeance over compensation prosecuted their wrongdoers for crime. Victims who preferred compensation over vengeance sued their wrongdoers for tort. Royal officers prosecuted wrongdoers for crime on the king's behalf when victims feared or chose not to do so.[8]

Further, as counterintuitive as it may seem to contemporary sensibilities, a major purpose of early criminal law was not to punish, but to drive the parties to compose the dispute.[9] The threat of punishment was accompanied by various procedural impediments to trial—e.g., benefit of clergy, flight to sanctuary—and opportunities to settle the dispute—e.g., agreements to make amends at a "loveday"—that were designed to encourage settlement rather than the pursuit of a conviction.[10] Indeed, evidence suggests that in the thirteenth century between 40 and 67 percent of "appeals"—cases brought by criminal charge—were settled.[11] Moreover, among those cases that were not settled, "the rate of jury acquittal remained enormously high throughout the period"[12] because

> the medieval jury's high acquittal rate reflected "deeply engrained notions of how social harmony was to be maintained through composition with, rather than ultimate rejection of, the offender." Strikingly, complaints about the acquittal rate were infrequent. Between the fourteenth and sixteenth century in England, not a

[8] David J. Seipp, *The Distinction between Crime and Tort in the Early Common Law*, 76 Bos. U. L. Rev. 59, 59–60 (1996).

[9] *See* Olson, *supra* note 6, at 73 ("dispute resolution—criminal or otherwise—is and ought to be focused upon concord and reconciliation").

[10] *See id.* at 74–75.

[11] Daniel Klerman, *Settlement and the Decline of Private Prosecution in Thirteenth-Century England*, 19 L. & Hist. Rev. 1, 16 (2002).

[12] Olson, *supra* note 6, at 74.

> single jurist nor chronicle writer complained that the jury conviction rate was too low.[13]

In point of fact, criminal law arose not to provide order, but predominantly to serve the financial interests of the Crown. The original difference between tort and crime was who got paid. The action was a tort if the payment went to the party that suffered harm at the hands of the defendant. It was a crime if the payment went to the king. This created a financial incentive for the Crown to continually expand the scope of actions that were considered crimes, which is precisely what the Norman kings of England did.

> The profits from justice also stemmed from the royal prerogative and constantly increased as the royal justice expanded its jurisdiction. In fact, the expansion of the king's justice in the period of its early development can be explained satisfactorily only by the royal need for money. Any case tried in the royal court netted the king a sizable fee, and all the profits from those actions that fell under the category of the king's pleas went into the royal hand.[14]

This financial incentive also accounts for the introduction of the concept of felony into English law, which resulted in the massive expansion of the scope of the criminal law. Felony originally referred to the feudal crime of betraying or committing treachery against one's lord. Such an offense, which was not necessary for and played no role in the maintenance of civic order, was an extraordinarily useful mechanism for raising royal revenue.

[13] *Id.* at 75–76.

[14] Bruce Lyon, A Constitutional and Legal History of medieval England 163 (1980). Lyon further points out that "[i]n the growth of this list [of crimes] we may be certain that although the king's concern for law and order was a cause, his chief interest was need of money; to increase his income the king only needed to use his prerogative and throw his jurisdiction over another offense." *Id.* at 189.

> Again royal greed seems to be the best explanation for the expansion of the concept of felony. Any crime called a felony meant that if the appellee was found guilty his possessions escheated to the king. The more crimes called felonies, the greater the income, and so the list of felonies continued to grow throughout the twelfth century. The fortuitous yet conscious combination of the royal prerogative with the concepts of the king's peace and felony gave royal justice a flexibility that enabled the royal court to spread its jurisdiction over all sorts of places and men and over almost any type of offense.[15]

Far from being necessary for the maintenance of social order, the introduction of criminal law tended to undermine it "by effectively destroying the system of community composition."[16] Motivated by the desire for revenue, the Crown took steps to ensure that offenders paid fines to the king in preference to restitution to their victims. Thus, it prohibited victims from making settlements that included an agreement not to prosecute, suspended the civil remedies of victims until after the criminal charge was resolved, and prevented victims from receiving stolen goods back until they gave evidence in a criminal proceeding.[17] As the Crown absorbed more and more of the resources that would otherwise have been available to pay restitution, the incentive to pursue settlement and voluntary composition declined, and was eventually entirely displaced. Without the ability to obtain compensation for their injuries, victims were left with nothing but the desire for vengeance—that is, for the punishment of those who had wronged them.[18] Whereas the underlying system of tort law

[15] *Id.* at 190.

[16] Richard E. Laster, *Criminal Restitution: A Survey of its Past History and an Analysis of its Present Usefulness*, 5 U. Rich. L. Rev. 71, 75 (1970).

[17] *Id.* at 76.

[18] As Richard Laster explains,

> When the king or overlord began to take their share of the victim's compensation, . . . the focus of the proceedings shifted from the victim to the

> had two important consequences that promoted social harmony and maintained social order: 1) it tended to restore the victim and eliminate his desire for violent revenge, and 2) it benefited [sic] the offender in that he bought back the "peace" and his place in society, . . . the creation of the criminal law appears to have generated greater social *disorder* precisely because victims were no longer "restored" to their original level of satisfaction and therefore became more likely to demand severe physical punishment.[19]

Thus, history suggests that the commonly held belief that criminal punishment is necessary for the preservation of social order has cause and effect reversed. Order was well-maintained by the underlying system of restitution/tort law until the advent of the criminal law with its punitive payments to the Crown rendered that system ineffective. The public's desire for criminal punishment arose not as a response to disorder, but to the disruptive consequences of the criminal law itself.

III. Psychology

If the criminal law disappeared, the underlying system of tort law would remain. Therefore, to show that criminal law is necessary for the preservation of a peaceful, orderly society, one would have to show both that a system of civil liability alone would not reduce interpersonal violence to an acceptable level and that the addition of criminal law and punishment would. Doing this requires a comparison of the relative effectiveness of civil and criminal liability as deterrents, which raises a question of human psychology.

criminal. The next step was for the king to take the entire compensative payment and thus effectively destroy the process of community composition and raise punishment to the level of satisfaction. *Id.* at 75–76.

[19] BRUCE L. BENSON, THE ENTERPRISE OF LAW: JUSTICE WITHOUT THE STATE 71 (1990).

Civil liability requires one who has wrongfully harmed another to pay financial restitution sufficient to restore the wronged party to the condition he or she would have been in had the wrongful action not occurred. In addition, when the wrongdoing is intentional or reckless, civil liability can include exemplary damages that greatly increase the amount that wrongdoers must pay their victims. Criminal punishment can consist in financial fines, physical pain, incarceration, or death. The question then is whether the ability to threaten people with financial penalties, pain, imprisonment, or death *in addition to* the requirement to pay restitution plus exemplary damages is necessary to reduce interpersonal violence to a level that permits a relatively secure life in society.

Although people generally assume that the additional punishment is necessary, there are good empirical reasons to doubt that this is the case.

First, recent psychological research has shown that the brain reacts to the prospect of financial loss in the same way that it reacts to the prospect of physical pain,[20] and further, that the fear of financial loss can be as effective a mechanism of "aversive learning" as fear of physical pain.[21] This at least suggests that the threat of financial loss may be a more effective deterrent than is generally thought.

Indeed, some evidence in support of this suggestion may be found in English legal history. For example, between the thirteenth and eighteenth centuries, those accused of serious crimes had to consent to the jury that would try them in order for the trial to proceed. If they did not, they would be imprisoned and subject to *peine forte et dure*, which consisted of being chained to the floor, fed

[20] Ben Seymour, Nathaniel Daw, et al., *Differential Encoding of Losses and Gains in the Human Striatum*, 27 J. NEUROSCIENCE 4826 (2007). *See also* Wellcome Trust, *Why Losing Money May Be More Painful than You Think*, at https://www.eurekalert.org/news-releases/580607.

[21] M. R. Delgado, C. D. Labouliere, & E. A. Phelps, *Fear of Losing Money? Aversive Conditioning with Secondary Reinforcers*, 1 SOCIAL COGNITIVE AND AFFECTIVE NEUROSCIENCE 250 (2006). *See also* Roxanne Khamsi, *Proof That Losing Money Really Is Scary*, NEW SCIENTIST DAILY NEWS, Oct. 18, 2006.

only bread and water on alternate days, and having ever larger and heavier stones placed on their chests until they either agreed to a jury or died. Because if one died without being convicted of a crime his or her property did not escheat to the Crown, many defendants chose to be pressed to death rather than risk a trial that could result in the impoverishment of their dependents.[22]

Second, contemporary psychological evidence casts doubt on the effectiveness of incarceration as a deterrent. Thus, although "[i]t has long been assumed that prison deters criminal offenders, ... recent research in the forensic sciences has shown that, contrary to popular belief, prison may in fact increase the likelihood that offenders will engage in further crime after they are released."[23] If in fact "incarceration is not just ineffective but even criminogenic,"[24] then there is at least reason to doubt that it is necessary to preserve an orderly society.

Once again, English legal history offers support for this possibility because imprisonment did not develop as a form of punishment under common law. Imprisonment was used to detain those awaiting trial but was regarded as inappropriate as punishment because "[i]t would force the offender to be idle, making it difficult for him to pay his restitution, and it would be costly to the community."[25] In a time where most of life consisted in hard work, remaining idle in prison was not considered highly punitive. Hence, at common law "fines and whipping became the usual forms [of

[22] *See* J. H. Baker, An Introduction to English Legal History 508–509 (4th ed. 2002).

[23] Eyal Aharoni, *Punishment Without Reason: Isolating Retribution in Lay Punishment of Criminal Offenders*, 18 Psychol. Pub. Pol'y & L. 599, 599 (2012) (citing M. K. Chen & J. M. Shapiro, *Do Harsher Prison Conditions Reduce Recidivism? A Discontinuity-based Approach*, 9 Am. L. & Econ. Rev. 1 (2007); J. Cid, *Is Imprisonment Criminogenic? A Comparative Study of Recidivism Rates Between Prison and Suspended Prison Sanctions*, 6 Eur. J. Criminology 459 (2009); & J. Grogger, *Certainty vs. Severity of Punishment*, 29 Econ. Inquiry 297 (1991)).

[24] *Id.*

[25] Benson, *supra* note 19, at 71.

punishment], imprisonment being relatively uncommon for this purpose before the time of George III."[26]

The assumption that criminal punishment is necessary to maintain an orderly society almost certainly derives from the worry that those without financial resources would not be deterred by the threat of civil liability—that in the absence of the threat of criminal punishment, "judgment-proof" individuals would have no reason to refrain from criminal activity. However, this worry is based on the improper assumption that a system of civil liability that functions in a world without criminal law would be identical to our current system of civil liability, which functions alongside a system of criminal law and punishment.

In our current dual system of criminal and civil liability, the threat of criminal punishment supplies the necessary element of deterrence. Hence, the system of civil liability need not and does not contain such an element. However, a system of civil liability that functioned without the deterrence provided by the threat of criminal punishment would be a very different system from the one that presently exists. Such a system would be more like the ancient system of tort law that the rise of criminal law displaced than the present one. The problem is that it is difficult for people to imagine what such a system would look like in contemporary circumstances. So here is where a bit of philosophical speculation can be of service.

IV. Philosophy

Philosophers love to engage in thought experiments. Apparently, I am no exception. So please indulge me by considering the following hypothetical legal system.

[26] Baker, *supra* note 22, at 513.

Imagine a society with no criminal law and no criminal punishment. In order to not strain credulity too greatly, imagine that the police function precisely as they do at present.[27] When citizens are threatened with harm, they may call on the police for protection, and if they have been the victim of a wrongful invasion of any of their legally protected interests, they may call on the police to apprehend those who have wronged them. However, in this society, citizens' legally protected interests are defined by the rules of tort law as it evolved through the common law process. Again, in order not to strain credulity, let us assume that the substantive rules of tort law in the hypothetical society are identical to those of our current society.

As in our current society, citizens would have to take out insurance policies to protect themselves against the possibility that they may be the victims of theft or personal injury by wrongdoers who are never apprehended. However, in cases in which the police do apprehend the wrongdoers, victims may bring private lawsuits against them to recover for the harm that they caused.[28]

The hypothetical system is similar to our current system of civil liability in that plaintiffs/victims are entitled to recover sufficient compensation to restore them to the position that they would have been in had the tortious conduct not occurred, plus, in the case

[27] This chapter is concerned exclusively with the question of whether criminal *law* is necessary to preserve a peaceful, orderly society. It is not concerned with whether the state is justified in supplying police services, which is an entirely different question. Therefore, for present purposes, one may assume that the state continues to supply the police who attempt to apprehend criminals. The absence of the criminal law does not entail the absence of government-supplied police. The question of whether the state is needed to supply police services will be addressed in Chapter 8.

[28] In this respect, our hypothetical legal system functions much like the actual English legal system, in which, until the late nineteenth century, criminal prosecutions were brought by private attorneys hired by the victims. "It has long been a common practice in England for crime victims to initiate criminal prosecutions. . . . England's common law considered a crime to be a wrongful act against a particular identified victim, as opposed to a wrongful act against the state. The common belief at the time, therefore, was that those in the best position to prosecute criminal cases were the victims themselves." Michael T. McCormack, *The Need for Private Prosecutors: An Analysis of Massachusetts and New Hampshire Law*, 37 Suffolk U. L. Rev. 497, 499–500 (2004).

of intentional wrongdoing, exemplary damages. However, in the hypothetical system, the amount of damages necessary to restore plaintiffs is understood to include both the costs that they bore in apprehending the defendant and the costs of bringing the lawsuit.

The hypothetical system is similar to our current system of civil liability in several other respects as well. Plaintiff's attorneys could be paid on a contingency fee basis in which their compensation is contingent on the success of the lawsuit and is deducted from the judgment. This would ensure that injured parties with limited resources would nevertheless have access to the court system. Juries would be free to set the amount of exemplary damages at whatever level they deem appropriate and would be permitted to consider the defendant's net worth in doing so. This would ensure that the system could discourage actions that the ordinary members of society find especially reprehensible as well as all intentional wrongdoing by wealthy defendants. Estates of those killed by others would be authorized to bring lawsuits for wrongful death,[29] and class action lawsuits could be brought to discourage frauds and other wrongful actions that impose small injuries on large numbers of people. And finally, defendants who have the resources to pay their judgments must do so—either in a lump sum or in installments paid over time that include appropriate interest payments—and this debt cannot be discharged in bankruptcy. Successful plaintiffs are entitled to take out liens on defendants' personal and real property and to garnish defendants' wages to satisfy the judgment.

The main difference between the hypothetical system and our current liability system concerns the way the hypothetical system treats defendants who do not have sufficient resources to pay their judgments—the so-called judgment-proof defendants. In the

[29] Just as automobile insurance policies include provisions to bring suit on behalf of the policy holder against negligent drivers, in the absence of public prosecution, life insurance policies would include provisions to bring wrongful death suits on behalf of the deceased. This would ensure that even those who kill isolated individuals without estates would be subject to liability.

hypothetical system, successful plaintiffs are entitled to restrain the liberty of defendants in a limited number of legally authorized ways until the judgment has been paid.

For example, plaintiffs may elect to sell their judgments to monitoring companies that take on the task of obtaining payment from the defendant. Thus, one who recovers a judgment of $100,000 against an indigent defendant might sell the right to collect the judgment to Acme Monitoring, Inc. for $65,000 in cash.[30] Acme Monitoring would then have charge of the defendant and could ensure that he works sufficiently to earn $25,000 per year for four years, which it would collect.

Monitoring companies would have the incentive to employ defendants in the most economically efficient way. Thus, those who are neither dangerous nor a flight risk can be lightly monitored and permitted to remain in society while working to pay off their judgment. Those who are a flight risk but present no danger to others and have marketable skills might be monitored by an electronic ankle bracelet and employed by companies that value their skills. In contrast, violent defendants who pose a danger to others might have to be confined in the equivalent of private prisons and employed at whatever low-skilled labor they are capable of.[31] Monitoring companies would release the defendants when they collected the full amount of the judgment. Further, such companies could be subject to whatever form of governmental regulation or inspection is required to guard against abuse of those in their charge.

On this point, it is essential to distinguish the type of monitoring facility being suggested from what are misleadingly called private

[30] There is nothing novel about this proposal. Many financial companies already purchase judgments from successful plaintiffs for lump sum payments. The most well-known of these may be J. G. Wentworth because of its television commercials; others such as Novation Settlement Solutions and Peachtree Financial Solutions do the same thing.

[31] The discount paid to the plaintiff would reflect the monitoring company's prospects of collecting the full amount of the judgment.

prisons today. Currently, the federal government and several states employ private contractors to house their inmates in private facilities. These are not true private prisons that are subject to the discipline of market competition, but are "privatized" prisons—prisons that the state grants private contractors the exclusive right to operate at taxpayer expense subject to government regulation and oversight. Use of such privatized prisons, many of which have been criticized for abusive practices, is definitely *not* what is being advocated.

In the present context, the relevant comparison is between state-imposed restrictions of liberty under the criminal justice system—the current system of state punishment, which includes both state-operated and privatized prisons—and privately imposed restrictions of liberty under the hypothetical civil liability system—the hypothetical monitoring companies. As a rule, there is no reason to believe that state provision of a service provides a superior product or results in less abuse than private provision of that service subject to government regulation and inspection, as the comparison of public and private schools illustrates.

Indeed, in the context of incarceration, there is good reason to believe that precisely the opposite is the case. The state-operated or privatized prisons are paid a fixed amount by taxpayers regardless of how they treat the inmates. The way to maximize profits under this incentive structure is to spend as little money and cut as many corners as possible. Further, state-operated systems have a high degree of immunity from tort suits brought by inmates alleging abuse by state employees.

In contrast, privately operated monitoring companies receive no taxpayer funding and can profit only by producing value in excess of their operating costs. This creates the incentive for them to increase the useful skills and productive capacities of their inmates. In addition, as private entities, they have no special immunity from lawsuits brought by those in their charge and are subject to whatever anti-abuse regulations the government sees fit to impose on the industry.

Of course, under the hypothetical system, plaintiffs could elect to monitor the defendants themselves if they thought it worthwhile, but they have no right to inflict gratuitous harm on them and are permitted to restrain their liberty only to the extent necessary to collect their judgment. However, plaintiffs would be free to bargain with defendants for alternative arrangements. For example, a vindictive plaintiff could offer to forgive all or a portion of the judgment if the defendant agreed to submit to some form of corporeal punishment or humiliation, while a compassionate or merciful plaintiff could forgive all or a portion of the judgment if the defendant agreed to reform or do good works.

In the hypothetical system, there is no state prosecution, no state-created criminal law, and no state-imposed punishment. To the extent that the state provides the courts, its role is that of a neutral referee in disputes between private parties. There are no punitive sentences, only restorative judgments; no state parole boards, only victims/plaintiffs with the discretion to release defendants from their debt obligations or not as they see fit. The system does not create an incentive to vindictively wreak harm on the defendants, but rather to employ them as productively as possible so that they can pay the judgments—i.e., to rehabilitate them. In short, the hypothetical system is not a punitive system. Its purpose is restitution, not punishment.

Would such a system deter harmful activity sufficiently to sustain a relatively peaceful society?

It certainly would not provide the economically optimal amount of deterrence. There will be many instances in which people who engage in predatory conduct get away with wrongdoing under the hypothetical system. But that is irrelevant because the same is true under a state-run system of criminal punishment. The relevant question is how the hypothetical system compares with a system of criminal punishment. Using the level of deterrence provided by our contemporary system of criminal law and punishment as a baseline, the question is whether the hypothetical system would provide a similar level of deterrence.

There is good reason to believe that it would.

Skepticism about the efficacy of the hypothetical system can arise from the belief that the threat of financial liability is unlikely to discourage hardened criminals from engaging in serious wrongdoing such as murder, rape, assault, or theft. But one must keep in mind that we are making a comparative assessment, and that even under our present highly punitive system with its threat of imprisonment and death such individuals are often not deterred. Further, in the hypothetical system, plaintiffs victimized by such hardened criminals are likely to receive extraordinarily large exemplary damage awards that would translate into the equivalent of long terms of confinement for defendants who have to work off the debt, and often into the analog of life sentences. In addition, the confinement permitted under the hypothetical system is less likely to be criminogenic because the only way to shorten one's term of confinement is to become more productive.

Skepticism may also arise from the belief that without state-supplied public prosecutors, there will be no guarantee that a sufficient number of prosecutions will be brought to provide adequate deterrence. However, once again, one must remember that we are making a comparative assessment. Public prosecutors have limited budgets. This requires them to make decisions about which offenses to expend their limited resources on and which offenders to prosecute. Further, these decisions are often influenced by political considerations that can diverge from the goal of maintaining social order. For example, current efforts to satisfy the political demand for the suppression of drug use, prostitution, and illegal gambling consume such a large share of available prosecutorial resources that relatively small amounts are left for the prosecution of crimes of violence, and even less for nonviolent property offenses. In contrast, under the hypothetical system, there is no limited collective prosecutorial budget. Each party that has suffered a loss at the hands of an offender has the incentive to pursue that party for restitution.

Indeed, there is historical evidence that supports the hypothetical system's ability to deliver the needed deterrence. Private prosecution was the norm for most of English history and adequately supplied the needed deterrence until the late eighteenth century. With the advent of the Industrial Revolution, the increasing urbanization of English society produced an increase in criminal activity that strained the ability of crime victims to bring effective prosecutions as individuals. As a result, private prosecution associations formed to allow individuals to share the costs of bringing prosecutions.

> Beginning in the mid-eighteenth century, private associations and organizations began to be formed across the country. These associations emerged out of agreements neighbors made with one another to prosecute any crime committed against them. Over time, the agreements became more formal. Associations drew up constitutions, membership lists, and rules that committed them to fund prosecutions on behalf of their members. Members paid entry fees and annual subscriptions which were used to help pay for the expenses involved in apprehending and prosecuting a suspect. Most associations had their own solicitor who represented the association in court and provided legal advice to members. The funds of an association were also used to pay informers and to advertise rewards.[32]

Thus, even under highly adverse conditions, private parties were able to achieve sufficient economies of scale to supply the deterrence necessary to maintain an orderly society.

[32] Mark Koyama, *The Law and Economics of Private Prosecutions in Industrial Revolution England*, 159 Public Choice 277, 287 (2014).

It is certainly the case that the hypothetical system will not deter any victimless crimes. There can be no civil lawsuit without a plaintiff, so there will be no deterrence of activities that do not harm others. But it is not clear that the suppression of voluntary drug use and consensual sexual or gambling activities is necessary to the maintenance of an orderly society. In fact, given the amount of violence engendered by the effort to supply black market goods, this may be a reason to believe that the hypothetical system is likely to be more successful than a system of criminal punishment in preserving a peaceful and orderly society.

V. Conclusion

I have argued only that criminal law is not necessary to preserve a peaceful, orderly society. But an implication of this argument is that criminal law is actually a significant impediment to that end. As noted above, there can be no "victimless torts." Criminal law is required for there to be the type of morals offenses that give rise to black markets that are violently maintained by criminal organizations and require invasive, oppressive, and violent police tactics to suppress. A body of law that gives us the violence and corruption associated with Prohibition, the war on drugs, and the suppression of vice is not one that is well-crafted for maintaining a peaceful, orderly society.

But the more significant effect of criminal law is that it promotes the desire for vengeance, not reconciliation. Tort law evolved as an alternative to violent revenge. The natural reaction to an assault, theft, or insult is to strike back. Tort law evolved to tame this reaction and channel it in a direction that reestablished peaceful interaction. The threat of having to pay compensation deterred violence *ex ante* and the actual payment of compensation *ex post* bought off the desire for revenge by the injured parties and allowed wrongdoers to regain their place in the community.[33] Under a system of civil liability, victims receive a benefit from the private prosecution of wrongdoers. They therefore become invested in resolving the dispute, and the recompense they receive drains their desire to impose harm on the other party. This is a system designed to compose disputes and draw the members of society together.

Criminal law arose not to provide order, but to amass revenue for the royal government. As the Crown extended the scope of the criminal law, it absorbed the wrongdoers' resources in the form of fines, leaving nothing to be gained by private prosecution. Without an economic incentive, the underlying restitution-based system waned, leaving the victims uncompensated and desiring revenge. The modern-day manifestation of this is the crowds outside high-profile criminal trials demanding "justice" in the form of conviction and harsh sentences. Perhaps the most pernicious effect of criminal law supplanting the pre-existing restitution-oriented system is the identification of justice with doing harm to others. This is a system designed to increase rancor and divide members of society into hostile groups.

Most people think it is obvious that criminal law is necessary to maintain a peaceful, orderly society. But most people believe there is no alternative. This is false. The alternative to a punitive system of criminal law that authorizes the state to impose harm on individuals to enforce its rules is a restitution-oriented system of tort law that authorizes enforcement only when one member of society has harmed another. I contend that when this is the basis of comparison, it is obvious not only that criminal law is not necessary to maintain a peaceful, orderly society, but that it is antithetical to that end.

[33] *See* Berman, *supra* note 3, at 55–56.

2

Market Failure, Regulation, and Invisible Gorillas

I. A Story about Market Failure and Invisible Gorillas

Many years ago, when I completed my graduate study in law and philosophy, I accepted a position as an assistant professor at Georgetown's business school. Not being trained as an economist, this was somewhat intimidating. During my first few faculty workshops, I noticed that my colleagues—social scientists and economists all—frequently talked about the need to remedy "market failure" when advocating for government regulation. Eventually, overcoming my embarrassment at not understanding the reference, I asked one of my colleagues what precisely it meant. With good-humored amusement at the naiveté of the new guy, he provided the following explanation.

In general, markets are good because they make everyone better off. When two parties engage in market exchange, each receives something that he or she values more than the thing he or she gives to the other party. After the exchange, both parties consider themselves better off. Both have gained from the trade, and the wealth (store of value) of society has increased. This is the case as long as the transaction imposes no costs on anyone else—as long as the contracting parties who receive 100 percent of the benefits of the transaction also bear 100 percent of its costs.

The problem is that there are cases in which the transacting parties do not bear all the costs of the exchange. In some cases, the exchange imposes costs on others who are not themselves parties to

Common Law Liberalism. John Hasnas, Oxford University Press. © Oxford University Press 2024.
DOI: 10.1093/9780197784631.003.0003

the transaction. These costs, which are external to the transaction—or in economic terminology, are negative externalities—are the social costs of private market activity. When the external or social costs are great enough to outweigh the private benefits received by the transacting parties, the transaction is detrimental to society as a whole. However, because the private benefits received by transacting parties exceed their private costs, they will proceed with the transaction.

As my more sophisticated colleague explained, in such cases, markets fail to deliver the socially optimal outcome. Therefore, government intervention is necessary to correct the market's failure to consider the social costs of private transactions or, again in economic terminology, to internalize unacceptable negative externalities.[1] This is the market failure argument for government regulation of the free market.[2]

My colleague illustrated this for me with what he described as a classic example from the Industrial Revolution. With the advent of the factory system, clothing and other consumer products could be manufactured more efficiently and sold at lower prices. This allowed consumers to obtain manufactured items that they valued more than the money they had to exchange for them, and factory owners to obtain money that they valued more than the items that they manufactured. Thus, both parties were made better off by the exchange. However, the factories were powered by coal, which, when burned, sent soot up their smokestacks and into the air. This descended upon the surrounding landowners'

[1] For a more precise account of the market failure argument, see Tyler Cowen, *Public Goods and Externalities: Old and New Perspectives, in* The Theory of Market Failure: A Critical Examination 1, 1–3 (Tyler Cowen ed., 1988) and Milton Freidman, Capitalism and Freedom 30–32 (1962).

[2] Please note that despite my use of the definite article, the argument described is not "the" market failure argument but one among a family of "market failure" arguments that identify ways in which markets fail to deliver economically optimal outcomes. The present chapter focuses exclusively on the version of the argument claiming that government regulation is necessary to prevent private transactions from imposing unbargained-for costs on the members of society.

property, imposing significant clean-up costs on them. The soot was a negative externality, and the clean-up costs were the social costs that the parties to the private transaction failed to take into consideration. Therefore, government regulation of the factories was necessary.

This explanation, which was perfectly logical, struck me, as one not long out of law school, as incredibly myopic. It was as though my highly sophisticated, PhD, social science colleagues had never heard of civil liability. Didn't they realize that the landowners in the proffered example could sue the factory owners for damages and/or an injunction? At a time when tort reform was one of the hottest political issues, how could they not notice that tort law was one of society's most powerful tools for regulating market activity?

I learned the answer a couple of decades later when I encountered the concept of inattentional blindness. Inattentional blindness is a psychological phenomenon that consists of the "failure to notice a fully visible, but unexpected object because attention was engaged on another task, event, or object."[3] Because for humans, conscious perception requires attention, it is possible for people to fail to perceive an object that is right in front of them when they are focused on something else.[4]

This feature of our psychology was famously demonstrated in what became known as the invisible gorilla experiment. In the experiment, subjects were asked to watch a video of two teams of three people each, one wearing white shirts and one wearing black shirts, passing a basketball back and forth while weaving in and out of each other's space. The subjects were asked to count the number of passes made by either the white-shirted team or the black-shirted team. In the middle of the video, a woman in a gorilla

[3] Daniel J. Simons, *Inattentional Blindness*, *Scholarpedia* (Apr. 30, 2007), http://www.scholarpedia.org/article/inattentional_blindness [https://perma.cc/4UKS-RNZY].

[4] Daniel J. Simons & Christopher F. Chabris, *Gorillas in Our Midst: Sustained Inattentional Blindness for Dynamic Events*, 28 Perception 1059, 1059–1074 (1999).

costume walks into the frame, stops and looks into the camera, and then walks out of the frame. Subsequent questioning showed that only half of the subjects noticed the gorilla. Further, none of those who failed to notice the gorilla believed there was one until the videotape was replayed for them.[5]

The invisible gorilla experiment shows that when human beings focus their attention on one aspect of their experience, they can become blind to what would otherwise be apparent to them. And this is true even when the humans involved have a PhD. Apparently, economists and social scientists can become so focused on a particular model of human interaction that they can fail to see features of reality that are right before their eyes. When it comes to public policy analysis, civil liability is an invisible gorilla.

Consider the model that underlies the market failure argument described above. In this model, the market is seen as the realm of unregulated voluntary transactions—the realm in which human beings interact free from any restraint other than self-interest.[6] Law is seen as a set of rules consciously created by the government to regulate voluntary transactions for the public good. In this model, the market and law are entirely separate and distinct realms. If you will indulge me, I will refer to this as the "academic model" of the relationship between law and the market. This model is depicted in Figure 2.1.

[5] *Id.* Although this version of the experiment may seem trivial, the phenomenon it identifies can constitute a significant danger in real-world contexts. For example, in a similar experiment, professional airline pilots operated a flight simulator in which flight console information was projected directly onto the cockpit windshield. The pilots could view both the console information and the external world simultaneously, but some of the pilots still attempted to land the plane when the runway was clearly obstructed by another airplane. When asked about it afterward, the pilots reported never being aware that there was a plane obstructing the runway. By their own reports and their actions, these pilots never saw the other airplane despite looking directly at it. Richard F. Haines, *A Breakdown in Simultaneous Information Processing*, *in* Presbyopia Research 171, 171–175 (1991).

[6] Implicit in the model is the operation of the basic rules of criminal law that prohibit violence and threats of violence as a means of achieving one's ends.

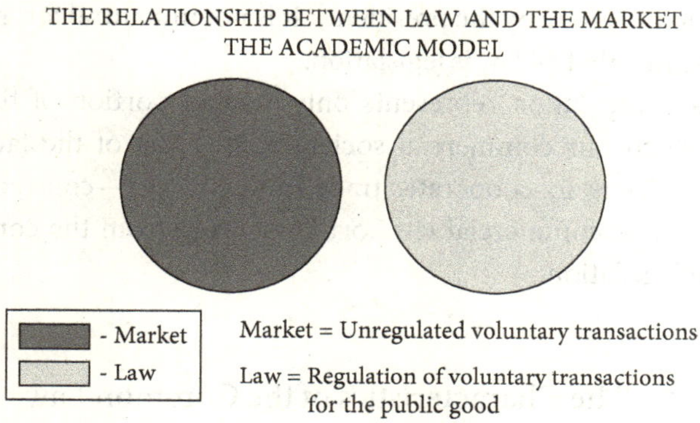

Figure 2.1 The academic model of the relationship between the law and the market, demonstrating the law and market as entirely separate.

The problem with this model is that it is based on gross misrepresentations of both the law and the market. To see how, let's consider the law first.

II. The Dual Nature of Anglo-American Law

The academic model considers the law to be rules purposely created by the government to advance the public good. This implies that it identifies law with legislation.

Legislation is law that is consciously created by those who exercise political power—in liberal democracies, by the political representatives of the community. Thus, in the United States, legislation is the output of the state legislatures and the federal Congress. And, indeed, legislation is the type of law that is most familiar to the ordinary citizen. Given that the legal education of most Americans began in elementary school with the *Schoolhouse Rock!* video of a bill singing its way through the House of Representatives and the

Senate to be signed by the president,[7] it is not unnatural for most of us to assume that all law is legislation.

In fact, legislation represents only a small portion of the law upon which our commercial society rests. Most of the law that allows citizens to cooperate, trade, and prosper—contract law, property law, commercial law, tort law—arose from the common law, not legislation.

A. The Characteristics of the Common Law

Common law is case-generated law—law that arises from the settlement of actual disputes. Common law is often unhelpfully and inaccurately referred to as "judge-made" law and is associated with rules of law consciously created by judges in appellate decisions. But this characterization is neither historically accurate nor representative of the contemporary common law system. For most of its history, the common law consisted of rules that were abstracted from a series of cases thought to represent just resolutions of past disputes, or, in the words of England's most famous legal commentator, William Blackstone, of "general customs; which are the universal rule of the whole kingdom, and form the common law, in its stricter and more usual signification."[8] More recently, the common law came to be understood as rules that are derived

[7] *See e.g.*, the Schoolhouse Rock! song "I'm Just a Bill." DAVID FRISHBERG, *I'm Just a Bill* (ABC Publishing 1973).

[8] 1 WILLIAM BLACKSTONE, COMMENTARIES ON THE LAWS OF ENGLAND 67 (1765). Harold Berman explains that

> [T]he common law of England is usually said to be itself a customary law. What is meant, no doubt, is that the royal enactments established procedures in the royal courts for the enforcement of rules and principles and standards and concepts that took their meaning from custom and usage. The rules and principles and standards and concepts to be enforced . . . were derived from informal, unwritten, unenacted norms and patterns of behavior.
>
> HAROLD BERMAN, LAW AND REVOLUTION 480–481 (1983).

from the examination of specific cases that constitute relevant precedents. Even today, judges are free to depart from precedent and announce new rules only in rare and exceptional cases. Thus, common law is the law that evolves over time from past experience. In contrast to intentionally created legislation, common law is "the result of human action, but not the execution of any human design."[9]

Tort law is the part of the common law that addresses personal injuries. If one party acts in a way that imposes unconsented harm on another, the injured party may bring a tort suit to recover damages, obtain an injunction to prevent the harmful activity, or both. The rules of tort law governing such lawsuits were not created by legislatures. They evolved from the needs of ordinary people to live together in peace.

This evolutionary process can be illustrated by two of the most ancient torts: battery and assault. In contemporary terminology, the law of battery forbids one from intentionally making "harmful or offensive contact" with another. This prohibits not only direct blows but also snatching a plate out of someone's hand[10] or blowing smoke in his or her face.[11] The law of assault forbids one from intentionally causing another to fear he or she is about to be battered, but it does not prohibit attempts at battery of which the victim is unaware or threats to batter someone in the future.[12] Why are the torts defined in this way? Why does battery bar not only harmful, but also offensive contact, and why doesn't assault bar attempts of which the victim is unaware or that are remote in time?

At the time these rules of law were evolving, one of the most urgent social needs was reducing the level of violence in society.

[9] Adam Ferguson, An Essay on the History of Civil Society 142–156 (2001) (1767).

[10] Fisher v. Carrousel Motor Hotel, Inc., 424 S.W.2d 627 (Tex. 1967).

[11] Leichtman v. WLW Jacor Comm'ns, Inc., 634 N.E.2d 697 (Ohio Ct. App. 1994).

[12] W. Union Telegraph Co. v. Hill, 150 So. 709 (Ala. Ct. App. 1933).

This meant discouraging people from acting in ways that were likely to provoke an immediate violent response. Quite naturally, then, when disputes arising out of violent clashes were settled, the community tended to hold parties who had taken such actions at fault. But what type of actions are these? Obviously, direct physical attacks on one's person are included. But affronts to one's dignity or other attacks on one's honor are equally if not more likely to provoke violence. Hence, the settlements that eventually coalesced into the law of battery forbid not merely harmful contacts but offensive ones as well. Furthermore, an attack that failed was just as likely to provoke violence as one that succeeded and thus equally in need of discouragement. But if the intended victim was unaware of the attack, it could not provoke a violent response, and if the threat was not immediate, the threatened party had time to escape, enlist the aid of others, or otherwise respond in a nonviolent manner. Hence, the settlements that eventually coalesced into the law of assault forbade only threats of an immediate battery of which the target was aware.

There is nothing unique about the development of assault and battery. A similar evolutionary process produced the torts of negligence (injuring others through carelessness), strict liability (injuring others by engaging in abnormally dangerous activities even while being careful), trespass and nuisance (interfering with the possession, use, and enjoyment of others' land), trespass to chattels and conversion (interfering with or depriving others of their private property), and defamation (publishing falsehoods that damage others' reputation), among others.

Notice that all of these torts require those who impose harm on others to compensate the injured parties for the damage they suffer. To the extent that these injuries are side effects of individuals pursuing their private transactions, one might say that the torts require individuals to internalize the negative externalities of their private pursuits.

B. The Characteristics of Legislation

As noted above, legislation is law that is consciously created by the political representatives of the community. Legislation supplants the common law. Thus, the state legislatures and the federal Congress can alter the rules of common law at will.

Two theoretical arguments are typically offered to show why this is a good thing. The first is that legislation is more democratic than the common law. The second is that legislation can be designed to proactively achieve the common good in a way that the common law cannot.

Legislation is more democratic because it is created by the people's elected representatives. Democratic theory holds that the people elect representatives to express their will in the legislature. In this way, everyone has a say in the creation of the law that they all must obey, and because legislation results from the votes of these representatives, it embodies the will of the people. Thus, we have, in Abraham Lincoln's famous phrase, a "government of the people, by the people, [and] for the people."[13]

Legislation can also function proactively. Unlike the common law that grows haphazardly and changes slowly, legislation can be scientifically crafted to address broad social problems and ensure that the law keeps pace with the rapidly changing technological and cultural conditions of modern society. Because legislators can recognize potential threats to society's well-being, they can craft legislation to avert harm before it occurs. Hence, legislation can operate preventatively in a way that common law, which arises in response to harm that has already occurred, cannot. And because legislation can address the full range of human activity, it can be used to enact consciously planned social policies designed to achieve the common good that cannot result from the decentralized common law process.

[13] Abraham Lincoln, Gettysburg Address (Nov. 19, 1863).

There is, however, good reason to believe that many of legislation's theoretical advantages over common law are chimerical. In the first place, political representatives are not ideal types who infallibly adhere to their constituents' wishes or selflessly pursue the common good. They are ordinary human beings functioning within the incentive structure of democratic government. They are neither more nor less virtuous than the ordinary person and are just as fallible, corruptible, responsive to incentives, and motivated to achieve their personal goals as anyone else.

As far as legislation being the democratic embodiment of the will of the people, there is little evidence that contemporary state or federal representatives make any effort to determine the majority of their constituents' views on or about any particular issue before casting their votes. Whatever objectives they are pursuing when they vote, it is clear that they are not endeavoring to craft the most accurate approximation of the desires of most of their constituents.

Further, although legislation has the potential to prevent future harm, politicians are rarely able to correctly identify the threats that need addressing in advance. As a matter of fact, almost all legislation is a reaction to harm that has already occurred. The New Deal legislation followed the Great Depression. The Patriot Act[14] followed the September 11, 2001 attacks. Dodd-Frank[15] was passed after the Great Recession. Megan's Law,[16] requiring public notification of the presence of convicted sex offenders, is named after Megan Kanka, who was murdered by a convicted sex offender living nearby. But to the extent that legislation is a reaction to past harm, it is not distinct from the common law, which operates

[14] Uniting and Strengthening America by Providing Appropriate Tools Required to Intercept and Obstruct Terrorism (USA PATRIOT Act) Act of 2001, Pub. L. No. 107-56, 115 Stat. 272 (2001).

[15] Dodd-Frank Wall Street Reform and Consumer Protection Act, Pub. L. No. 111-203, 124 Stat. 1376 (2010).

[16] Megan's Law, Pub. L. No. 104-145, 110 Stat. 1345 (1996).

prospectively after the initial decision. Further, even when long-term threats can be identified, the institutional incentives inherent in democratic politics frequently make it difficult to enact legislation addressing them. Federal legislators have been aware for decades that Social Security, Medicare, and Medicaid are heading toward insolvency.[17] Yet short-term political considerations consistently prevent them from enacting legislation to address this long-term threat. Hence, the inherent limitations on human knowledge and the institutional structure of democratic government make it very difficult to realize the theoretical benefits of effective preventative legislation.

Finally, although it is true that legislation presents the opportunity to implement social policies designed to achieve the common good, it also presents the opportunity to implement policies that advance the interests of some over others in derogation of the common good. Unfortunately, the incentive structures operative within representative government frequently favor the latter outcome. In recent decades, political science scholars and public choice economists have demonstrated *ad nauseam* the myriad opportunities for governmental rent-seeking: the process by which special interests sway legislation to favor them at the expense of the general public. This chapter is not the proper venue to rehearse the specifics of public choice research on matters such as concentrated benefits and dispersed costs, voting paradoxes, agenda control, special interest lobbying, and interest group politics in general. It is enough to observe that there are many forces at work within the political process that can skew legislation away from the attainment of the common good. This is not a matter of corruption, although

[17] The Social Security Administration itself predicts Social Security funds will be depleted by 2033, Soc. Sec. and Medicare Bd. of Trs., *A Summary of the 2023 Annual Reports*, Soc. Sec. Admin. tbl.10, https://www.ssa.gov/oact/trsum/ (last visited Sept. 8, 2023), and Medicare by 2031, Soc. Sec. and Medicare Bd. of Trs., *A Summary of the 2023 Annual Reports*, Soc. Sec. Admin. tbl.12, https://www.ssa.gov/oact/trsum/ (last visited Sept. 8, 2023).

that may be present as well, but of institutional incentives. Even the most honest politicians will often find themselves bound to favor the parochial interests of their constituents over the good of society as a whole.

As an illustration, consider the case of George Mitchell, who retired as Senate majority leader in 1994, respected by all sides as a man of great integrity. In an exit interview, he was asked to explain what made the long hours and aggravating work of Senate majority leader worthwhile. In answer, he recounted how, because of his influential position, he was able to get the Clinton administration to reverse an order requiring the federal government to purchase only recycled paper—presumably a measure that would serve the common good—in order to protect the jobs of workers in paper mills in his home state of Maine.[18] He then related how, a few weeks later, a mill worker came up to him "shaking with emotion" to tell him how much saving his job meant to the worker, and how that moment was "indelibly imprinted on [his] mind" and was what "makes all the aggravation worthwhile."[19] When the legislator with the highest reputation for integrity tells you that what makes the possession of power worthwhile is the ability to thwart the common good to protect one's parochial interest, you should believe him.

Despite any abstract theoretical advantages, legislation is law that is produced by political forces. Describing it as law that is consciously created by the political representatives of the community should not hide the fact that legislation consists of the law that is produced by ordinary human beings with limited knowledge and virtue functioning in the rough and tumble of real-world politics. This process can produce just law that benefits society as a whole or exploitative law designed to provide rents to some at the expense of

[18] *All Things Considered: An Exit Interview with George Mitchell* (NPR radio broadcast Oct. 17, 1994).

[19] *Id.*

society as a whole. But regardless of the character of the legislation produced, in the real world, legislation is always law that reflects the politically dominant interest.

III. The Market

Economists engaged in theoretical work often explore what would happen if people were free to interact with no external restraints. To do this, they assume a realm in which self-interested individuals engage in unregulated voluntary transactions. There is absolutely nothing wrong with this—such theorizing is an effective way of discovering and studying the relationship between abstract concepts. It is no different than when physicists assume that space is a perfect vacuum in order to discover and study the relative motion of objects. But physicists do not believe that space is actually a perfect vacuum. Similarly, economists do not (or should not) believe that there actually is a realm of unregulated voluntary transactions.

In the real world, human conduct is always subject to some form of regulation. The most powerful force regulating human interaction is our ethical and religious beliefs. Whether due to fear of divine retribution, faith-based adherence to scripture, rational commitment to abstract principles, or simply societal indoctrination, human beings regularly restrain their pursuit of self-interest to conform to their society's ethical and religious traditions. This alone provides the lion's share of the regulation necessary for society to function.

A second powerful regulatory force is custom. When the members of a community follow a customary practice, others must conform to this practice to interact with them. Customary practices of reciprocity (helping those who help you, exchanging gifts, contributing to joint projects to receive the benefits) and hospitality (expectations of largess from hosts and respectful treatment from guests) greatly discipline how people deal with each other.[20] Similarly, it is impossible to transact business with others without conforming to the customary practices within the particular industry or trade. Indeed, the binding force of such "course of dealing" and "trade usage" is recognized in contemporary commercial law.[21]

In the countries of the British Commonwealth and the United States, individuals' conduct is also regulated by common law civil liability, as described in Section II(A) above. Individuals are discouraged from intentionally engaging in harmful conduct and incentivized to exercise care not to inadvertently harm others by the threat of having to pay damages, and they can be prevented from taking actions that create a high risk of serious harm by the availability of injunctions.

Finally, individual conduct can be regulated by legislation,[22] which, as noted in Section II(B) above, is the law that is consciously created by the political representatives of the community.

But if human interaction is always subject to some form of regulation—if there is no such thing as the realm of unregulated voluntary transactions—then what do we mean when we talk about the market? We cannot mean human interaction free from

[20] A particularly good illustration of the force of custom is supplied by almost all pick-up sports. How teams are chosen, how the rules of the sport are altered and enforced, how disagreements are resolved, and when the game ends are determined by the custom of the location. To enter and participate in a game, one must abide by the customs of the schoolyard.

[21] *See* U.C.C. § 1-303 (Am. L. Inst. & Unif. L. Comm'n 2012) (defining a course of dealing as "a sequence of conduct concerning previous transactions between the parties to a particular transaction that is fairly to be regarded as establishing a common basis of understanding for interpreting their expressions and other conduct," and a usage of trade as "any practice or method of dealing having such regularity of observance in a place, vocation, or trade as to justify an expectation that it will be observed with respect to the transaction in question").

[22] For the purposes of this chapter, the term "legislation" should be understood capaciously to encompass not merely the statutes that are enacted, but also the administrative rulemaking and agency regulatory actions that are taken pursuant to statutory authority. Thus, legislative regulation includes all regulation emanating from both the legislature and the executive branch agencies.

all regulation. We must mean human interaction free from *politically generated* regulation.[23]

Note that the first three regulatory forces described above—ethics, custom, and common law—are nonpolitical in nature. They are all emergent orders in which rules evolve as a result of human interaction but are not the output of any identifiable human will. Although these rules impose restrictions on individuals' conduct, they are not politically generated and do not subject individuals to the will of those invested with political power.[24] In contrast, legislation is inherently political in nature. It emerges from the political process and is the conscious creation of those who wield political power.

Thus, for the market to be a meaningful concept—for it to refer to something that can exist in reality—it must refer to the realm of human interaction free from politically generated regulation. Correctly understood, the market is not the realm of unregulated voluntary transactions, but the realm of voluntary transactions regulated by ethics, custom, and common law (civil liability).

IV. The Relationship between Law and the Market Revisited

We are now in a position to appreciate what is wrong with the academic model of the relationship between law and the market.

[23] There are at least two good reasons for this. First, it accords with the way we usually use the term. When political theorists talk about the "free market," they are usually talking about the market free from government interference. That is what the term "laissez-faire" typically refers to. Second, this usage is consistent with the purpose of the market failure argument. The basic tenet of liberalism holds that state action that restricts individual liberty needs justification. The market failure argument is designed to provide such justification. If the purpose of the argument is to justify politically generated restrictions on market activity, then the most natural way to understand what is meant by the market is human interaction free from politically generated restrictions.

[24] Such restrictions on individual liberty are perfectly consistent with a liberal society. Liberalism requires justification for state restrictions on individual liberty, not that individuals live in a society with no restraints on their free will of any sort. Such a state of being would not qualify as a society at all.

Recall that in that model, the market is seen as the realm of unregulated voluntary transactions in which individuals interact with no restraint on their self-interest, and law is seen as rules consciously created by the government to regulate voluntary transactions for the public good. But neither of these characterizations is accurate.

The realm of unregulated voluntary transactions is a theoretical construct with no referent in reality. In the real world, the market is the realm of human interaction free from political regulation by the government—that is, the realm of voluntary transactions regulated by ethics, custom, and common law civil liability. Similarly, the characterization of law as rules consciously created by the government to achieve the public good is an idealized conception of legislation, which is only part of the law. In the real world, law consists of both common law and legislation, which is correctly understood as rules consciously created by the government to advance the politically dominant interest.

Note that when the nature of both the law and the market are correctly understood, they constitute overlapping rather than distinct realms. Common law, which is part of the law, is also part of the market. It is one of the market's internal regulatory forces.

This suggests that the actual relationship between law and the market is quite different from that depicted in the academic model. In what I will, again with your indulgence, call the "real-world" model of human interaction, the relationship between law and the market could be depicted in Figure 2.2.

V. The Market Failure Argument Revisited

Given this understanding of the relationship between law and the market, let us reconsider the story of the market failure argument with which this chapter began. That argument claimed that because there was no regulation on self-interested human action

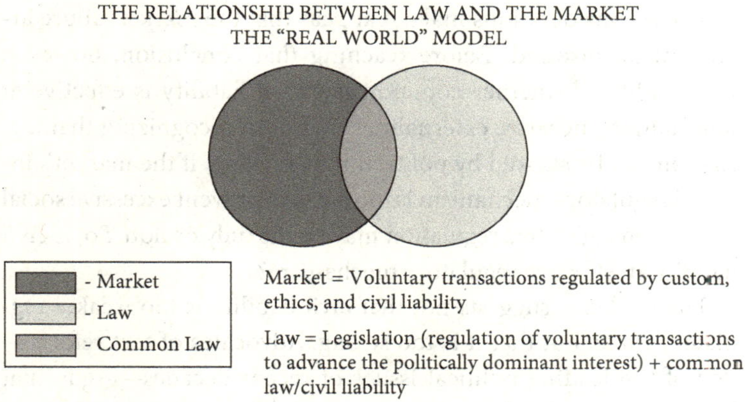

Figure 2.2 The real-world model of the relationship between the law and market, demonstrating the law and market as overlapping, with their shared area being common law.

in a market, private parties acting rationally would impose deleterious social costs on third parties, and that politically generated government regulation was necessary to internalize these negative externalities.

But we have seen that, correctly understood, the market is not a regulation-free zone, but comes with its own internal regulatory mechanisms. People's ethical beliefs and customary practices are designed to reduce the degree to which their actions cause harm to others (negative externalities), and common law civil liability evolved to address the harmful actions (negative externalities) that are not suppressed. To employ economic terminology, we have seen that regulation is endogenous to the market. We have also seen that although it is possible that legislation will be designed to properly internalize negative externalities to advance the public good, it is also possible, and appears far more likely, that it will be designed to serve politically powerful interests at the expense of the public good.

These considerations make it appear that the market failure argument is unsound. Before reaching that conclusion, however, we should ask whether common law civil liability is effective at internalizing negative externalities. For even recognizing that legislation can be skewed by political rent-seeking, if the market's internal regulatory mechanism is too weak to prevent excessive social costs, then legislative regulation may be the only option. So, is civil liability an effective regulatory mechanism?

The evidence suggests not that civil liability is too weak a regulatory force, but that it is too strong. Advocates of tort reform—one of the leading political issues of recent decades—argue that our current civil liability system puts such a great premium on safety that it discourages not only unreasonably dangerous activities, but also those whose benefits greatly outweigh the risks. They claim that the threat of civil liability is forcing playgrounds to close,[25] making football helmets unaffordable to high schools and Pop Warner leagues,[26] driving manufacturers of small aircraft and diving boards out of business,[27] causing physicians to engage in defensive medicine by ordering expensive and unnecessary tests,[28] and requiring needless warning signs on simple products such as ladders and children's costumes.[29] Further, they claim that the current system awards damages out of proportion to the harm or wrong done. Thus, the availability of punitive damages for minor harms, e.g., hundred-million-dollar judgments for selling a BMW

[25] *Lawsuits Take School's Swing Sets Away from Kids*, Faces of Lawsuit Abuse (June 15, 2018), https://www.facesoflawsuitabuse.org/2018/06/lawsuits-take-schools-swing-sets-away-from-kids/ [https://perma.cc/WGH3-P5XS].

[26] Alan Schmadtke, *Helmet Companies Facing Tough Times*, Chi. Trib. (Oct. 16, 1988), https://www.chicagotribune.com/news/ct-xpm-1988-10-16-8802080430-story.html [https://perma.cc/S2XU-2SQN].

[27] Debra Rae Anderson, *The Cost of Frivolous Lawsuits is No Joke*, Minneapolis Bus. J. (Aug. 10, 1997), https://www.bizjournals.com/twincities/stories/1997/08/11/editorial2.html [https://perma.cc/RLT5-UP9H].

[28] Eric D. Katz, *Defensive Medicine: A Case and Review of Its Status and Possible Solutions*, 3 Clinical prac. & cases emergency med. 329 (2019).

[29] *See* Anderson, *supra* note 27.

without informing the buyer that it has been repainted,[30] class action lawsuits that aggregate small wrongs into large judgments, e.g., the half-million-dollar settlement for Subway selling foot-long sandwiches that were less than twelve inches long,[31] and damages for speculative injuries, e.g., decades of medical monitoring for exposure to toxic substances,[32] cause businesses to overinvest in precautions and be reluctant to pursue innovations that carry even a slight risk of harm.

Perhaps the advocates of tort reform are correct. Perhaps contemporary tort law is indeed too highly regulatory. In the present context, it is not to my purpose to attempt to defend tort law against such criticism. But it is to my purpose to note that if tort law is indeed too strong—if it is so powerful a regulatory force that it suppresses not only socially deleterious, but also useful, productive activities, then it cannot possibly be the case that civil liability is not an effective regulatory mechanism.

The failure to acknowledge the effectiveness of civil liability in public policy debates is a glaring example of inattentional blindness. For the past several decades in the United States, the Democratic Party has vociferously argued that greater legislative regulation is necessary to protect the public against the dangerous

[30] BMW of N. Am., Inc. v. Gore, 517 U.S. 5591 (1996).

[31] In re: Subway Footlong Sandwich Marketing and Sales Practices Litigation, 316 F.R.D. 240 (E.D. Wis. Feb. 25, 2016).

[32] *See* Richard Bourne, *Medical Monitoring without Physical Injury; The Least Justice Can Do for Those Industry Has Terrorized with Poisonous Products*, 58 SMU L. Rev. 251, 252 n.10 (2005). ("The first state supreme court decision to hold that medical monitoring damages should be awarded was *Ayers v. Township of Jackson*, 525 A.2d 287 (N.J. 1987), which upheld an award of legal damages for future medical costs. *Id.* at 312. A number of other courts have taken the same position. *See, e.g.,* Abuan v. Gen. Elec. Co., 3 F.3d 329, 334 (9th Cir. 1993); *In re* Paoli R.R. Yard PCB Litig., 916 F.2d 829, 852 (3d Cir. 1990); Hagerty [v. L & L Marine Servs., Inc.], 797 F.2d 256; Herber v. Johns-Manville Corp., 785 F.2d 79, 83 (3d Cir. 1986); Burton v. R.J. Reynolds Tobacco Co., 884 F. Supp. 1515, 1523 (D. Kan. 1995); Merry v. Westinghouse Elec. Corp., 684 F. Supp. 847, 849 (M.D. Pa. 1988); Potter v. Firestone Tire & Rubber Co., 863 P.2d 795 (Cal. 1993); Bowerman v. United Illuminating, 23 Conn. L. Reptr. 589 (Conn. Super. Ct. 1998)".)

excesses of the market.[33] Nevertheless, in 2000, Ed Rendell, the chair of the Democratic National Committee, explicitly recognized that "trial lawyers paved the way for America's safety advances," stating "[80] to 90 percent of those safety advances come from litigation."[34] One might wonder how one mind could hold two such discordant thoughts until he or she remembers the invisible gorilla. Tort law is public policy's invisible gorilla.

VI. The Market Failure Argument Revised

Because the market failure argument mischaracterizes both the law and the market, it is clearly unsound. But perhaps its flaws can be remedied. Perhaps it can be saved by a more realistic account of both.

Let's begin with the understanding that the market comes with its own powerful internal regulatory mechanism—that ethics and custom reduce the social costs of private transactions, and that common law civil liability effectively internalizes many if not most of the negative externalities that nevertheless occur. But let's also recognize that civil liability is not a panacea, and there may remain many negative externalities that escape its grasp. Let's further observe that legislation is an imperfect tool for internalizing negative externalities, that in many cases political interests can sway it from its intended purpose. But let's also recognize that if there are social costs that do not respond to ethics, custom, or common law civil liability, an imperfect tool may be the best tool available for reducing them. Thus, there may be cases in which, even with all its imperfections, legislation is a more effective tool for addressing social costs than civil liability.

[33] This continues right up until the present day. *See infra* note 69 and text accompanying note 69.

[34] Ceci Connolly, *Democrats Have No Argument with Trial Lawyers*, WASH. POST, April 9, 2000, at A6.

With this in mind, let's revisit the story with which this chapter began, which can be rewritten as follows. In general, markets, which are places where human beings engage in voluntary transactions regulated by ethics, custom, and common law civil liability, are good because they make everyone better off. When two parties engage in market exchange, each receives something that he or she values more than the thing he or she gives to the other party. After the exchange, both parties consider themselves better off. Both have gained from the trade, and the wealth (store of value) of society has increased. Further, transactions that impose unwanted costs on third parties are discouraged by society's ethical beliefs, customary practices, and the threat of civil liability.

The problem is that there are cases in which the transacting parties engage in exchanges that impose unwanted costs on third parties which are not adequately discouraged by ethics, custom, and civil liability. These costs, which are external to the transaction, or, in economic terminology, are negative externalities, are the social costs of market activity. When the social costs outweigh the private benefits received by the transacting parties, the transaction is detrimental to society as a whole. However, because the private benefits received by the transacting parties exceed their costs, they will proceed with the transaction.

In such cases, markets fail to deliver the socially optimal outcome. This result suggests that there may be a role for legislative regulation of the market, if politically generated legislation can be tailored to internalize the negative externality rather than serve politically powerful special interests. Therefore, legislative regulation of the market is justified when (1) the market's internal regulatory mechanisms cannot internalize the negative externality or cannot do so as effectively as legislative regulation; (2) there is reason to believe that the political factors that skew legislation away from the public interest and toward politically dominant special interests can be controlled well enough for the legislative regulation to internalize the negative externality more effectively than civil liability;

and (3) the harm from the failure of such controls is not greater than the harm of the negative externality itself.

This version of the market failure argument may well be sound. But note that its application requires a series of empirical investigations and a comparative analysis. To begin with, it requires an examination of the rules of tort law and an evaluation of how effective civil liability is at internalizing any particular negative externality. For example, if an industrial enterprise expels waste products that enter or impair the enjoyment of another's land, an investigation of whether the aggrieved party has the ability to collect damages or obtain an injunction against the polluting activity must be undertaken.

Next, there must be an examination of how likely it is that the political process will produce legislation that effectively internalizes the externality. In the case of industrial pollution, this would include consideration of (1) whether politicians can amass the technical and economic knowledge necessary to identify the optimal level of tax or regulation to apply; and (2) the probability that highly capitalized manufacturers and/or politically connected environmental organizations will skew the political process away from the optimal tax or regulation.

Finally, with this information in hand, there must be a comparative assessment to determine which of the two regulatory mechanisms will most effectively and efficiently internalize the externality. If civil liability does not reduce the social costs of private transactions to the optimal level, we must ask whether legislation would get us closer to that level or whether the influence of politically powerful special interests would take us further away. In doing so, we must be cognizant that legislation affords highly capitalized interests the ability to free themselves from common law civil liability by influencing politicians to enact tort reform legislation.[35]

[35] *See infra* Part VII(B)(ii. The BP Oil Spill) for a specific illustration of this phenomenon.

VII. The Comparative Assessment

Assuming that the revised market failure argument is sound, the question arises as to how often it will justify governmental regulation of the market. How often will legislation be more effective than common law civil liability? I offer some general considerations and a couple of specific examples that bear upon this question.

A. General Considerations

Let's begin with the relative costs and limitations of the two regulatory mechanisms. To be effective, regulation via legislation must overcome significant impediments to both its implementation and its enforcement. To begin with, it is difficult and expensive to move regulatory legislation through the political system. To legislatively internalize a negative externality, an advocate of government regulation must

1) propose a bill regulating individual conduct to protect the safety of the public or other public interest;
2) steer the bill through the legislature, dealing with the bill's opponents lobbying for its amendment or defeat;
3) set up the regulatory agency (e.g., get offices, hire staff, obtain an operating budget, etc.);
4) begin the regulatory rule-making process;
5) deal with the lobbying of regulated parties trying to obtain the rules most favorable to their interests and most damaging to their competitors;
6) promulgate the regulations;
7) create an enforcement agency (e.g., hire inspectors, create a schedule of penalties, set up an appeals process); and
8) monitor the regulated environment to determine whether changing conditions require new rules or revisions to the existing ones.

This process can, and often does, produce complex and arcane regulations that are collected in state or federal compilations. The Code of Federal Regulations contained 188,343 pages at the end of 2021.[36] Compliance with such regulations is typically beyond the competence of the layperson and requires the aid of legal counsel. And once the regulations have been enacted, they must be enforced. But political enforcement is subject to several limitations. In the first place, all regulatory agencies have limited budgets. State regulations apply to all businesses operating within the state. Federal regulations are national in scope and apply to the tens of millions of businesses that operate in the United States. Because they are funded by politically apportioned state or federal revenues, no regulatory agency has unlimited resources for enforcement, and almost all such agencies functioning in the United States claim to be woefully underfunded. This underfunding requires most agencies to engage in enforcement triage, pursuing a subset of violators while ignoring others. Further, the required enforcement priorities are determined by politically appointed directors who can be driven by ideology and/or the lobbying efforts of well-connected special interests, rather than an objective assessment of what best promotes the public interest. This can leave ordinary citizens, who cannot organize to influence the regulatory agencies, exposed to the damage of unaddressed social costs.

In addition, regulatory violations carry legislatively fixed financial penalties. Although a fine of $100,000 may be substantial for an individual entrepreneur, it may constitute a relatively small budget item for a large, highly capitalized corporation. If the prescribed penalty is less than the gain the corporation can obtain by violating the regulation, the corporation could regard the penalty merely as a cost of doing business. In such a case, the regulatory agency

[36] Office of the Federal Register, *Code of Federal Regulations Total Pages 1938–1949, And Total Volumes and Pages 1950–2021* (2002).

will be unable to effectively internalize the problematic negative externality.

Compare this scenario with the mechanics of reducing the social costs of private transactions through common law civil liability. To begin with, there is no need to develop a new set of regulations. The principles of civil liability have been stable for more than a century and are easily captured in three basic rules:

1) Do not intentionally harm others.
2) Exercise the degree of care that a reasonable person would use to avoid causing harm to others by his or her actions.
3) If you engage in actions that impose a risk of harm on others that cannot be reduced by being careful, compensate anyone your actions injure.

These rules are easily understood by the layperson and do not require thousands of pages of official publications to record them.[37] In fact, if they are generalized and translated into economic terminology, they are simply an injunction to internalize social costs. To wit, when one or more parties act in ways that impose unconsented-to harm on another party (that create a negative externality), the injured party may sue to recover damages or enjoin the damaging activity (to internalize the externality).

With regard to enforcement, the general complaint about civil liability is not that it provides too little enforcement but that it provides too much. The civil liability system releases an army of regulators to police private transactions. They are called plaintiff's attorneys. Unlike regulatory agencies, they are not funded by taxpayers and they do not have limited budgets. They work on commission and collect their fees directly from successful regulatory

[37] Although if you do want to go into detail about how these general rules are instantiated in particular torts, I recommend TORTS IN A NUTSHELL, the latest edition of which runs 609 pages.

actions, i.e., as a percentage of the judgments they recover for their clients. They cannot be captured by the regulated entities. If a corporation tries to buy one off with a settlement, others come flooding in with additional enforcement actions. They function as individual entrepreneurs free from any controlling central authority whose ideological or partisan preferences can sway them from their enforcement mission.

Further, in contrast to regulatory agencies over which the unorganized public can exert little control, plaintiff's attorneys are fawningly responsive to the ordinary citizen. Tort law is poor person's law. Because the contingency fee system allows the lawyers to be paid out of the judgments they obtain, no injured party has to be able to pay attorney's fees to have his or her day in court. Plaintiff's attorneys will pursue enforcement actions on behalf of even the most destitute individual if he or she has a good case. Those old enough to remember commercial television will recall the plaintiff's-attorney ads declaring: "If you have a phone, you have a lawyer."[38] These days, you don't even need a phone.[39]

Finally, civil liability has rarely been accused of imposing financial penalties that are too small to effectively internalize social costs. Quite the opposite: for half a century, regulated entities have complained about overdeterrence—about the awards being too large. Civil liability awards are not prescribed by legislation and can be as large as is necessary to cause the regulated entities to absorb 100 percent of the costs they impose on others. Indeed, in the case of intentionally undertaken harmful action, additional exemplary (i.e., punitive) damages can be awarded to ensure that corporations do not treat the awards as a cost of doing business. This can be a

[38] Long Forgotten Videos, *Saiontz & Kirk—Free Injury Hotline—1995 Commercial*, YouTube (Aug. 23, 2019), https://www.youtube.com/watch?v=8ez_Hu5SkOU [https://perma.cc/QBF4-RYAG].
[39] Saiontz & Kirk, P.A., *Saiontz & Kirk: You Have a Lawyer*, YouTube (June 10, 2019), https://www.youtube.com/watch?v=QGE4mPJzRDU [https://perma.cc/UJG6-XCJ3].

particularly effective way of encouraging more socially responsible behavior. Corporations tend to be more responsive to multimillion-dollar judgments than they are to hundred-thousand-dollar regulatory fines.[40]

For an interesting illustration of how comprehensive a regulatory mechanism civil liability can be, consider the case of Ralph Gentles. Mr. Gentles, a Jamaican immigrant to New York City who needed employment, obtained a job walking the sidewalks of Staten Island looking for broken pavement that could endanger pedestrians. Whenever he discovered a dangerous condition, he recorded it on a detailed street map. Mr. Gentles was not a city inspector and was not paid with taxpayer money. He was paid by a consortium of plaintiff's attorneys called the Big Apple Pothole and Sidewalk Protection Corporation. Because the city cannot be held liable for injuries due to unsafe conditions unless it is on notice of their existence, the consortium pays people like Mr. Gentles to create these sidewalk surveys, which it then turns over to the city's transportation department. This enables the attorneys to bring the more than 1,700 negligence suits filed each year against the city for sidewalk accidents.[41]

I can understand why some may argue that a liability system that incentivizes this type of lawsuit is overly regulative. However, in the context of the comparative assessment we are required to make, that is immaterial. We are asking how likely it is that social costs that are not internalized by civil liability will be effectively internalized by legislative regulation. If, in fact, civil liability already provides too much regulation, it seems unlikely that there will be many such examples.

[40] As previously discussed, civil liability is not limited to retrospectively awarding damages for harm already done, but can also, like legislative regulation, act prospectively to prevent harm by granting injunctions against dangerous actions in the future.

[41] This account comes from an episode of "All Things Considered," *National Public Radio*, Sept. 6, 1995.

B. Specific Examples

i. McDonald's Coffee

The only tort case most of the public has ever heard of is the infamous McDonald's coffee cup case. This case has been inaccurately caricatured as one in which a little old lady spilled hot coffee on herself in a moving car and collected millions. The actual facts of the case are as follows.

Stella Liebeck was a seventy-nine-year-old woman who was a passenger in her grandson's car when they went through a McDonald's drive-through. Ms. Liebeck ordered a cup of coffee, and her grandson pulled over and stopped the car so that she could add cream and sugar. She held the Styrofoam cup between her knees while attempting to remove the lid. In doing so, she accidentally spilled the contents of the cup on her lap. This caused third-degree (full thickness) burns on her thighs, buttocks, and groin.

McDonald's corporate policy was to hold its coffee at between 180 and 190 degrees Fahrenheit. At 190 degrees, spilled coffee can cause third-degree burns in less than three seconds. At 180 degrees, it can cause such burns in twelve seconds. But at 160 degrees, it takes twenty seconds or more to produce third-degree burns. McDonald's records showed that in the ten years preceding Stella Liebeck's injury, there had been at least seven hundred cases in which McDonald's customers had suffered mild to third-degree burns due to coffee spills, and that McDonald's had settled claims arising from such burn injuries for more than $500,000.

On the basis of these facts, the jury concluded that McDonald's was knowingly exposing its customers to an unreasonable risk of burn injury. It awarded Ms. Liebeck $200,000 in compensatory damages, which were reduced 20 percent to $160,000 due to her negligence in opening the cup, and $2.7 million in exemplary damages, which was the amount of profit McDonald's made on coffee in two days. The exemplary damages award was reduced by the trial court to $480,000, producing a total award of $640,000.[42]

Fallible human beings sometimes spill things, including cups of coffee. Sometimes, restaurant waiters or employees at fast food restaurants spill coffee on customers. Sometimes, restaurant customers spill the coffee they purchase on themselves or others. Whichever is the case, it is reasonable to view burn injuries from extremely hot coffee as a negative externality of the private exchange of money for brewed coffee. In this case, the burn injuries are literally a spillover effect of the private transaction.

During the decade in which McDonald's was settling seven hundred coffee-spill burn-injury lawsuits, no federal or state regulatory agency issued any rules governing the safe temperature for serving hot beverages to the public. The Consumer Products Safety Commission never considered whether restaurants should be handing its customers products that could cause third-degree burns in three seconds.[43]

The day after the verdict was announced in Stella Liebeck's lawsuit, the McDonald's she patronized began serving coffee at 158 degrees Fahrenheit.[44] All major retailers now serve coffee at temperatures between 165 and 180 degrees.[45] The McDonald's handbook for franchisees now calls for holding coffee between 170 and 180 degrees, ten degrees cooler than previously mandated.[46]

[42] This account of the case is taken from Kevin G. Cain, *And Now the Rest of the Story . . . The McDonald's Coffee Lawsuit*, 11 J. Consumer & Com. L. 14 (2007) and Andrea Gerlin, *A Matter of Degree: How a Jury Decided That a Coffee Spill Is Worth $2.9 Million*, Wall St. J., Sept. 1, 1994, at A1.

[43] *See Final and Proposed Rules*, U.S. Consumer Product Safety Comm'n, https://www.cpsc.gov/Regulations-Laws--Standards/Rulemaking/Final-and-Proposed-Rules [https://perma.cc/Q5HR-AQ2R] (last visited July 31, 2021).

[44] Gerlin, *supra* note 42, at A1.

[45] Alan Farnham, *Woman Sues Dunkin' Donuts Over Hot Cider; A Look Behind Beverage Suit Tsunami*, ABC News (Feb. 24, 2014), https://abcnews.go.com/Business/dunkin-donuts-sued-hot-apple-cider-burns/story?id=22656060 [https://perma.cc/H4J9-QQ4A].

[46] Hilary Stout, *Not Just a Hot Cup Anymore*, N.Y. Times (Oct. 21, 2013), https://www.nytimes.com/2013/10/21/booming/notjustahotcupanymore.html [https://perma.cc/36EX-FR9G].

Starbucks serves its coffee at between 150 and 170 degrees by corporate specification.[47] The cups in which to-go coffee is served have been redesigned to have sculpted lids with a raised opening for sipping and zarfs—cardboard sleeves around the cup that insulate one's fingers from the heat.[48]

The McDonald's coffee cup case became famous because it was thought to illustrate that the civil liability system provides too much safety regulation. And perhaps that is the case. Perhaps regulating the temperature at which coffee is served in order to prevent serious burn injuries is indeed too much regulation. However, our present concern is to compare legislation to civil liability as a regulatory mechanism. If the state and federal regulatory agencies tasked with protecting consumer safety provided no regulation and the civil liability system provided too much regulation, this case serves as evidence against the claim that legislation is necessary to remedy the market's failure to internalize the social costs of private transactions.

ii. The BP Oil Spill

On April 20, 2010, British Petroleum's (BP) Deepwater Horizon offshore drilling rig exploded and sank into the Gulf of Mexico. The explosion killed eleven members of the drilling crew, seriously injured seventeen others, and resulted in the discharge of 3.19 million barrels of oil into the waters of the Gulf until the blown oil well was capped eighty-seven days later on July 15, 2010.[49] The oil well

[47] *See* Starbucks Corporation, WPS Starbucks FY16 Beverage Resource Manual 031516 (2013), https://studylib.net/doc/25255636/wps-starbucks-fy16-beverage-resource-manual-031516 [https://perma.cc/L5H6-QUEU]. *See also* Hayley Peterson, *Three Reasons Why You Should Order Your Starbucks Drink "Extra Hot,"* Bus. Insider (Dec. 16, 2013), https://www.businessinsider.com/starbucks-drink-extra-hot-2013-12 [https://perma.cc/3S9U-N7AE].

[48] Stout, *supra* note 46.

[49] *Deepwater Horizon—BP Gulf of Mexico Oil Spill*, EPA, https://www.epa.gov/enforcement/deepwater-horizon-bp-gulf-mexico-oil-spill [https://perma.cc/2RNZ-Q6XL] (last updated Dec. 4, 2020).

over which the Deepwater Horizon was positioned was located on the seabed almost a mile below the surface of the water.[50]

Why was BP drilling for oil a mile deep in the Gulf of Mexico? The answer is not because that is where the oil is. Oil companies are not interested merely in getting oil out of the ground; they are interested in getting oil out of the ground at the lowest cost relative to the amount for which it can be sold. It is difficult and extremely expensive to drill for oil a mile underwater. So why was BP there?

One of the major expenses of drilling for oil in deep water is the cost of liability insurance. The potential exposure to liability from injured parties is great. An oil leak in the Gulf of Mexico could cause damage to a vast array of parties, such as shoreline landowners, boaters, fishers and shrimpers, and maritime transportation companies. Further, the difficulty in capping leaks deep underwater makes such drilling an abnormally dangerous activity subject to strict liability for any harm that it causes.[51] Liability insurers charge oil companies who want to drill in such deep water inordinately high rates and want assurances that all reasonable precautions are being taken. If the risk is great enough, liability insurance can be unobtainable and oil companies have to self-insure. Hence, the threat of common law civil liability is both an exceptionally strong disincentive to drilling for oil deep underwater, and an exceptionally strong incentive for any company that nevertheless engages in such drilling to exercise all possible care.

[50] Richard Pallardy, *Deepwater Horizon Oil Spill*, ENCYCLOPEDIA BRITANNICA (Nov. 2, 2020), https://www.britannica.com/event/DeepwaterHorizonoilspill [https://perma.cc/4LZZ-PFBJ].

[51] Indeed, one of the purposes of the tort of strict liability is to send a signal that the activity is inappropriate to the location and to create an incentive to do it somewhere else. *See* Indiana Harbor Belt R. Co. v. Am. Cyanamid Co., 916 F.2d 1174, 1177 (7th Cir. 1990) ("By making the actor strictly liable—by denying him in other words an excuse based on his inability to avoid accidents by being more careful—we give him an incentive, missing in a negligence regime, to experiment with methods of preventing accidents that involve not greater exertions of care, assumed to be futile, but instead relocating, changing, or reducing (perhaps to the vanishing point) the activity giving rise to the accident").

This incentive structure posed a problem for the federal government, which had declared "the subsoil and seabed" of the Gulf of Mexico to be "a vital national resource reserve held by the Federal Government for the public, which should be made available for expeditious and orderly development."[52] To spur this development, the federal government divided the seabed into oil and gas leases, which it wanted to sell to oil companies, and from which it could collect 12.5 percent royalties on all the oil and gas the companies extracted.[53] But if common law civil liability discouraged drilling for oil at great depths, who would buy the leases and develop the seabed? The problem for the federal government was that the existence of common law safety regulation was antithetical to its pro-development, revenue-generating public policy.

Fortunately for the government, a solution to this problem was at hand in the form of tort reform legislation. Thus, in 1990, Congress passed the Oil Pollution Act (OPA), which included Section 2704, which limited oil companies' liability for spills to the clean-up cost plus $75 million, unless the company had been grossly negligent.[54] Although $75 million may sound like a lot to us, it is not that much to companies whose budgets run into the billions. The liability cap lowered the financial risk of drilling for oil in deep water sufficiently to make it economical for BP (and other oil companies) to

[52] Outer Continental Shelf Lands Act, 43 U.S.C. § 1332(3) (2006).

[53] 30 U.S.C. § 226.

[54] This abbreviated account of the advent of § 2704 of the OPA is slightly disingenuous in that it suggests more intentionality on the part of Congress than actually existed. The bill that was to become the OPA was originally introduced in response to the *Exxon Valdez* oil spill to provide better compensation to the victims of such spills than could be obtained under the 1977 Clean Water Act Amendments, which contained a $50 million liability cap per facility. *See* Keith J. Jones, *Drill Baby . . . Spill Baby: How the Oil Pollution Act's Economic-Damage Liability Cap Contributed to the Deepwater Horizon Disaster*, 40 Envtl. L. Rep. News & Analysis 11132, 11133 (2010). Nevertheless, as the bill worked its way through the legislative process, oil industry lobbyists convinced Congress to include § 2704 with the $75 million liability cap. *See id.* at 11132–11133. The difference is immaterial in the present context because the effect of lobbying on legislative regulation is one of the factors that must be considered when making a comparative assessment between it and common law civil liability. See *supra* § VII(A).

engage in this extremely risky activity. As explained by economist Michael Greenstone, the OPA

> fundamentally distorts a company's decision making. Without the cap, executives would have to weigh the possible revenue from a well against the cost of drilling there and the risk of damage. With the cap, they can largely ignore the potential damage beyond cleanup costs. So they end up drilling wells even in places where the damage can be horrific, like close to a shoreline.[55]

So, the answer to the question of why BP was drilling for oil a mile underwater in the Gulf of Mexico is that the OPA's liability cap allowed BP to run "serious risks in its operations . . . [and] focus on the potentially enormous financial rewards of accessing millions of gallons of oil, all the while knowing that its potential liability would be limited to a dollar amount that it could easily pay with little impact to the company's bottom line."[56]

Having undermined the regulatory effect of common law civil liability with its tort reform legislation, the federal government established the Minerals Management Service (MMS) to regulate offshore oil drilling for safety.[57] The MMS did a famously bad job of this

[55] David Leonhardt, *Spillonomics: Underestimating Risk*, N.Y. TIMES MAG. (June 6, 2010), https://www.nytimes.com/2010/06/06/magazine/06fob-wwln-t.html [https://perma.cc/YH55-YXUU].

[56] Jones, *supra* note 54, at 11134. *See also* Andrew F. Popper, *Capping Incentives, Capping Innovation, Courting Disaster: The Gulf Oil Spill and Arbitrary Limits on Civil Liability*, 60 DEPAUL L. REV. 975, 990 (2011). ("Companies participating in high-risk activities including offshore drilling should have every incentive to maximize safety. Statutorily capped liability has exactly the opposite effect. It is now fair to conclude that the cap on liability for offshore drilling played a meaningful role in the decisions that led to this disaster. Oil spills are not completely preventable. However, there are ways to lessen risk—and they can be costly. It is only logical that a company will not incur those costs if it already knows the limits of its liability and has already programmed those costs into its pricing structure. . . . If a cap is set below the amount of expected damage, this not only violates the victim's right to compensation but also vitiates the full internalization of risks associated with an activity.")

[57] The Minerals Management Service (MMS) no longer exists, having been reconstituted as the Bureau of Ocean Energy Management, Regulation, and

for at least three reasons. In the first place, the MMS was massively underresourced. Between 1982 and 2007, the number of offshore oil leases increased by 200 percent and oil production increased by 185 percent, while MMS inspectors decreased by 36 percent. In 2010, the MMS budget was the same as it had been in the 1980s, which was before the agency was tasked with regulating deep-water drilling. The MMS did not even have enough money in its budget to provide transportation to the deep-water rigs to conduct surprise inspections, and could not retain knowledgeable employees, who could earn much more working for the oil industry.[58]

Secondly, federal statutes gave the MMS conflicting missions. The MMS was charged with both (1) promoting the development of the underwater oil fields and collecting royalties, and (2) regulating the oil companies' conduct for safety.[59] Inevitably, the first mission overwhelmed the second. Congress was pushing to raise royalty revenue and increase domestic oil production. Enforcing safety standards would interfere with those objectives. Responding to these incentives, the MMS continually turned a blind eye toward unsafe practices and regularly accepted industry representations of safety.[60] Thus, "because MMS willingly accepted industry representations that a spill was 'unlikely' and the resulting consequences 'minimal,' MMS accepted a role as cheerleader and booster for the drilling industry, consistently choosing oil production over environmental protection."[61]

Finally, the MMS presents a textbook example of a regulatory agency being captured by the regulated industry. Prior to the BP

Enforcement (BOEMRE) following the BP oil spill for reasons that will become apparent. *See* text accompanying notes 58–66. The agency was responsible for regulating the extraction of gas and mineral resources on federal lands, including offshore drilling in the Gulf of Mexico.

[58] *See* Rebecca M. Bratspies, *A Regulatory Wake-up Call: Lessons from BP's Deepwater Horizon Disaster*, 5 Golden Gate U. Envtl. L. J. 7, 51–52 (2011).

[59] Federal Oil and Gas Royalty Management Act of 1982, 30 U.S.C.A. § 1701 (1983).

[60] *See* Bratspies, *supra* note 58, at 52–53.

[61] *Id.* at 30.

disaster, an Interior Department Inspector General report detailed how MMS regulators "accepted gifts, steered contracts to favored clients and engaged in drug use and illicit sex with employees of the energy firms."[62] A subsequent inspector general investigation into the BP disaster turned up examples of "egregious misconduct" by MMS inspectors who "were routinely treated to golf tournaments, hunting trips, fishing expeditions, sporting tickets and other expensive perks by the oil companies MMS was supposed to be regulating."[63] As an MMS district manager who testified as part of the inspector general's investigation explained,

> Obviously we're all oil industry . . . We're all from the same part of the country. Almost all of our inspectors have worked for oil companies out on these platforms. They grew up in the same towns. Some of these people, they've been friends with all their life. They've been with these people since they were kids. They've hunted together. They fish together.[64]

This relationship resulted in a "culture of deference"[65] to the oil industry such that MMS regulators acted as though their evaluations "should always be a green light to proceed."[66]

The BP oil-spill disaster is often cited as an example of regulatory failure. Although that is undeniably true, it is important to specify

[62] Derek Kravitz & Mary Pat Flaherty, *Report Says Oil Agency Ran Amok*, WASH POST (Sept. 11, 2008), https://www.washingtonpost.com/wp-dyn/content/article/2008/09/10/AR2008091001829_pf.html [https://perma.cc/6KUL-GMPC]. *See also* John McQuaid, *Anatomy of the BP Oil Spill: An Accident Waiting to Happen*, YALE ENV'T 360 (May 10, 2010) ("MMS has also been plagued by scandals in recent years, including one in which eight employees were disciplined for partying, having sex with, and receiving expensive gifts from their energy industry counterparts"), https://e360.yale.edu/features/the_gulf_of_mexico_oil_spill_an_accident_waiting_to_happen [https://perma.cc/P4UV-B5ZM].

[63] Bratspies, *supra* note 58, at 53.

[64] *Id.*

[65] *Id.*

[66] *Id.* at 54.

what type of regulation failed. It was not the market's internal regulatory system of common law civil liability. This was obviously working effectively; otherwise, there would be no explanation for the liability cap built into the OPA. Tort reform legislation is only passed when the threat of civil liability is preventing the achievement of some politically desired goal.[67] Apparently, the market's internal regulatory forces were privileging safety and protection of the environment over politically popular economic development. Hence, from the government's point of view, deregulation was required.

On the other hand, the BP disaster is a classic example of the failure of legislative regulation. Congress legislatively freed the oil industry from the discipline of the market—from having to balance the potential reward of drilling in deep water against the magnitude of the risk of doing so. It then created a regulatory agency to protect the public and the environment against the unreasonably risky behavior that such legislation would encourage. It invested that agency with conflicting missions, failed to provide adequate funding for it to carry out its duties, left the revolving door to industry employment wide open, and tolerated a culture of widespread corruption within the agency. That is a pretty good tally of the ways legislative regulation can fail.[68] In comparison to protecting the environment with poorly paid government regulators who can profit from shirking their responsibilities, plaintiff's attorneys working on contingency fees who cannot be bought off, do not require public funding, and get paid only if they do their regulatory job well look pretty good.

[67] This is a particular illustration of the more general observation that politicians only pass legislation to achieve ends that cannot be attained on the market. This gives rise to what I call "Hasnas's rule of thumb": If you want to know how markets work, look at legislation.

[68] Indeed, this case seems likely to become a mainstay of future textbooks on public choice economics.

VIII. Conclusion

Returning to the story with which this chapter began, once my more experienced colleague acquainted me with the market failure argument, I encountered it everywhere. Almost all of our workshops and conferences would begin with an advocate of government regulation explaining how the proposed regulation was necessary to prevent parties to private transactions from imposing social costs on the public. This line of reasoning appeared to be the lingua franca of economic analysis.

Nevertheless, for many years, I found the ubiquity of the market failure argument mystifying. I did not understand why such otherwise brilliant people would completely ignore the civil liability system. Even more baffling was the fact that many of those who relied on the market failure argument were also advocates of tort reform legislation. How, I wondered, could one simultaneously argue that legislation was required to remedy the defects of the unregulated market and that tort reform legislation was needed to cure the overregulation of the market?

It was not until I encountered the invisible-gorilla experiment and learned about inattentional blindness that I finally understood. Apparently, an intensive enough focus on one's theoretical model of the world can make one unable to see the way the real world departs from it even when the divergence is directly before one's eyes.

In this chapter, I have argued that the market failure argument, as it is usually presented, is obviously unsound. I have also argued that it could be revised in an interesting way. I have suggested that if we begin with a realistic depiction of the market as the realm of voluntary transactions regulated by ethics, custom, and civil liability, we could then attempt to identify types of private transactions whose social costs are not prevented or internalized by these regulatory mechanisms. And to the extent that we can identify such transactions, we could ask whether it is possible to craft politically generated legislation that would internalize these remaining negative externalities without being diverted from that goal by politically dominant or well-connected special interests. I have also introduced abstract considerations and specific examples that cast doubt on the prospects for such legislation.

I think that exploring the questions raised by the revised market failure argument would be fascinating and fruitful. Unfortunately, I detect no interest in undertaking such an exploration in the vast majority of my social science colleagues. Wherever I look, I continue to encounter the version of the argument derived from the academic conception of the law and market as entirely separate realms. Indeed, as I sit down to write these words, I find that economist Alan Blinder has a column in the *Wall Street Journal* explaining that

> [O]ne of the most important ideas we teach every economics student is that unfettered markets systematically get it wrong in the presence of externalities—cases in which the decisions of some people or businesses have important effects on third parties who have no say in the decision. . . . Negative externalities are often more spectacular—and more worrisome. The classic example is pollution. If firms aren't charged for the pollutants they spew into the atmosphere, they will emit too many. For over a century, economists have advocated a straightforward fix for this market failure: Tax polluters for the damages they inflict on others . . . [but where] this is impractical . . . [t]he best compromise may be an enforced mandate.[69]

The academy is the home of the market failure argument. The call for legislation to internalize negative externalities is proclaimed by the political science and economics professoriate and echoes through the halls of our finest universities. This takes place as the

[69] Alan S. Blinder, *Individual Choice is a Bad Fit for Covid Safety*, Wall St. J., Aug. 13, 2020, at A15.

universities that employ these professors and from which these calls emanate vigorously petition the government for legislative protection against civil liability for coronavirus infections. I am probably unable to come up with a better example of inattentional blindness than this. Tort law truly is the invisible gorilla.

3
Two Theories of Environmental Regulation

Most analyses of environmental regulation begin by referring to "The Tragedy of the Commons."[1] This one is no exception. Garrett Hardin's seminal article is usually cited for its account of how pollution and environmental degradation result from the tendency of human beings to overexploit resources held in common—what he calls the tragedy of the commons.

But "The Tragedy of the Commons" also has much to tell us about what are, and what are not, effective means of avoiding such potentially tragic consequences.

In this chapter, I extrapolate from Hardin's article to draw some conclusions regarding environmental regulation. Specifically, I argue that there are two distinct forms of environmental regulation, and that proper public policy analysis requires a comparative assessment of which constitutes the more effective means of combating any particular environmental problem.

I begin in Section I by describing the three basic lessons of "The Tragedy of the Commons." In Section II, I briefly rehearse the familiar application of the first of these lessons to demonstrate the causes of environmental degradation and pollution. In Section III, I apply the second of these lessons to demonstrate that environmental protection is correctly understood as a public policy problem, not an ethical one. In Section IV, I apply the third lesson to demonstrate that there are two potentially effective approaches

[1] Garrett Hardin, *The Tragedy of the Commons*, 162 Science 1243 (1968).

Common Law Liberalism. John Hasnas, Oxford University Press. © Oxford University Press 2024.
DOI: 10.1093/9780197784631.003.0004

to environmental regulation: common law privatization, and legislative restriction of access. I argue that common law privatization, which is frequently more effective, is typically and improperly ignored by public policy analysts. I conclude by suggesting that the sound public policy analysis of environmental issues must include a comparative assessment of the two approaches to environmental regulation.

I. The Lessons of "The Tragedy of the Commons"

"The Tragedy of the Commons" teaches three distinct lessons. The first, that commonly held resources will be overexploited,[2] is the one most frequently associated with the article. The other two—that the tragedy of the commons cannot be remedied by appealing to the consciences of those exploiting the resource[3] and that the only solutions to the tragedy are to privatize or restrict access to the resource[4]—are equally important, if less frequently remarked upon.

Hardin's most famous observation is that holding valuable resources in common presents a collective action problem even when the resources are renewable ones. Any renewable resource has a carrying capacity—a maximum number of individuals that can utilize the resource indefinitely without permanently damaging the ability of the resource to replenish itself. As long as the number of individuals exploiting a resource remains below the carrying capacity, the resource will continue to exist and provide benefit. Once the carrying capacity is exceeded, however, the resource will be totally consumed by the present users and yield no future benefit. When such a resource is held in common, the individuals utilizing it gain 100 percent of the benefit of their activities for

[2] *See id.* at 1244.
[3] *See id.* at 1246–1247.
[4] *See id.* at 1245.

themselves, but share the costs of their activities with all other users of the resource. As a result, it is in each individual's rational self-interest to continue to expand his or her use of the resource, despite the fact that if all do so, the carrying capacity of the resource will be exceeded and the resource destroyed. This is the tragedy of the commons.

Hardin illustrates this point with the example of herdsmen grazing their livestock on a common pasture.[5] As long as the number of livestock remains below the pasture's carrying capacity, the grass will have time to regrow between grazings. Yet each herdsman knows that if he adds an animal to his herd, he will gain the entire benefit of the sale of the animal for himself, but share the costs the animal imposes on the pasture with all other herdsman. Therefore, it always makes sense for him to add the animal. Since all herdsman reason in this way, the group continues to add animals to the pasture until its carrying capacity is exceeded and the pasture is destroyed.

Hardin's second point is that the tragedy of the commons cannot be remedied by appealing to the consciences of those exploiting the resource. At first blush, one might think that the destruction of commonly held resources can be avoided simply by acquainting those exploiting the resource with the situation and calling upon them to exercise self-restraint. Hardin points out, however, that people vary in their receptiveness to appeals to act against their own interests. The more scrupulous or public-spirited among those exploiting a resource may well respond to an appeal to their conscience to restrict their usage, and hence their personal gain, in order to preserve the resource for all. But the less scrupulous will reason that because the others are exercising self-restraint, they can expand their use of the resource without having to fear the resource's destruction. Thus, they will do so, gaining a competitive advantage over their more conscientious brethren. Over time,

[5] *See id.* at 1243.

this competitive advantage will flush the more scrupulous out of the marketplace. As a result, only those who are not receptive to appeals to conscience will be left exploiting the resource, which they will do until the resource's carrying capacity is exceeded and the resource is destroyed. As Hardin puts it, in a commons, conscience is self-eliminating.

This may be illustrated with Hardin's own example of herdsmen utilizing a common pasture. Imagine that the herdsmen hold a meeting at which the danger of exhausting the pasture is explained and all are called upon to voluntarily refrain from adding animals above a certain number to their herds. The herdsmen, who vary in how receptive they are to such appeals, can be ranked on what may be called a "conscientiousness scale." At the top of the scale are the most conscientious herdsman—those who regard their word as their bond or who are committed to the common good as a matter of principle. In the middle of the scale are the ordinarily conscientious herdsmen—those who normally keep their agreements and are usually willing to do their part in projects to achieve the common good. And at the bottom of the scale are the least conscientious herdsmen—those who are motivated primarily by self-interest and participate in projects to achieve the common good only to obtain benefits for themselves.

At first, all the herdsmen voluntarily limit their herds. However, before long, those at the bottom of the conscientiousness scale reason that because the other herdsmen are exercising self-restraint, they can increase the size of their herds without overgrazing the pasture. They do so, and reap gains relative to their more conscientious fellows. Some of the herdsmen in the middle of the conscientiousness scale are willing to limit their personal gain as long as everyone does so, but not if it means that others will gain at their expense. As they become aware of the actions of their lower-ranked brethren, they too begin to add animals to their herds in order to avoid being a "chump." Soon, enough herdsmen are violating the limit so that those even higher up on the scale, who would not abandon their self-restraint unless a significant number of others do, also begin to increase the size of their herds. Before long, the only herdsmen observing the limit are the most conscientious, for whom doing so is a matter of principle. But these herdsmen are placed at such a competitive disadvantage that eventually they can no longer operate profitably. At that point, the only herdsmen utilizing the pasture are those who are not receptive to an appeal to their conscience for self-restraint. Conscience has been eliminated from the pasture.

Hardin's third point is that the only solutions to the tragedy of the commons are to privatize the commonly held resource or to restrict access to it. Hardin published his essay in the journal *Science* because he was arguing that there are problems for which there are no technological solutions.[6] His point was that as long as the incentive structures of an open-access commons remain operative, the resource will be destroyed regardless of any technological progress human beings may make. Hardin contended that the only way to avoid the tragedy is to alter the incentive structures, and that there are only two ways to do this—privatize the commons or restrict access to it.

Privatizing the commons means giving those utilizing the resource an ownership interest in a portion of it. As owners, individuals have the right to exclude others from using their portion of the resource. This means not only that an individual's effort to preserve his or her portion of the resource cannot be defeated by costs imposed by others, but also that the individual cannot export his or her costs onto others, all of whom have a similar ownership interest. With regard to his or her portion of the former commons, each individual reaps 100 percent of the benefit of using the resource, but also bears 100 percent of the costs of doing so. Under these conditions, it is not in anyone's rational self-interest to exceed the carrying capacity of his or her portion of the resource. Hence,

[6] *See id.* at 1243.

privatization aligns the interests of individuals exploiting the resource with the common good of its preservation. Using economic terminology, privatization internalizes the social cost of using the resource.

In the example of the pasture, privatization means assigning each herdsman a portion of the pasture as his private property. Since only the individual herdsman can graze animals on his land, he does not have to fear that animals from other herds will overgraze and destroy his portion of the pasture. However, because he must graze his animals exclusively on his own land, he bears the entire cost his animals impose on the pasture. To remain in business, therefore, he must ensure that his herd does not exceed the carrying capacity of his portion of the pasture. Because all the herdsmen utilizing the privatized pasture have the same incentives, the carrying capacity of the pasture as a whole will not be exceeded, and the pasture will be preserved.

Restricting access to the commons means enlisting a coercive agency to limit the amount of use individuals can make of a common resource. This may be done by empowering some agency to impose financial penalties or other sanctions on any party using more of the resource than he or she is allotted. As long as the fine (properly discounted by the probability of the violation going undetected) is large enough or the alternative sanction frightening enough, the cost of overexploiting the resource will outweigh the benefit that may be obtained by doing so. When the enforcement mechanism is sufficiently effective, the incentives of the individuals exploiting the resource are altered so that it is no longer in anyone's rational self-interest to exceed his or her allotment. Hence, the carrying capacity of the resource will not be exceeded and the resource will be preserved.

Again using Hardin's example of the pasture for illustrative purposes, the herdsmen could collectively hire a "regulator" empowered to impose fines or other sanctions on any herdsman found to be grazing animals beyond his allotment on the pasture.

Although unscrupulous herdsmen may be tempted to add animals to their herd in excess of their allotment, fear of the sanction the regulator will impose causes them to resist the temptation. As a result, their more scrupulous colleagues are not tempted to exceed their allotment by the knowledge that others are gaining at their expense. The regulator's threat of coercion supplies what the bald appeal to conscience lacks, and the agreed-upon limits are observed.

II. Lesson One Applied: Environmental Degradation and Pollution

The first lesson of "The Tragedy of the Commons," that commonly held resources will be overexploited, may be applied in a perfectly straightforward manner to the problem of environmental degradation—the depletion of valuable natural resources—and, in a slightly less straightforward manner, to the problem of pollution—the spoliation of such resources by the admixture of destructive waste products. Little explanation is necessary with regard to environmental degradation. To the extent that natural resources are held in common, they are subject to the logic of "The Tragedy of the Commons." Consider, for example, the depletion of fishing stocks. This is merely Hardin's parable of the herdsmen transferred to the sea. When fisheries are open to all, each fisherman gains the full benefit of all the fish he takes but shares the cost of the depletion of the fishery with all other fishermen. Should any of the fishermen elect to restrict his take to allow the fishery to regenerate, his effort will be thwarted by other, less enlightened or less conscientious fishermen who simply increase their take. Hence, it is in every fisherman's interest to take as many fish as he or she can regardless of the effect this will have on the future usefulness of the fishery.

As another example, consider the problem of deforestation. When woodlands are held in common, as they are in vast swaths of the western United States, each logger gains the full benefit of every tree he or she harvests but shares the cost of deforestation with all other loggers and the public at large. No logger will invest resources in replanting trees because there is no guarantee that they will not be harvested by other loggers. Hence, it is in each logger's interest to clear as much land as he or she can and move on to the next forest, leaving nothing behind for future generations.

A similar account may be given with regard to the loss of species. Consider the African elephant. To the extent the herds are open to hunting by all, the elephant is a commonly held resource. Anyone killing an elephant gains the full benefit of the sale of its ivory tusks for himself or herself but shares the costs of the reduction in the size of the herds with everyone else. Restraining oneself from killing an elephant does not give that animal time to reproduce, but merely means that it will be killed by another hunter who will reap the gain from the sale of its tusks. This will continue until no elephants remain.

Further, endangered species are subject to the tragedy of the commons even if they have no commercial value in themselves. Farmers and ranchers kill gray wolves because they gain the full benefit of the livestock they thereby protect. Developers eliminate the habitat of snail darters because they gain the full benefit of the increased value of their property. Oil companies disrupt the mating patterns of caribou because they gain the full benefit of the oil they extract. Yet these parties share the cost of the loss of species with the world at large. Further, voluntarily refraining from their profit-making activity will not save any animals since others will move in to exploit the opportunities they forgo.

The story is slightly different with regard to pollution, where the problem arises not because something is being removed from the commons, but because something is being put into it. The logic, however, is entirely the same. Consider water pollution. Like any other resource, a river has a carrying capacity. As long as the waste that is discharged into it remains below a certain level, the river's flow is able to purify it.[7] Factories operating along the river frequently generate sludge or toxic chemicals as byproducts of their manufacturing processes. Paying others to dispose of such waste is a cost to the factories that can be avoided by discharging it into the commonly held river. By doing so, the factory reaps 100 percent of the benefit of avoiding this cost, yet shares the cost of the spoliation of the river with the world at large. Therefore, it is always in the factory owner's interest to discharge the waste into the river. And because all factory owners operating along the river reason in the same way, each increases the amount of waste he or she discharges into the river until the carrying capacity is exceeded.

The story is the same for air pollution. Factories, power plants, and automobiles produce soot, sulfur dioxide, ozone, and greenhouse gases as undesirable byproducts of their operation. Discharging them into the commonly held atmosphere provides factory, utility, and car owners with the full benefit of reduced waste-disposal costs while sharing the cost of the spoliation of the air with the world at large. Hence, it is in their interest to discharge the pollutants into the air regardless of the deterioration in overall air quality.

III. Lesson Two Applied: Protecting the Environment Is a Public Policy Problem

The second, but frequently overlooked, lesson of "The Tragedy of the Commons" is that in a commons, conscience is self-eliminating. The incentive structures of a commons are such that those who respond to appeals to their conscience—appeals to do

[7] In *The Tragedy of the Commons*, Hardin notes the old saying that "[f]lowing water purifies itself every 10 miles." *Id.* at 1245.

the right thing—are placed at a competitive disadvantage to those who do not. Over time, this competitive disadvantage eliminates the conscientious from the commons, leaving only the unscrupulous exploiting the commonly held resource. What this tells us is that environmental problems are problems of collective action—that is, public policy problems.

Many important ethical issues concern the discovery and application of the proper standards for individual action—the proper way for individual entities, whether human or corporate, to behave. Public policy issues concern the proper standards for collective action—the proper rules and decisions that will govern the actions of all members of a particular community or society. For example, the question of whether an individual woman should have an abortion is purely an ethical question. The question of whether any women should be permitted to have an abortion—of whether abortion should be legally banned—is a public policy question. "The Tragedy of the Commons" demonstrates that environmental problems are public policy problems that cannot be resolved by exhorting individuals to behave more ethically.

Recognizing that environmental problems are public policy problems is far from a trivial observation, for it implies that a significant portion of contemporary environmental activism is misguided. Over the past half-century, public awareness of and concern over environmental problems has skyrocketed. Air pollution, water pollution, the plight of endangered species, acid rain, pesticide use, the increasing generation of nonbiodegradable waste, the depletion of the ozone layer, and global warming are examples of environmental problems that have generated considerable public alarm. Environmental activists have reacted with calls for individuals, corporations, and even nations to alter their behavior. Individuals have been exhorted to drive smaller, less comfortable automobiles, purchase more expensive organic foods, and alter their lifestyle to reduce their "carbon footprint"; corporations to adopt profit-reducing programs of corporate social responsibility or sustainable development;[8] and nations to voluntarily restrain their industrial development and accept slower economic growth to reduce their greenhouse gas emissions. These are direct appeals to the consciences of individual parties to place the common good ahead of self-interest.

In calling on individual actors to behave better, activists are treating environmental problems as ethical problems—problems that arise because individuals either do not understand how or are unwilling to behave in the ethically proper way. Hardin's second lesson teaches that treating environmental problems as ethical problems is not only futile but self-defeating. Individuals who bear the discomfort of driving smaller cars or incur the expense of purchasing a hybrid in an effort to combat smog merely reduce the demand for oil, which keeps its price low enough for less conscientious citizens to indulge their desire to drive oversized SUVs. Firms that reduce their profit margins by adopting programs of corporate social responsibility or sustainable development create opportunities for less scrupulous entrepreneurs to capture their market share by employing less costly, but more environmentally damaging technology and make them ripe for takeover by new management promising to make the corporation "lean and mean." Nations whose citizens experience slower material welfare gains due to restriction on industrial development facilitate other nations' effort to attract the displaced industries by offering a less regulated business environment. In all such cases, conscientious parties bear the costs of efforts to protect the environment that are rendered ineffective by the actions of their less conscientious counterparts who profit at their expense.

The second lesson of "The Tragedy of the Commons" is that environmental problems are public policy problems—collective action

[8] Sustainable development is defined as "development which meets the needs of the present without compromising the ability of future generations to meet their own needs." World Commission on Environment and Development, Our Common Future, delivered to the General Assembly, U.N. Doc. A/42/427 (Aug. 4, 1987).

problems that must be addressed systemically. Hence, it is counterproductive to address such problems by exhorting individuals to more ethical behavior. As simple as this lesson is, it is one that many have not learned, at least if we are to judge by the literature and activities of many contemporary environmental activist groups.

IV. Lesson Three Applied: Two Theories of Environmental Regulation

Once it has been recognized that environmental problems are public policy problems that cannot be resolved by ethical appeals, it becomes clear that the only solution lies in the systemic reform of the incentive structure under which individual parties act. Hardin's third lesson is that in the context of commonly held resources, there are only two ways to alter incentives to align individuals' personal interests with the preservation of the resource: privatize the resource or restrict access to it. Unfortunately, half of this lesson is frequently overlooked by contemporary public policy analysts.

To assert that there are *only* two ways to resolve environmental problems is also to assert that there *are* two ways to resolve environmental problems. This implies that determining the optimal solution to environmental problems requires a comparative assessment. If environmental problems may be resolved either by privatizing the commonly held resource or by restricting access to it, the question of which approach will be more effective is always in play. Yet the conventional public policy analysis of environmental issues typically ignores the possibility of privatization.

The conventional analysis views decreasing environmental quality as an instance of market failure needing correction by legislation. This analysis derives from the classic market failure argument described in Chapter 2. Applying the first lesson of "The Tragedy of the Commons," the conventional approach observes that because the environment is a commons, private contacting parties personally bear only a small fraction of the costs their activities impose upon it, and hence, on all other members of society. The conclusion that is drawn is that environmental damage is a social cost of market activity that requires legislation such as the Clean Air Acts and Clean Water Acts to internalize the negative externalities.

Note that environmental legislation is a mechanism for restricting access to the commons. The Clean Air and Clean Water Acts restrict the amount and type of things that may be dumped into the nation's air and waters. In general, environmental legislation employs the coercive power of government to threaten individual market actors with sanctions if they overutilize the protected common resource.[9] Hence, the conventional analysis appears to assume that restricting access is the only solution to environmental problems.

The suppressed premise in the conventional analysis is that privatization is not a viable solution to environmental problems. This is not an unnatural assumption. After all, one cannot build fences around air or water. Nevertheless, it is an inappropriate one that rests on an overly narrow conception of privatization. Obviously, rights cannot be assigned to air, water, migratory animals, and other vagrant environmental resources in the same way they are assigned to land. But privatization is not limited to the creation of entitlements to tangible objects. Privatization refers to any assignment of rights that gives individuals a personal interest in preserving a resource. At its most general, the distinction between restricting access and privatizing consists in the difference between punishing those who pursue personal gain by overexploiting a commonly held resource and assigning rights in a way that causes individuals pursuing personal gain to act in ways that preserve the resource.

[9] The exception to this is cap-and-trade legislation, discussed *infra* at pp. 89–90, which is a hybrid form of legislation that combines restricting access—the cap—with privatization—the trading.

To the extent that it is possible to assign rights in such a way, the conventional public policy analysis of environmental issues is unsound. Demonstrating that in a commons, market forces produce socially suboptimal outcomes does not demonstrate that legislation designed to restrict access to the commons is required. It demonstrates only that *either* such legislation *or* an assignment of private rights to the commons is necessary, and that a comparative assessment of the effectiveness of each approach must be made.

To what extent is it possible to assign rights so as to privatize the environment? What mechanism can be used to make such assignments? The fact that the answers to these questions are not obvious is another example of the inattentional blindness discussed in Chapter 2—of the public policy community's intense focus on legislative solutions turning the operation of the common law into an invisible gorilla.

In Chapter 2, we saw that Anglo-American law is an amalgam of common law and legislation. Common law consists of rules that evolve over time in response to actual interpersonal conflicts. It forms without a guiding human intelligence and is a result of human action, but not human design. In contrast, legislation is the law that is consciously created by the political representatives of the community—law that reflects the politically dominant interest. The different mechanisms that give rise to each type of law are reflected in the different ways that they address environmental problems.

A. Common Law as a Privatization Mechanism

Common law is a mechanism by which human beings privatize commons. The rules of customary and common law arise from the process of settling actual disputes among the members of society. These rules are responses to the type of activities that bring human beings into conflict in the contemporary social environment. The conflicts engender efforts to resolve them in ways that restore peaceful interaction; the trial-and-error process of the common law discovers rules that do this successfully. When the conflicts arise from activities that overexploit a commonly held resource, the rules that result usually align individual incentives with the mutually beneficial use of the resource—that is, they privatize the resource.

Under the proper conditions, resources held in common may be used by the members of a community with little or no conflict. As long as human exploitation of a commonly held resource remains below the resource's carrying capacity, individuals may use as much of the resource as they wish without destroying others' ability to do the same. In such circumstances, conflicts over the use of the resource do not develop, and hence, neither do common law rules. The resource remains a commons.

However, when human activity approaches the carrying capacity of commonly held resources, conflicts develop over their use. As the grass in Hardin's pasture becomes relatively scarce, different herdsman will want to graze at the same location at the same time. In very primitive circumstances, such conflicts can give rise to violence. But resolving conflicts through violence tends to be expensive and highly disruptive to the life of the community in which it occurs. Hence, the violence itself produces an incentive to find alternative, more peaceful means of conflict resolution. In more civilized circumstances in which such alternatives have been found, the conflicts typically produce efforts at negotiated settlements or compositions that evolve into the practices that comprise the customary law. In relatively modern circumstances, they produce lawsuits heard before third-party decision-makers, the results of which are abstracted into the rules of common law. The rules specify how parties are permitted to act, creating entitlements that we call property rights.

In a society of hunter-gatherers, land would be held in common. In wandering across the countryside in search of game, fruit, and vegetables, the members of the community would have no reason to dispute the possession of a particular piece of ground. With no conflict to resolve, no rules of common law would evolve and the land would remain a commons. Should the community begin agricultural cultivation, the situation would change. Individuals who invest time and effort into planting would not take kindly to others who appropriate the crop that springs from their work. Because some portions of land are more fertile than others, different individuals will want to cultivate the same portions. The conflicts that result will have to be resolved, and the rules that result from these resolutions will almost assuredly create a mechanism by which individuals can exclude others from interfering with their use of the land. When this mechanism takes effect, the commons in land will be privatized.

The economist Harold Demsetz supplies what has become the classic example of this process with his description of the evolution of property rights among the Native American peoples of the Labrador Peninsula.[10] Before the fur trade brought by the Europeans, the members of the indigenous tribes treated the land on which they hunted as a commons. In hunting fur-bearing animals to supply themselves with food and furs, they did not approach the land's carrying capacity for such species. All hunters could satisfy their needs without undermining other hunters' ability to do the same. Hence, no conflicts developed. With the advent of the fur trade, the number of animals being hunted increased dramatically, approaching the carrying capacity of the land. The scarcity of game brought hunters into conflict, which was resolved by adopting the custom of blazing the trees with their crests to mark off individual hunting territories. The recognition and enforcement of this custom removed the fur-bearing game from the commons, effectively privatizing it.

[10] Harold Demsetz, *Toward a Theory of Property Rights*, 57 AM. ECON. REV. 347 (1967).

To the extent that private property reduces the incidence of social conflict, the common law is an engine of its creation. Independently of any consideration of real property, almost all of what we call intangible property arose through the common law process. Commercial instruments such as promissory notes, bills of lading, bills of exchange, stocks, and bonds all emerged from the Law Merchant—the customary commercial law that arose out of the settlement of actual disputes by medieval merchants.[11] Similarly, intellectual property such as trademarks, trade secrets, and copyright are all products of the common law. The same creative process is currently at work producing private rights in cyberspace.[12]

However, the property rights that evolve through the common law process are not the idealized, conceptually pristine rights to exclusive use and control that philosophers like to discuss. Rather, they are a subtle, nuanced bundle of rights that extend only as far as necessary to facilitate peaceful social interaction. Demsetz's own example provides an interesting illustration of this. Included in the anthropological evidence of Native American practices that he supplies is the observation that hunters could enter others' privatized territories to hunt for meat as long as they left the fur and tail behind for the territory's "owner." Because it was the animals' fur that had increased in value, disputes arose over the possession of the pelt, rather than the animal itself. Hence, the solution that evolved privatized the pelts, but not the meat, which was all that was necessary to prevent conflict.

Common law property rights generally reflect this. The essential element of the right to property is the right to exclude others. Yet one may not convey an enclosed estate to another and then exclude the owner from crossing one's property to access that estate. In such cases, an easement of necessity permits what would otherwise be a

[11] *See* HAROLD BERMAN, LAW AND REVOLUTION 349–350 (1983).

[12] *See* Bruce Benson, *The Spontaneous Evolution of Cyber Law: Norms. Property Rights, Contracting, Dispute Resolution and Enforcement without the State*, 1 J. L. ECON. & POL'Y 269 (2005).

trespass.[13] It is not difficult to see why the common law would carve out such an exception to the right to control one's property since a contrary rule that permitted an owner to convey land to another and then deprive him or her of the ability to use it would invite, rather than reduce, conflict.

Similarly, the common law doctrine of adverse possession is at odds with the idealized conception of property. Adverse possession allows one to acquire ownership of another's property by making open and notorious use of it for a prescribed period of time if the owner takes no action to stop the usage.[14] To the philosopher, it may seem unjust that an interloper may acquire good title to another's property merely by making continuous unauthorized use of it. But the common law evolves in ways designed to reduce conflicts, not effect perfect justice. One who makes open and notorious use of property sends a message to the public that he or she has title to the property. An owner who takes no action to contradict that message invites the public to deal with the interloper as though he or she held title—an invitation that sows the seeds of future conflict. The common law rules of property evolved a duty for owners to prevent misleading messages about who holds title because such a duty reduces the potential for disputes.[15]

[13] *See* RESTATEMENT (THIRD) OF PROPERTY § 2.15 (2000). This rule, which applies when the two estates had once been held by the same owner, "can be traced back in the common law at least as far as the 13th century." *Id.* at cmt. 1.

[14] EDWARD H. RABIN ET AL., FUNDAMENTALS OF MODERN PROPERTY LAW, 4th ed. (2000), 789.

[15] Carol Rose makes this point by stating that property owners have a duty to "make and keep their communications clear" because

> clear titles facilitate trade and minimize resource-wasting conflict. If I am careless about who comes onto a corner of my property, I invite others to make mistakes and to waste their labor on improvements to what I have allowed them to think is theirs. I thus invite a free-for-all over my ambiguously held claims, and I encourage contention, insecurity, and litigation—all of which waste everyone's time and energy and may result in overuse or underuse of resources. But if I keep my property claims clear, others will know that they should deal with me directly if they want to use my property. We can bargain rather than fight; through trade, all items will come to rest in the hands of those who value them most.

Carol Rose, *Possession as the Origin of Property*, 52 U. CHI. L. REV. 73, 81–83 (1985).

Hence, the common law does not produce conceptually perfect property rights, merely the degree of privatization necessary to channel human interaction away from conflict and toward cooperation. However, that degree of privatization is often all that is needed to escape the tragedy of the commons. A good illustration of this is provided by the medieval open-field system of agriculture, in which the common law process produced an amalgam of individual rights and group control. Rural villages were usually organized around two or three large common fields bordered by hedges or fences. Large-scale decisions regarding the management of these fields, such as what to plant, which portion to leave fallow, etc., were made collectively by the group. But individuals had private rights to harvest the crops on various noncontiguous strips scattered throughout the fields, as well as other private rights to use the common field.[16] This produced fields that have been described as "marble cake[s] of group and individual property rights."[17] Yet this semi-privatized marble cake was sufficient to properly align individual incentives with the preservation of the resource.[18]

Indeed, in some circumstances, common law privatization does not produce individualized property rights at all. Sometimes, all that is necessary to align incentives is a set of rules governing the resource's use that provides benefits to all members of the relevant group. In cases in which a group that is exploiting a resource is capable of self-management, the common law may produce

[16] For a good account of the private "common rights" that evolved at customary and common law, *see* Jane Buck Cox, *No Tragedy of the Commons*, 7 Environmental Ethics 53–55 (1985).

[17] Robert C. Ellickson, *Property in Land*, 102 Yale Law Journal 1388 (1993).

[18] Robert Ellickson writes: "Most economic historians regard the open-field system as an efficient institution during its prime in the high Middle Ages. Medieval farmers, recognizing that efficient boundary locations varied, devised a clever way to change land boundaries on a seasonal basis. The agricultural activities for which there were efficiencies of scale—harvesting, fencing, shepherding—were performed jointly on commonly accessible land according to explicit bylaw or implicit contract ('the custom of the manor'). The small agricultural events that lacked returns to scale—planting, weeding, thinning—were stimulated through the direct material incentives of private land ownership." *Id.* at 1391.

group, rather than individual, property rights. Specifically, under circumstances in which "the administrative costs of customary management are low relative to those of an individual property system,"[19] the common law process tends to produce a managed commons rather than individual entitlements.[20] Thus, the common law produced not fully privatized avenues of transportation, but "roads and waterways [that] were 'managed commons,' where customary practices ameliorated congestion and external harms, and where alternative property regimes might not have been worth the expense, so long as the country was relatively undeveloped."[21]

Carol Rose provides an interesting illustration of the subtlety of the common law process of privatization with her account of the development of common law water rights during the nineteenth century.[22] She notes that although the value of river water increased in England and the United States, the reasons for its increase in England and the eastern United States were different than the reasons for its increase in the western United States. In England and the eastern United States, the main value of the water was as a source of power, which, with the advent of the Industrial Revolution, was in increasing demand. This use did not decrease the amount of water in the river, but did affect its flow. In the

[19] Carol Rose, *The Comedy of the Commons: Custom, Commerce, and Inherently Public Property*, 53 U. Chic. L. Rev. 744 (1986).

[20] Carol Rose notes that many theorists believe that there is a "natural history of property rights when resources are growing scarcer: a stage 1 of plenty, where any given resource is unowned, unmanaged, and open to all; a stage 2, where the resource is less plentiful and is appropriated by a group and subjected to somewhat diffuse common-property arrangements, often customary; and a final stage 3, in which the resource is scarce enough to be subject to full-blown individualized property rights." Carol Rose, "Energy and Efficiency in the Realignment of Common Law Water Rights," in Carol Rose, Property and Persuasion 164 (1994). Rose points out, however, that property rights do not necessarily evolve in this order, arguing persuasively that the process can stop at stage 2, and that stage 2 and stage 3 can often be reversed. Her point, which I believe to be correct, is that common law evolution tends to find the most apt solution in the particular circumstances, whether this fits scholars' theoretical models or not.

[21] Rose, *The Comedy of the Commons*, *supra* note 19, at 745.

[22] *See* Carol Rose, *Energy and Efficiency in the Assignment of Property Rights*, *in* Property and Persuasion: Essay on the History, Theory, and Rhetoric of Ownership 163 (1994).

western United States, the main value of the water came from its use in mining operations and for irrigation, the demand for which was increasing with rising population. These uses extracted water from the rivers, decreasing its amount.

The common law rules that evolved in England and the East only partially privatized the water. Riparian owners received only the right to prevent unreasonable uses of the water—uses that would destroy its value to downstream users by obstructing its flow. Otherwise, the river remained an open commons. But this level of privatization was all that was required to preserve the value of the resource, which was its flow. In contrast, the rules that evolved in the western United States fully privatized water by recognizing individual, tradeable rights to it.[23] In the West, full privatization was necessary to internalize the social cost of appropriating river water to prevent it from being totally consumed. Although the common law process produced different rules in different locations, the rules that evolved provided precisely the degree of privatization necessary to avoid the tragedy of the commons.

In sum, the common law privatizes commons not by erecting fences around resources, but by aligning the incentives of individuals with their preservation. It is not unreasonable to think of the common law process as a legal version of Adam Smith's invisible hand. It erects a structure of rules within which individuals pursuing their own legal interests also advance the general good.

B. Legislation as a Mechanism for Restricting Access

Because it is intentionally created, legislation can be used in a variety of ways. With regard to matters that impact the environment,

[23] For a fuller account of the development of water rights in the western United States, see Terry Anderson and P. J. Hill, *The Evolution of Property Rights: A Study of the American West*, 18 Journal of Law and Economics 1, 177–178 (1975).

legislation may be used to preserve commons, to "commonize" private property, to restrict access to commons, and in some cases to privatize commons. However, generally speaking, legislation is a mechanism by which human beings preserve and restrict access to the commons.

Governments regularly use legislation to preserve commons. State and federal parks are examples of land that is maintained as commons by legislative action. From the point of view of the nonindigenous Americans living east of the Mississippi in the early nineteenth century, the land encompassed by the Louisiana Purchase constituted a commons. The federal government set the terms under which this land could be reduced to private ownership, but in so doing legislatively designated large portions of it to be preserved as commonly held public land. A large percentage of the western United States still consists of such public land. Similarly, legislation guarantees that the lands under the coastal waters of the United States are preserved as commons shared by the state and federal governments.[24]

Having preserved a commons in land, government then protects it against overexploitation by restricting access to it. State and federal legislation[25] determines the nature of the use that can be made of public land and conditions under which individuals may undertake such use. Legislation banning snowmobiles and dune buggies from national parks and oil drilling in the Arctic National Wildlife Refuge serve as good examples of managing the commons by legislatively restricting access to it.

The electro-magnetic spectrum is a commons. With the advent of radio and the demands placed on it by the increasing number of broadcasters, it became a commons that was approaching its carrying capacity. Congress addressed this by passing the Radio Act

[24] *See* Submerged Lands Act of 1953, 43 U.S.C.A. §§ 1301–1315 (West 2007).

[25] For purposes of concision, the term "legislation" is being used to encompass regulations issued by administrative agencies.

of 1927, which ensured that the spectrum remained a commons by prohibiting private ownership of broadcast channels, and required a federal license to broadcast.[26] By limiting the number of licenses issued and the use rights granted by each license, the legislation was designed to preserve the value of the commonly held spectrum by restricting access to it.

The rivers and other waters of the United States, which were partially privatized by the common law, remained a commons with respect to the introduction of pollutants that did not obstruct the water's flow. As the amount of pollutants discharged into these waters increased over the course of the twentieth century, they began to undermine the value of the water as a resource—that is, they began to approach the water's carrying capacity. Congress responded with the Clean Water Acts,[27] which set limits on the types and amounts of pollutants that may be discharged into the navigable waters of the United States—a clear example of managing a commons by restricting access. Similarly, the atmosphere over the United States is a common resource that was being damaged by its overexploitation as a waste-disposal medium. Congress addressed this by legislatively restricting access to the atmosphere in the Clean Air Acts.

In addition to preserving resources as commons, legislation is often used to "commonize" private property. The most obvious example of this is when government exercises the power of eminent domain to take private property for a public use—for example, condemning private property to build an open access roadway. However, legislative commonization is not always so direct.

Whenever legislation transfers the management of property from private to public hands, it essentially returns the property to the commons. For example, the Clean Water Act gives the

[26] Radio Act of 1927 47 U.S.C.A. § 83, repealed by ch. 652, § 602(a), 48 Stat. 1102 (West 2007).

[27] Federal Water Pollution Control Act of 1948, 33 U.S.C. § 466 (1948), subsequently amended by The Clean Water Act 33 U.S.C. § 1251–1387.

Army Corps of Engineers the power to prevent dredging, filling, or building on wetlands, which is defined as land that is saturated by surface or ground water frequently enough to support vegetation adapted for life in saturated soil conditions.[28] When the Corps finds that private property includes a wetland, it can prevent the owner from making any productive use of that portion of his or her property. By removing the owner's right to control the property, the legislation effectively commonizes it, simultaneously restricting access to it as a means of preventing its destruction.

A similar example of legislative commonization is supplied by the Endangered Species Act. When a plant or animal is placed on the endangered species list, any alteration to its habitat that may threaten its survival is prohibited. When endangered species are found on private property, the law prohibits the owner from altering his or her land, once again passing control of the property from private to public hands. By preventing the private owner from managing the property and restricting access to it, the law has again effectively commonized the property.

Legislation may also be crafted to simultaneously restrict access and partially privatize a commons. For example, cap-and-trade environmental legislation establishes an upper limit, or cap, on the amount of a pollutant that may be discharged into a commons and creates and distributes tradeable permits to discharge specified amounts of the pollutant, the total of which is equal to the cap. The legislation also bars anyone from discharging the pollutant into the commons without such a permit. Those who wish to discharge the pollutant into the commons must now pay for the right to do so. Those who reduce the amounts they discharge below the level allowed by the permits they hold may sell their unused allotment to others, reaping rewards from their reduction in pollution. The cap restricts access to the commons; the ability to buy and sell pollution permits aligns the incentives of individuals with the reduction of

[28] *See* Definition of Waters of the United States, 40 C.F.R. 230.3 (2006).

pollution, privatizing the commons with respect to the discharge of the regulated pollutant.

Finally, legislation can privatize commonly held property. The Homestead Act of 1862, which allowed citizens to gain ownership of public land by working on it for a specified number of years, is probably the preeminent example of this type of legislation. However, any legislation that auctions off commonly held resources, such as the FCC auction of wireless airwaves, has this character. Thus, legislation *could* be employed to address environmental problems by privatizing the commons. However, there are very few examples of such legislation. Although in recent years there has been a greater utilization of the hybrid cap-and-trade legislation, it is nevertheless the case that environmental legislation is almost always designed to preserve the commons by restricting access to it.

C. The Comparative Assessment, or Why Doing Nothing Is Doing Something

Anglo-American law provides two distinct models of environmental regulation: the common law model of privatization, which aligns individual incentives with the preservation of the resource, and the legislative model, which preserves the commons by punishing individuals who overexploit the resource. Therefore, good environmental management requires a comparative analysis of the two models to decide which measures are most appropriate for the protection of various resources. Such comparative analyses rarely take place, however. Why?

When a threat to an important environmental resource is identified, there is a virtually irresistible desire to do something about it. But the common law model of regulation is a decentralized, evolutionary model. The rules evolve in response to actual conflicts through a process of trial and error. This implies that the rules do not evolve until the problem is acute enough to give rise to conflicts. Although the common law process typically produces practical, effective rules that have been informed by human experience, it does not produce them right away. As a result, there can be a considerable delay between the initial recognition of an environmental problem and the development of the common law regulation that addresses it. Further, the rules that arise through the common law process are not crafted by any identifiable guiding intelligence. They evolve. They are not created. Hence, no particular human being is acting directly to solve the problem. For these reasons, allowing the common law regulatory process to work can appear to be doing nothing.

From the perspective of those concerned about protecting the environment, however, doing nothing is not an option. Without a good understanding of the evolutionary mechanism of the common law, it is natural to assume that doing something means doing something *intentionally*. And in the legal context, doing something intentionally means enacting legislation. Comparative analyses of the common law and legislative approaches to environmental regulation are rarely made because the common law approach is frequently associated with simply failing to address the problem.

This is unfortunate because there are many situations in which common law regulation is likely to be the more effective approach. If I may be forgiven for using a sports analogy, addressing environmental problems can be like playing defense in soccer. When confronted with an attacking player, a defender must decide whether to attempt to tackle the ball away or maintain his or her position between the attacker and the goal. Under certain circumstances, such as when the attacker is going in on a breakaway, the right play is to attempt the tackle. In most situations, however, the proper play is for the defender to maintain his or her position, doing no more than impeding the attacker's progress and creating time for his or her teammates to get into an effective defensive alignment. This type of play requires great patience and self-control by the defender, who must resist the temptation to "do something" by tackling the ball. Although a successful tackle would stop the attack, an unsuccessful tackle could spell disaster by allowing the attacker a clear shot at the goal. When playing properly, a defender may appear to be standing still, but he or she is not doing nothing. The defender is creating time for a dynamic defensive system to adjust to a threat. Similarly, in the context of environmental regulation, those who have the patience and self-control necessary to resist the temptation to immediately pass laws restricting access to a common resource may appear to be standing still legislatively, but they are not doing nothing. They are creating time for the dynamic common law regulatory system to adjust to a new environmental threat.

Two of the most potent common law weapons against pollution are the torts of trespass and nuisance. One is liable for trespass whenever one intentionally causes something to enter another's land[29] and for nuisance whenever one interferes with the private use and enjoyment of another's land.[30] To the extent that one exploits the commons in air, rivers, or other bodies of water in ways that one knows will either deposit pollutants on another's land or negatively impact the value of that land, one may be sued for trespass or nuisance. Such liability judgments shift the cost of the polluting activity back onto the polluter, thereby internalizing the social cost of exploiting the commons, effectively privatizing it.[31] Such lawsuits have been used to curtail the dumping of sewage and industrial waste into rivers[32] and the air.[33] To what extent can such

[29] *See* Restatement (Second) of Torts § 158 (2000).

[30] *See* Restatement (Second) of Torts § 821D (2000).

[31] When a polluter exploits a commons in a way likely to cause an unreasonable level of harm to the land of another, the landowner may obtain an injunction to terminate the activity. See W. Page Keeton, et. al, Prosser and Keeton on Torts 631 (5th ed. 1984).

[32] *See*, e.g., Sammons v. City of Gloversville, 175 N.Y. 346 (1903); Whalen v. Union Bag & Paper Co. 208 N.Y. 1 (1913).

[33] *See*, e.g., Boomer v. Atlantic Cement Co., 257 N.E. 2d 870 (1970). It has been suggested that the continued development of such common law environmental causes

privatization via lawsuit replace legislation designed to restrict access?

Acid rain damages forests, buildings, and the aquatic life in lakes and streams. It is caused by industrial activity that releases sulfur dioxide and nitrogen oxides into the atmosphere. The federal government addressed this problem legislatively in the 1990 Clean Air Act Amendments by directly limiting emissions of nitrogen oxides and adopting a cap-and-trade program for the emission of sulfur dioxide. By all accounts, this approach has been quite effective, achieving the required reductions in emissions at lower than anticipated costs. Could the same or more reductions have been accomplished through common law nuisance suits?[34] Would such

of action could provide most of the environmental protection now afforded by federal environmental law. *See* H. Marlow Green, *Common Law, Property Rights and the Environment: A Comparative Analysis of Historical Developments in the United States and England and a Model for the Future*, 30 CORNELL INT'L L. J. 541 (1997).

[34] What would such lawsuits look like? How can there be a lawsuit when those whose property has been damaged do not know which polluter to hold responsible? But the common law has encountered this problem before and has already evolved a response to it: market-share liability. In cases in which the plaintiff has been damaged by a product produced by several manufacturers but cannot identify the particular manufacturer who caused his or her injury, the plaintiff may join all available manufacturers as defendants. As long as the defendants constitute a substantial share of the market for the offending product, the plaintiff can recover damages from each defendant in proportion to the defendant's share of the market for the product at the relevant time. *See Sindell v. Abbott Laboratories*, 26 Cal. 3d 588 (1980).

What if an individual property owner's damage is too slight to make it worthwhile to pursue a lawsuit? But the common law has encountered this problem before and has already evolved a response to it: the class action lawsuit, which allows the joinder of many small claims of damage presenting essentially the same factual issues into one suit. Won't polluters merely regard lawsuits as a cost of doing business to be absorbed and continue with their polluting activities? Perhaps, but the common law has encountered this problem before and has already evolved a response to it: the injunction. In trespass and nuisance suits, a plaintiff can sue not merely for damages, but for an injunction that orders the defendant to refrain from the activity that is causing the plaintiff's injury

The essential characteristic of the common law is that it learns. At any point in time, there are interpersonal wrongs that it does not adequately address. But it is precisely these inadequacies that spur the legal innovations that produce new procedures and remedies. I can describe how the common law would be likely to handle lawsuits over acid rain because the problems that beset such suits are similar to those that have arisen and been resolved in the past. I cannot, however, predict how the common law will address novel environmental problems that present entirely new challenges. This is precisely the reason for advocating common law environmental regulation: to learn how to

suits have been a more or less costly way of addressing the acid rain problem? We don't know because no comparative analysis of the alternative approaches has been done. Waiting for the common law solution was seen as doing nothing, rather than as giving a mechanism for internalizing social costs on the basis of actual experience time to operate.

Tort reform is currently a high-profile political issue. A broad coalition of business and intellectual interests is actively lobbying Congress and the state legislatures to pass legislation curtailing the ability of plaintiffs to recover damage judgments. Tort reform advocates typically accuse plaintiffs' attorneys of employing creative and expansive interpretations of the common law to undemocratically overregulate the business environment in ways that have never been approved by voters. They claim that liberal discovery rules and low evidentiary thresholds for establishing a cause of action coupled with the availability of class action lawsuits, joint and several liability, and punitive damages force businesses to bear too large a share of the cost of protecting the public against injury. But, of course, plaintiff's attorneys are just as clever and creative when the injury is due to pollution as they are when it is due to defective products. There is every reason to believe that they will seek ways to adapt the law of trespass and nuisance to emerging environmental threats. If the tort reform advocates are correct, and if the problem with the contemporary tort system is that it is too highly regulative, refraining from legislative efforts to solve environmental problems in order to allow this system to operate can hardly be regarded as doing nothing.

In this chapter, I am arguing only that with regard to any particular environmental issue, proper public policy analysis requires a comparative assessment of the efficacy of common law privatization and legislative restriction of access. I nevertheless believe that such assessments will usually favor the common law approach

align private incentives with the preservation of resources that are not easily reduced to physical possession.

over the legislative one. This is because of both the incentives inherent in each approach and the mechanism by which each creates regulations.

Common law privatization functions by changing the incentive structure so that it is in individuals' self-interest to act in ways that preserve the relevant environmental resource. This minimizes problems of enforcement. Because individuals benefit from behaving responsibility, common law solutions tend to be self-enforcing. Furthermore, because the rules that align the incentives grow out of the settlement of real-world disputes, they are informed by the way human beings actually behave. Hence, they are rarely undermined by the type of unanticipated consequences that beset theoretically constructed solutions. Finally, the self-correcting nature of the common law process renders it flexible enough to adapt to any such unanticipated consequences or changes in conditions that tend to undermine the efficacy of the rules. To the extent that the rules do not properly align individual incentives, the resulting conflicts give rise to increased litigation, which abates only when a more effective set of rules is found.

In contrast, legislatively restricting access to common resources leaves the incentive to overexploit the resource intact and attempts to punish those who respond to it. In this situation, individuals can always benefit from undetected cheating, which creates considerable enforcement problems—a fact evidenced by the Environmental Protection Agency's employment of armed agents in its Criminal Investigation Division.[35] Further, this state of affairs also creates a powerful incentive for individuals to engage in rent-seeking—the expenditure of resources to influence legislators or regulators to draw up the rules restricting access in ways that favor their interests over those of their competitors or the common good. Thus, regulations under the Clean Air Act Amendments of 1970 were written to require the installation

[35] *See United States v. Knott*, 106 F. Supp. 2d 174, 180 (D. Mass. 2000).

of scrubbers in the smokestacks of coal-burning power plants rather than to establish maximum ambient levels for pollutants (even though requiring scrubbers had greater costs and left the air dirtier) in order to protect the interests of coal miners in West Virginia, which was represented by Robert Byrd, one of the most powerful US senators. Requiring the air to be cleaned after the coal was burned neutralized the economic advantages of the cleaner-burning coal mined in the western United States over the dirty-burning coal mined in West Virginia.[36] Finally, because legislation is abstract in nature and formed in response to political influences rather than the practical demands of human interaction, it frequently produces counterproductive unanticipated consequences. A good illustration of this is the global food crisis in 2008, which was due, in part, to legislative mandates for the use of biofuels in the United States and several other countries despite the fact that the production of ethanol is environmentally more damaging than burning fossil fuels.[37]

The common law also provides a flexible and adaptive method of creating environmental regulations. As the technological and social conditions of life in society change in ways that give rise to new sources of conflict, the trial-and-error process of common law evolution creates a feedback loop that helps human beings learn what rules most effectively resolve such conflicts. As such, the common law functions as a discovery process. This is extremely important when dealing with emerging threats to environmental resources

[36] *See* IAIN MCLEAN, PUBLIC CHOICE: AN INTRODUCTION 71–76 (1987).

[37] The *Washington Post* reported that

> [A] study published in Science magazine Feb. 29 concluded that greenhouse-gas emissions from corn and even cellulosic ethanol "exceed or match those from fossil fuels and therefore produce no greenhouse benefits." By encouraging an expansion of acreage, the study added, the use of U.S. cropland for ethanol could make climate conditions dramatically worse. And the runoff from increased use of fertilizers on expanded acreage would compound damage to waterways all the way to the Gulf of Mexico.

Steven Mufson, *Siphoning Off Corn to Fuel Our Cars*, WASH POST, April 30, 2008 at A8.

that are not easily privatized, such as air, water, endangered species, biodiversity, the ozone layer, and perhaps even climate stability. Through trial and error based on real-world experience, the common law learns what most effectively aligns the incentives of various human actors. Thus, it teaches us how best to privatize resources that cannot be reduced to physical possession. How else could we learn that riparian rights were the proper way to privatize rivers in England and the eastern United States, but that tradable water rights were needed in the western United States?

In contrast, legislation tends to be a rather rigid, all-eggs-in-one-basket method of creating environmental regulations, and one that is quite opaque to feedback. Given the nature of the political process, it can be crucially important to get the legislation restricting access to the commons right on the first try. This is because, once enacted, such legislation tends to become entrenched as the groups that benefit from it resist change. For example, it would be quite difficult to change the requirement of smokestack scrubbers in coal-burning power plants while Robert Byrd remained a powerful senator. Hence, legislation restricting access to the commons frequently cannot be changed without considerable political struggle, regardless of its effectiveness. Yet because legislation necessarily consists of rules that have run the gauntlet of special interest lobbying, political logrolling, and partisan compromising, there is reason to doubt whether its initial configuration will represent the most effective way of protecting the environment. In addition, because legislation supplants the common law, employing it to restrict access to the commons terminates the common law learning process. Thus, in opting for legislative rather than common law solutions to environmental problems, we are abandoning our opportunity to learn from experience, and betting our environmental future on the suitability of abstract rules generated by an explicitly political process. We are also abandoning a self-correcting regulatory mechanism for one that can be changed only through political struggle.

These considerations lead me to believe that the legislative approach will be preferable to the common law approach only where it is impossible to align incentives or in emergency situations in which the time lag associated with common law privatization is intolerable and there is reason to believe the legislative process could react more rapidly. To return to the soccer analogy, legislation is likely to be the superior option only in situations comparable to an attacker going in on a breakaway or when time is running out in the game. Ordinarily, however, giving the common law time to teach us how to privatize a common resource will be a more effective way of preserving it than utilizing the political process to legislatively restrict access to it. In most cases, doing nothing *legislatively* is doing something very significant indeed.

D. How One Woman Saved the Seahorse, or How to Do Something while Doing Nothing

In support of my contention that common law privatization will usually be a superior approach to environmental problems than legislatively restricting access, consider the following illustrative example.[38]

The seahorse, once plentiful, has recently come under threat of extinction. Many people in China believe the seahorse to have beneficial medicinal and aphrodisiac properties. With China's economic liberalization and greater participation in world trade, demand for seahorses sharply increased. As a result, the global supply of seahorses fell precipitously.

Prior to the 1980s, the waters off the coast of the Philippines were plentifully stocked with seahorses. The Philippine seahorse fishery was a commons that all seahorse fishermen were free to

[38] The information on which this illustration is based is taken from the PBS science show *Nova*, "The Kingdom of the Seahorse," broadcast on April 15, 1997.

exploit. However, as Philippine fishermen increased the number of seahorses they caught to meet the increased demand from China, the take began to approach the carrying capacity of the fishery.

Handumon is a village in one of the most impoverished regions of the Philippines. For much of its population, the sale of seahorses constituted the only source of income beyond subsistence fishing. By the mid-1990s, the population of seahorses in these waters was rapidly declining. One reason for this was the harvesting of pregnant seahorses, each of whom carried large numbers of young, before they could give birth. No fisherman was willing to forgo harvesting pregnant seahorses because doing so merely meant another fisherman would take the seahorse and the first would have relinquished an immediate benefit for no resulting gain, a clear example of the tragedy of the commons at work.

At this time, Amanda Vincent, a marine biologist concerned about the preservation of the seahorse, came to Handumon. After living in the community for a while and observing their practices, she showed the local fishermen how to construct netting with mesh small enough to contain adult seahorses, but large enough to allow newly born fish to escape to the open sea. Armed with this knowledge, the fishermen built personal floating cages in which they placed any pregnant seahorses that they found. They then allowed the seahorses to give birth before removing them from the water for sale. Similarly to the Native Americans in Demsetz's account, the custom evolved of treating the cages as private property acquired by the labor invested to gain possession of the fish they contained.

Encouraged by this experience, the fishermen agreed to one of Vincent's suggestions to place a portion of the reef near their village off-limits to all fishing in an attempt to increase the seahorse population in the surrounding waters. In effect, they created a commons informally managed by the community, with individual members of the community having the right to take a share of the surplus it generated.[39] This practice was successful at further increasing the local seahorse population.

This situation was stable until word of the increased population of seahorses near Handumon spread up and down the Philippine coast, causing fishermen from surrounding islands and villages to begin to "poach" seahorses from Handumon's preserve. In response, the Handumon villagers began patrolling the waters around the preserve to keep the poachers out. In addition, to further increase the security of the resource and its yield, the Handumon fishermen, with Vincent's help, began to organize fully privatized seahorse farms.

Eventually, fishermen from surrounding areas came to Handumon to learn what the villagers were doing and copied their techniques. As a result, the seahorse population of the entire region is rapidly recovering.

In my opinion, this story provides an interesting modern-day illustration of the customary/common law process of privatization at work. Note, however, that it is not a tale of the purely spontaneous evolution of property rights, as Demsetz's account of the native peoples of the Labrador Peninsula purports to be. Amanda Vincent, who played a significant role in the process, was an outsider who came to Handumon because of her desire to save the seahorse. But she came as a researcher, not a regulator. As her account of the Handumon project makes clear, to advance her goal, she had to enter into the life of the community, earn the trust of the fishermen, and learn through a process of trial and error how best to align the interests of the fishermen with the preservation of the species. As one who invested her own time, effort, and resources

[39] This arrangement has much in common with the medieval common-field system of agriculture and is a good example of Carol Rose's second stage in the evolution of private property, in which "the resource is less plentiful and is appropriated by a group and subjected to somewhat diffuse common-property arrangements, often customary." Carol Rose, *Energy and Efficiency in the realignment of Common Law Water Rights, in* PROPERTY AND PERSUASION 163, 164 (1994). *See supra* note 20.

into a speculative project to realize the environmental value of species preservation, it would be fair to call Amanda Vincent an environmental entrepreneur.

The presence of such an entrepreneur does not mean that the common law process is not at work. Even in the most primitive systems, there always must be individuals who first advance the ideas that gain customary acceptance. In a sense, every plaintiff's attorney working on a contingency fee who argues for a novel interpretation of the common law is operating as an entrepreneur. Saying that the common law process does not involve intentional law-making does not imply that it involves no intentional action *by individuals.* It involves constant intentional action by individuals trying to solve social problems. Its distinguishing feature is the open-ended, trial-and-error feedback mechanism it employs to select among these intentionally crafted solutions. Common law privatization requires that we do nothing collectively through legislation, not that we do nothing individually.

Contrast the Handumon project with the effort to protect endangered species by maintaining them as a common resource and legislatively restricting access to them. Examples of this approach are embodied in the Endangered Species Act (ESA) in the United States and the worldwide Convention on International Trade in Endangered Species of Wild Fauna and Flora (CITES). ESA radically restricts access to endangered species. Under the act, once a species has been declared endangered, any effort to "harass, harm, pursue, hunt, shoot, wound, kill, trap, capture, or collect" any member of that species is prohibited.[40] Further, one harms an endangered species whenever one modifies its habitat in a way that impairs the animals' "essential behavioral patterns, including breeding, feeding, or sheltering."[41] CITES indirectly restricts access to endangered species by banning international trade in

[40] 16 U.S.C. §1532(19).
[41] 50 CFR § 17.3 (1994).

protected animals and their byproducts. Each attempts to preserve endangered species by protecting each and every member of such species. Under ESA and CITES, actions like those undertaken by the Handumon fishermen that involved killing and selling individual animals would be blatantly illegal.

In contrast to the Handumon situation, which was marked by an increasing degree of voluntary cooperation, the legislative approach is beset with significant enforcement problems. For example, the ban on trade in ivory from the tusks of African elephants caused the price of ivory to skyrocket. This created such strong incentives for poachers to kill protected elephants that the "international effort to halt the illegal killing of elephants for their ivory tusks has all but collapsed in most of Africa, leaving officials and advocates alarmed about the survival of the species."[42] Similarly, because the ESA prohibits the alteration of private property on which a member of an endangered species is found, it effectively commonizes the property, rendering it valueless to its owner. This creates strong incentives for property owners to ensure that no such animal is found on their property. As a result, property owners secretly kill the members of endangered species found on their land frequently enough for the practice to have been memorialized in the expression "shoot, shovel, and shut up."[43]

The legislative approach also tends to produce negative unintended consequences. For example, to avoid the commonization of their property that results from the presence of a member of an endangered species, landowners often destroy habitat that is attractive to such animals.[44] This "preemptive destruction" of habitat

[42] Marc Kaufman, *Increased Demand for Ivory Threatens Elephant Survival*, WASH. POST, Feb. 27, 2007, at A10.

[43] Stephen Polasky & Holly Doremus, *When the Truth Hurts: Endangered Species Policy on Private Land with Imperfect Information*, 35 J. ENVTL. ECON. & MGMT. 22, 42 (1998).

[44] *See* Dean Lueck & Jeffrey A. Michael, *Preemptive Habitat Destruction Under the Endangered Species Act*, 46 J. L. &. ECON. 27 (2003). See also, Jonathan H. Adler, *Money or Nothing: The Adverse Environmental Consequences of Uncompensated Land Use Controls*, 49 BOSTON COLLEGE LAW REVIEW 301, 319–332 (2008).

tends to undermine efforts to preserve the endangered species.[45] Indeed, the commonization of private property effectuated by the ESA and CITES can directly undermine otherwise successful conservation efforts. For example, in 1968, the Cayman Turtle Farm, Ltd. was formed as an effort to save the endangered green turtle. In a manner similar to the Handumon project, the Cayman Turtle Farm raised green turtles, released a certain percentage into the wild, and killed the remainder to sell their meat and other byproducts. This program was remarkably successful, increasing the stock of green turtles in the Caribbean from five thousand to eight hundred thousand. However, in 1978, the green turtle was placed on the endangered species list in the United States, resulting in a ban on the importation into and transshipment through the United States of all green turtle products. This destroyed the economic viability of the farm. As a result, the demand for such products is again supplied by poachers who illegally kill green turtles in the wild.[46]

In addition, compared to the Handumon experience, the legislative approach has been relatively ineffective. Over the thirty-five years the ESA has been in effect, very few species that have come under its protection have recovered.[47] The United States Fish and Wildlife Service itself reports only twenty-two of the nearly two thousand listed species as recovered.[48]

[45] *See* David S. Wilcove et al., *Quantifying Threats to Imperiled Species in the United States*, 48 Bioscience 607 (1998).

[46] The account of the Cayman Turtle Farm is taken from Robert J. Smith, *Private Solutions to Conservation Problems*, in The Theory of Market Failure: A Critical Examination 341–360 (Tyler Cohen, ed., 1988).

[47] *See* Jonathan H. Adler, *Money or Nothing: The Adverse Environmental Consequences of Uncompensated Land Use Controls*, 49 Boston College Law Review 301, 335 (2008). *See also*, Joe Kerkvliet & Christian Langpap, *Learning from Endangered and Threatened Species Recovery Programs: A Case Study Using U.S. Endangered Species Act Recovery Scores*, 63 Ecological Econ. 499, 500 (2007) and Ike C. Sugg, *Caught in the Act: Evaluating the Endangered Species Act, Its Effects on Man and Prospects for Reform*, 24 Cumb. L. Rev. 1, 42–44 (1993).

[48] *See* U.S. Fish and Wildlife Service Web site, https://ecos.fws.gov/ecp/report/species-delisted

However, the most damaging aspect of the legislative approach is its exclusivity. Legislation restricting access to endangered species ensures that the species remain in the commons. As such, it prohibits all efforts at privatization. This terminates the common law learning process and stifles environmental innovation. In essence, it outlaws the flexible common law approach that welcomes experimentation and rewards successful adaptation to circumstances and enthrones one that rigidly adheres to a politically acceptable, predetermined course and is highly resistant to change. The perverse incentives and negative unanticipated consequences of ESA are not recent discoveries. However, given the political influence of environmental interest groups and the general public's pro-environmental attitude, it can hardly be surprising that efforts to reform ESA that opponents could paint as attempts to weaken protection for endangered species would be unlikely to meet with success.

In describing her efforts in Handumon, Amanda Vincent stated,

> In general terms, there are two approaches to conservation. Quite a number of people feel it very important to protect the individuals of a species very closely by putting up fences or by putting trade bans on them. The other approach is . . . just accepting that those animals cannot all be protected, not each and every one of them. You need to work towards ensuring that the population survives and just some individuals will be killed and will die. The latter approach . . . is more sustainable, and so we need to work very hard to integrate what people need with what the animals themselves need and build a future for both.[49]

The most negative aspect of addressing environmental problems by legislatively restricting access to the commons is that it outlaws the latter, more sustainable approach.

[49] *Nova*, "The Kingdom of the Seahorse" (PBS television broadcast, April 15, 1997).

I offer this comparison of the common law and legislative approaches to protecting endangered species as an example of the superiority of the common law approach. However, there is nothing unique about endangered species. In general, human beings produce better results when they are free to try many things and learn from their mistakes than when they rigidly apply abstract first principles to practical problems. This is why I believe that with regard to environmental matters, a comparative assessment of the efficacy of common law privatization and legislative restriction of access will usually favor the former.

V. Conclusion

"The Tragedy of the Commons" holds three great lessons for those concerned with preserving environmental values: that commonly held resources will be overexploited, that such overexploitation cannot be remedied by exhorting individuals to behave more responsibly, and that such overexploitation can be avoided only by privatizing or restricting access to the resource. In this chapter, I have argued that only the first of these lessons has been fully learned. Almost all contemporary considerations of environmental issues begin with the recognition of the tragedy of the commons. In contrast, the latter two lessons have been, at best, partially absorbed. The second lesson appears to have been completely ignored by many environmental activists who wage extensive public relations campaigns to persuade people to curtail their exploitation of environmentally sensitive common resources. And half of the third lesson is regularly ignored by public policy analysts who argue directly from the tragedy of the commons to the conclusion that legislation is required to restrict access to common resources, failing even to consider the alternative of common law privatization.

There can be no gainsaying the significant improvements in environmental quality wrought by the environmental legislation of the past five decades. This is because legislatively restricting access to common resources is an effective way of avoiding the tragedy of the commons. But whether legislatively restricting access is effective or not is not the relevant public policy question. The relevant question is whether legislatively restricting access is more effective than the alternative approach of allowing the common law process of privatization to operate. In some cases, it may well be, but there is good reason to believe that in many, if not most, it is not. To the extent that this is true, sound public policy analysis must include a comparative assessment of legislative and common law environmental regulation.

Comparative assessments that suggest common law regulation to be the superior alternative pose a difficult practical challenge. For the superior outcome can be achieved only if politicians can be induced to refrain from preempting it through legislation. This suggests that the ultimate lesson of "The Tragedy of the Commons" may be the one that is most difficult to learn—that with regard to environmental regulation, as with so many other things, patience is a virtue.

PART II
APPLICATIONS

I believe that focusing on the role the common law plays in regulating human behavior can shed light on some otherwise intractable philosophical problems. Two of these are (1) providing a nontheological grounding for the concept of natural rights, and (2) identifying the proper scope of freedom of speech. I turn my attention to these in this part of the book.

In Chapter 4, I review the conception of natural rights associated with the political thought of John Locke and Robert Nozick, show that it is a powerful tool for analyzing the proper scope of state authority that is unfortunately bereft of a firm philosophical grounding, and then argue that an understanding of the process by which the common law evolved can supply the needed grounding. In Chapter 5, I argue that the apparently never-ending implacable debate over the extent to which the state may properly restrict speech arises from the failure to consider the effect of the common law and can be resolved by doing so.

4
Empirical Natural Rights

With the publication of *Anarchy, State, and Utopia* in 1974, Robert Nozick breathed new life into the natural rights tradition of political philosophy. By opening his book with the statement "Individuals have rights, and there are things no person or group may do to them (without violating their rights),"[1] Nozick stimulated two distinct lines of philosophical investigation: a future-oriented inquiry into the implications that the existence of fundamental individual rights holds for morally acceptable public policy, and a backward-looking inquiry into the sources of and foundations for these rights. In this chapter, I propose to pursue the latter line of inquiry.

To this end, I will begin with a brief overview of natural rights political philosophy in Section I. Because Nozick explicitly adopts John Locke's conception of natural rights as his own, I will first survey both Locke's and Nozick's rights-based arguments for limited government. I will then suggest that although both arguments are quite powerful, their persuasive force can be no greater than that of the underlying arguments for the existence of the natural rights upon which they rest. I will conclude Section I by suggesting that neither Locke nor Nozick has supplied an adequate version of the necessary underlying arguments.

Rather than attempting to supply this lack myself, in Section II, I will offer an alternative conception of natural rights as rights that naturally evolve in the state of nature. I will then argue that these "empirical natural rights" form a good approximation of the

[1] Robert Nozick, Anarchy, State, and Utopia ix (1974). (Hereinafter, ASU. Future references to this work will be identified by page number in parentheses in the text.)

Common Law Liberalism. John Hasnas, Oxford University Press. © Oxford University Press 2024.
DOI: 10.1093/9780197784631.003.0005

negative rights to life, liberty, and property on which both Locke and Nozick rest their arguments and that such arguments are normatively well-grounded. I will conclude by suggesting that empirical natural rights can serve as an alternative grounding for rights-based arguments for limited government that would be more persuasive to those not already committed to a classical liberal position than the traditional conception of natural rights advanced by Locke and Nozick.

I. The Natural Rights Tradition

A. Locke and Nozick

Natural rights political philosophy derives both the justification for and the limitations upon political authority from the natural rights of individual human beings. Natural rights are the pre-political rights individuals possess in the absence of established political authority, that is, in the state of nature. A natural rights–based argument for limited government has several familiar and easily identifiable features. It begins by identifying the rights individuals possess in the state of nature. It proceeds by presenting a list of the inconveniences inherent in life in that state, and arguing that to escape these inconveniences, individuals delegate some of the power derived from their natural rights to the exclusive use of a civil government. It then identifies the powers so delegated to conclude that a government that exercises these powers *and only these powers* is morally justified. Different versions of this argument can be generated by different lists of natural rights, different conceptions of the state of nature, different methods of delegation, and different lists of delegated powers.

In *Anarchy, State, and Utopia*, Robert Nozick advanced an argument for a severely limited form of government, his minimal state, that explicitly mirrored several of the features of John Locke's version of natural rights theory. Accordingly, it will be worthwhile to conduct a brief review of Locke's theory and highlight its similarities to (and differences from) Nozick's. Doing so will also explain why both theories share the characteristic of being enormously influential to some and wholly unpersuasive to others.

Let us begin with a consideration of what Locke meant by the state of nature. This can best be done by contrasting it with the perhaps more familiar account of the state of nature given by Thomas Hobbes. Hobbes believed that human nature was such that in the absence of "a common power to keep them all in awe," human beings would behave so as to create a state of war "of every man against every man" in which "men live without other security than what their own strength and their own invention shall furnish them."[2] Hobbes's state of nature, therefore, was a world in which the utter want of personal security meant that there could be no industry, commerce, art, or learning; one in which life was necessarily "solitary, poor, nasty, brutish, and short."[3] For Hobbes, the state of nature consisted not merely in the absence of an organized central authority, but in the absence of any mechanism of social control—the absence not merely of *government*, but of *governance*.

This is not Locke's conception of the state of nature. Professor A. John Simmons argues persuasively that Locke's state of nature was not intended as an empirical description of human behavior, but as the specification of a normative condition—"the condition of men living together without *legitimate* government."[4] If this is the case, then the state of nature implies neither the absence of civil government since one may be subject to an illegitimate one, nor the absence of governance since human beings may make whatever interpersonal agreements or private arrangements they wish (within the law of nature) to provide for their personal security and comfort.

2 Thomas Hobbes, Leviathan 106–107 (Herbert Schneider ed., 1958) (1651).
3 *Id.* at 107.
4 A. John Simmons, *Locke's State of Nature*, 17 Political Theory 449, 451 (1989).

And since Locke makes it clear that "men may make [promises and compacts] one with another, and yet still be in the state of nature,"[5] even if his state of nature is regarded as an empirical condition, it is one that is consistent with a high degree of cooperative behavior.

The distinction between Hobbes's and Locke's conception of the state of nature is reflected in the different rights they ascribe to human beings in that condition. Hobbes's war of all against all is an entirely lawless state. Under such conditions, the only right of any relevance and hence the only natural right human beings possess is the right of self-preservation.[6] In contrast, Locke's state of nature, although it lacks a normatively binding human law, is not lawless. It is governed by the law of nature, which obligates human beings to act for the preservation of mankind, and hence, not to "take away, or impair the life, or what tends to the preservation of the life, the liberty, health, limb, or goods of another" (STG §6). Thus, the law of nature entails the existence of natural rights to life, liberty, and property. Life, because the preservation of mankind requires individuals not to take their own or others' lives; liberty, because "all men are by nature equal," and hence possess the "equal right . . . to [their] natural freedom, without being subjected to the will or authority of any other man" (STG §54); and property, because "every man has a property in his own person" that entitles him to "[t]he labour of his body, and the work of his hands" such that whatever "he removes out of the state that nature hath provided, and left it in, he hath mixed his labour with, and joined to it something that is his own, and thereby makes it his property" (STG

[5] John Locke, Second Treatise of Government §14 (C. B. MacPherson ed., Hackett Publishing 1980) (1690). (Hereinafter, STG. Future references to this work will be identified by section number in parentheses in the text.)

[6] *See* Thomas Hobbes, Leviathan 109 (Herbert Schneider ed., 1958) (1651):

> The Right of Nature, which writers commonly call *jus naturale*, is the liberty each man has to use his own power, as he will himself, for the preservation of his own nature—that is to say, of his own life—and consequently of doing anything which, in his own judgement and reason, he shall conceive to be the aptest means thereunto.

§27). In Locke's state of nature, human beings are invested with a rich panoply of rights.

Although human beings are obviously much better off in Locke's state of nature than in Hobbes's, their ability to enjoy the exercise of their natural rights is still far from secure. This is due to the absence of "an established, settled, known law" to serve as "the common measure to decide all controversies between [men]" (STG §124), "a known and indifferent judge, with authority to determine all differences according to the established law" (STG §125), and any organized "power to back and support the sentence when right, and to give it due execution" (STG §126). It is to escape these inconveniences and thereby secure the "mutual preservation of their lives, liberties and estates" (STG §123) that human beings delegate some of the power they derive from their natural rights to a civil government.

The method of delegation, for Locke, is clearly consent,[7] although the difficult question of what constitutes consent will not be addressed here. The amount of power delegated is that necessary to alleviate the inconveniences of the state of nature and secure individuals' lives, liberties, and estates. This requires each individual to relinquish all of his or her right to punish those who transgress the law of nature (STG §130) and that portion of his or her right "to do whatsoever he thinks fit for the preservation of himself, and others within the permission of the law of nature" (STG §128), that is required for the preservation of civil society.

The consensual delegation of these powers establishes both the legitimate authority of civil government and the limits of that authority. The delegation of the right to punish gives the civil government the exclusive power to redress actions that violate the law of nature, that is, that "take away, or impair the life, . . . liberty, health,

[7] "Men being, as has been said, by nature, all free, equal, and independent, no one can be put out of this estate, and subjected to the political power of another, without his own consent" (STG §95).

limb, or goods of another" (STG §6). The government is thus empowered to establish human criminal laws in support of the law of nature and vested with the exclusive authority to adjudicate and apply criminal punishment. The delegation of a portion of the right to liberty gives the civil government the power to establish general regulatory laws designed to achieve the common good. But because no individual possesses a right to act in contravention of the law of nature, no such power can be delegated to the government, and hence, the government has no power to make any law, criminal or otherwise, that is contrary to the injunction to preserve mankind. Thus, the power of civil government "in the utmost bounds of it, is limited to the public good of society" (STG §135). Further, because the delegation of power is consensual and "no rational creature can be supposed to change his condition with an intention to be worse," the government is obligated to use its delegated power "to secure everyone's property, by providing against those three defects above mentioned" (STG §131). Thus, civil government

> is bound to govern by established standing laws, promulgated and known to the people, . . . by indifferent and upright judges, who are to decide controversies by those laws; and to employ the force of the community at home, only in the execution of such laws, or abroad to prevent or redress foreign injuries, and secure the community from inroads and invasion. And all this to be directed to no other end, but the peace, safety, and public good of the people. (STG §131)

Turning now to Nozick's argument for the state, we find that it is virtually identical to Locke's with regard to its conception of the state of nature and the list of rights individuals possess therein. With regard to the state of nature, Nozick is seeking a conception that constitutes "the best anarchic situation one reasonably could hope for" because "if one could show that the state would be superior to even this most favored situation of anarchy, . . . it would justify the state" (ASU, 5). Nozick believes that Locke's conception in which individuals who are free from legitimate political authority are both bound to behave morally and able to cooperate on the basis of contractual agreements and communal arrangements meets this criterion. Accordingly, he explicitly adopts Locke's conception of the state of nature as one in which only government, not governance, is lacking (ASU, 9–10).

Further, although Nozick never explicitly identifies the rights individuals possess in the state of nature,[8] we may safely assume that the set of rights that Nozick ascribes to such individuals is either coextensive with or encompasses Locke's natural rights. In adopting Locke's conception of the state of nature, Nozick specifically cites Locke's characterization of it as being governed by the law of nature that requires "that no one ought to harm another in his life, health, liberty, or possessions" (ASU, 10, citing STG §6). This, along with the substance of Nozick's extended discussion, strongly suggests that he believes that individuals in the state of nature possess the same substantive rights to life, liberty, and property that Locke argues for. If Nozick's list of rights differs from Locke's at all, it is by including an additional procedural right not to be punished for violating others' rights unless one's guilt has been established by a reliable and fair process.[9]

Nozick's argument begins to depart from Locke's when it comes to the method by which individuals delegate their power to the state and the specific powers that are delegated. Like Locke, Nozick recognizes that individuals' rights are not secure in the state of nature. Unlike Locke, however, he does not argue that individuals

[8] With the possible exception of the right to punish, Nozick deals with rights exclusively on the generic level. It is worth noting that Locke too fails to provide an exhaustive or authoritative list of individuals' natural rights, although he does discuss several specific rights (e.g., the right to preserve oneself and others by means within the law of nature, the right to execute the law of nature, the right to pursue innocent delights) which I have subsumed in the traditional trilogy of life, liberty, and property.

[9] *See* ASU, 102. Nozick suggests but never explicitly affirms that such natural "due process" rights exist. *See* ASU, 101, 107.

ever directly consent to the authority of a civil government in order to secure them. Rather, Nozick contends that human beings in the state of nature will use their ability to contract with one another to hire private protective associations to secure their rights for them. He then makes the empirical claim that because of the special nature of the services protective associations provide, market forces will result in the rise of one dominant protective association in any given geographical area.[10] To this, he adds the normative assertion that the dominant association may legitimately prevent any competitor from taking action against its clients on the basis of any guilt-determination procedure of which the dominant association does not approve[11] as long as it provides its competitors' clients with in-kind compensation in the form of its own protective services.[12] But once a dominant protective association thus

[10] Nozick regards the provision of protective services as what economists call a network industry, one in which the value of the good increases as the number of users increases. He argues that

> [t]he worth of the product purchased, protection against others, is *relative*: it depends upon how strong the others are. Yet unlike other goods that are comparatively evaluated, maximal competing protective services cannot coexist; the nature of the service brings different agencies not only into competition for customers' patronage, but also into violent conflict with each other. Also, since the worth of the less than maximal product declines disproportionately with the number who purchase the maximal product, customers will not stably settle for the lesser good, and competing companies are caught in a declining spiral. (ASU, 17)

Hence, "[o]ut of anarchy, pressed by spontaneous groupings, mutual-protection associations, division of labor, market pressures, economies of scale, and rational self-interest there arises something very much resembling a minimal state or a group of geographically distinct minimal states" (ASU, 16–17). For an interesting attempt to refute this argument, see Bryan Caplan and Ed Stringham, *Networks, Law, and the Paradox of Cooperation*, 16 Rev. Austrian Econ. 309–326 (2003).

[11] It may do this either because its clients have a procedural right to have their guilt determined by a reliable and fair procedure that the dominant protective association is authorized to exercise for them or because nonclients do not have the right to punish the association's clients on the basis of guilt-determination procedures that the association deems unreliable or unfair (ASU, 107).

[12] This is because it is morally permissible to prohibit activities that impose risks on others only if "those who are *disadvantaged* by being forbidden to do actions that only *might* harm others [are] compensated for these disadvantages foisted upon them in order to provide security for the others" (ASU, 82–83).

suppresses its competitors and provides its services to all persons in a geographical area, it has all the necessary attributes of a civil government (ASU, 22–23). Therefore, Nozick concludes that a civil government can spontaneously arise through a series of morally legitimate steps, i.e., those that do not violate any of the rights individuals possess in the state of nature. For Nozick, then, individuals delegate their power to the state indirectly by consensually creating an entity that evolves into a state through unplanned, but morally legitimate human interaction.

Nozick's method of delegation transfers less power and produces a more severely limited state than does Locke's. Like Locke, Nozick sees individuals as delegating their right to punish rights-violators to what becomes the civil government, thus empowering it to establish (rights-protecting) criminal laws and to adjudicate and apply criminal punishment.[13] Unlike Locke, however, Nozick does not see individuals as delegating a portion of their right to liberty sufficient to empower the government to establish regulatory laws for the common good. Beyond relinquishing their right to punish, individuals delegate none of their right to liberty and only that portion of their right to property necessary for the state to supply protective services to those entitled to receive them as compensation.[14] The exceedingly spare nature of this delegation strictly limits the power of the state to that necessary to protect the rights of its citizens. Hence, Nozick's argument provides a justification for "the night-watchman state of classical liberal theory" (ASU, 25) that provides police, adjudicative, and national defense services, and nothing more.

[13] Individuals also delegate their "due process" right to be tried by reliable and fair procedures, if they have such a right. *See supra* note 9.

[14] Nozick does not explicitly state that individuals delegate a portion of their right to property, but this is the clear implication of his claim that "the dominant protective agency must supply the independents—that is, everyone it prohibits from self-help enforcement against its clients on the grounds that their procedures of enforcement are unreliable or unfair—with protective services against its clients" (ASU, 112; see generally, ASU, 110–113).

B. The Arguments' Persuasive Force or Lack Thereof

Natural rights arguments for limited government have a powerful but limited appeal. Their power comes from their argumentative structure. Their limitations come from the foundations on which this structure rests.

Natural rights arguments are structurally valid arguments. Given their assumptions about individuals' pre-political moral entitlements, they provide cogent justifications for both government power and its limitations. If individuals are truly vested with natural rights, then government can function morally and command obedience only to the extent that it does not violate them. Both Locke's and Nozick's arguments chart a well-reasoned course from Lockean natural rights to morally legitimate limited government. Locke's consent-based argument rests on the fundamental moral propositions that one who consents to what would otherwise be an invasion of a protected interest has not been wronged and that one is morally bound by one's freely undertaken agreements. These propositions imply that to the extent that one's obligation to obey political authority has been voluntarily assumed, no underlying right has been violated and one is morally bound to obey political authority. The intuitive appeal of these underlying propositions is so great that Lockean social contract theory has maintained a strong hold on popular imagination in the United States since the nation's inception. Nozick's argument, which rests partially on the binding force of voluntary agreement and partially on a philosophically sophisticated account of morally legitimate human interaction, can exert a similar hold on the philosophical imagination. If Nozick's contentions regarding individuals' procedural entitlements and the conditions under which risky behavior may be restrained when compensation is paid are correct, then he, too, provides a cogent justification for moving from a Lockean state of nature to a limited civil government. Arguments such as these can be extremely persuasive to those who believe that individuals do, in fact, have pre-political Lockean rights.

This statement, however, indicates the limitations of the arguments' power as well. For as effective as they may be at deriving limited government from Lockean natural rights, their appeal to those not antecedently committed to the existence of such rights is only as powerful as the underlying arguments for the rights themselves. These underlying arguments, however, are much less compelling than those they support.

For Locke's or Nozick's argument to gain purchase, natural rights theorists must first establish not only that natural rights exist in a generic sense, but also that the set of legitimate natural rights is coextensive with Locke's rights to life, liberty, and property. Establishing the first of these propositions has presented a notoriously difficult challenge.[15] But even if it could be overcome, establishing the second may prove equally formidable. Even natural rights theorists do not agree about what natural rights exist, as the earlier discussion of Hobbes and Locke illustrates. To establish that Lockean rights constitute *the* set of natural rights, a natural rights theorist would have to produce an argument robust enough to counter Hobbesian arguments that yield a more limited set of rights, yet not so robust that contemporary liberals can extend

[15] Loren Lomasky explains this difficulty as consisting in

> those ills endemic to any account that attempts to base moral status and obligation on "nature": on some characteristic that all and only those beings who are moral claimants possess and which is sufficient to justify their moral claims. Natural rights theories are a subclass of such nature-based theories. They routinely are embarrassed by the absence of any characteristic *universally* shared by those beings they wish to single out as rights holders, possessed *only* by them, shared *equally* by them (else rights possession would be an analog function admitting of degree rather than all-or-nothing), and which can credibly be taken as *justifying* the preferred moral status that is ascribed to rights holders. All such attempts to ground rights—or morality in general—in nature fail because the class of moral claimants does not coincide with the class possessing property Φ, where Φ is the alleged natural basis of rights.

LOREN E. LOMASKY, PERSONS, RIGHTS, AND THE MORAL COMMUNITY 37–38 (1987)

its logic to yield positive welfare rights to fundamental goods or services such as healthcare or a minimally decent standard of living. Whether natural rights theorists can ultimately meet these challenges remains an open question. It is clear, however, that neither Locke nor Nozick have done so.

Locke's "disturbing paucity of foundational work in the *Second Treatise*" has been noted by Professor Simmons, who points out that although "[t]he content of parts of the natural law and the rights defined by it receive considerable attention . . . very little is said about why these are our duties and rights."[16] Nozick, himself, explicitly recognizes both Locke's and his own failure to provide a firm grounding for natural rights when he declares at the beginning of *Anarchy, State, and Utopia* that the "task is so crucial, the gap left without its accomplishment so yawning, that it is only a minor comfort to note that we here are following the respectable tradition of Locke, who does not provide anything remotely resembling a satisfactory explanation of the status and basis of the law of nature in his Second Treatise" (ASU, 9). Nevertheless, the arguments that Locke and Nozick do provide are worth examining for what they reveal about the limitations on the persuasive force of natural rights theory.

Locke provides at least two lines of argument for the law of nature from which he derives his natural rights: one theological and one secular. The theological argument defines the law of nature as God's will with regard to human behavior that human beings can discover by the powers of reason God impressed into their nature for that purpose.[17] When the law of nature is understood in this way, demonstrating the existence of the law of nature requires Locke to establish that God exists, that God created human beings

[16] A. John Simmons, The Lockean Theory of Rights 15 (1992).

[17] "[T]his law of nature can be described as being the decree of the divine will discernable by the light of nature and indicating what is and what is not in conformity with rational nature, and for this very reason commanding or prohibiting." John Locke, Essays on the Law of Nature 111 (W. von Leyden ed., Clarendon Press, 1988) (1676).

as essentially rational creatures, that there is a normative duty to obey the commands of one's creator, and that reason allows human beings to derive the general principles of moral conduct from their knowledge of divine and human nature—none of which is an easy task.[18] The secular argument defines the law of nature as the law of reason commanding what is in the best interest of humanity. When it is understood in this way, Locke believes that the law of nature can be derived from the formal proposition that it is irrational to treat equals unequally and the substantive proposition that all human beings are of equal moral worth. This allows Locke to argue that the duty to preserve any human life logically entails the equal duty to preserve everyone's life, and hence the duty to preserve mankind by refraining from actions that impair the life, liberty, and property of others (STG §6).[19]

Nozick provides an argument that grounds rights not in the law of nature, but directly on Kantian moral theory, identifying them as reflections of "the underlying Kantian principle that individuals are ends and not merely means" (ASU, 30–31). Nozick accepts the Kantian proposition that every human being possesses inherent moral value, i.e., a dignity, that all others are required to respect. Rights, he argues, protect this dignity. By doing so, they "express the inviolability of other persons" (ASU, 32) and "reflect the fact of our separate existences. They reflect the fact that no moral balancing act can take place among us; there is no moral outweighing of one of our lives by others so as to lead to a greater overall social good. There is no justified sacrifice of some of us for others" (ASU, 33).

[18] A good account of Locke's theological argument for the law of nature can be found in SIMMONS, *supra* note 16, at 23.

[19] The argument Locke presents in §6 of the *Second Treatise* is not truly secular since he supports his contentions that human life has value and that all human lives are equally valuable on the basis of the claim that they are all equally the workmanship of God. However, the argument itself is logically severable from its theological support. Any argument for the value of human life and for human moral equality can serve as well. Hence, it is not inappropriate to regard Locke as providing a secular grounding for his natural rights.

Thus, Nozick believes that an individual's rights must be respected because the failure to do so "does not sufficiently respect and take account of the fact that he is a separate person, that his is the only life he has" (ASU, 33).

To the extent that Locke's or any natural rights argument has a theological basis, the limits of its appeal are patent. To begin with, establishing the existence of natural rights on this ground requires first establishing the existence of God, a proposition at least as difficult to substantiate as the one it is being offered to prove. Indeed, Locke does not even attempt to make such an argument, merely assuming the existence of God at the beginning of his *Essays on the Law of Nature*.[20] But even given this assumption, Locke must still prove that there is a duty to obey God's will. Although this may seem obvious at first, it is not. For, with Humean hindsight, we know that the *fact* that God commands something does not in itself imply that human beings *ought* to obey. What, then, is the source of this obligation? For Locke, the source of human moral obligation is the law of nature. But because the obligation to obey God is being offered to prove that the law of nature exists, the law of nature cannot serve as the source of the obligation without rendering the argument circular. And if Locke simply identifies divine commandment as the property that makes something morally obligatory, he runs directly into the naturalistic fallacy.[21] Finally, even if these problems could be surmounted, Locke would then face the task of establishing that his version of the law of nature correctly embodies God's will. Since he cannot rely on revelation, he can do this only

[20] "God shows Himself to us as present everywhere and, as it were, forces Himself upon the eyes of men as much in the fixed course of nature now as by the frequent evidence of miracles in time past, I assume there will be no one to deny the existence of God, provided he recognizes either the necessity for some rational account of our life, or that there is a thing that deserves to be called virtue or vice." Locke, *supra* note 17, at 109.

[21] The naturalistic fallacy is the improper identification of a normative property with a natural property, or more precisely, "the fallacy that results from construing the 'is' of attribution as an 'is' of identity, and thus supposing, for example, that because pleasure is (attributive 'is') good, good is identical with pleasure." See George Edward Moore, The Encyclopedia of Philosophy 5:379 (Paul Edwards ed., 1967).

by demonstrating that it is entailed by the respective natures of God and human being. Given the obvious difficulty of providing a compelling account of God's nature and the philosophical debate not only about what constitutes human nature, but about whether there even is such a thing,[22] the prospects of Locke (or any natural rights theorist) providing a convincing demonstration of this point must be considered remote.

Locke's secular argument does not fare much better. In this case, however, the difficulty is not so much with the substance of the premises as with whether they lead to the desired conclusion. There will be little disagreement either with the formal proposition that equals should be treated equally or with the substantive claims that human life has value and that human beings are equal in some morally significant respect. The difficulty for Locke is to establish that the respect in which human beings are equal is one that gives rise to a duty to preserve mankind that entails all and only the rights to life, liberty, and property that he endorses. In this respect, Locke's argument is both too weak and too strong.

Locke's argument is strong enough to establish a duty to preserve every human life and this would seem to entail a duty not to kill others or deprive them of the things necessary to preserve their lives. Whether it is strong enough to establish Locke's extensive rights to liberty and property would depend on whether these rights are truly necessary for the preservation of life in society. Although Locke assumes that they are (STG §6), there appears to be little reason for this. Clearly a right to some freedom of action and a modest right to keep those things necessary to maintain life could be established, but this falls far short of rights to one's "natural freedom, without being subjected to the will or authority of any other man" (STG §54) and to keep "whatever [one] hath mixed his labor with" (STG §27). The life of all may be very well preserved

[22] *See* Margaret MacDonald, *Natural Rights*, *in* THEORIES OF RIGHTS 29–30 (Jeremy Waldron ed., 1984).

consistently with great restrictions on personal liberty and severely limited rights to personal possessions. Hence, Locke's argument is too weak to persuade those not already committed to a classical liberal conception of rights.

The more serious problem with Locke's secular argument, however, is that it is much too strong. This is because the duty to preserve every human life that it entails can give rise to positive welfare rights as easily as it can the classical negative rights to life, liberty, and property. A duty to equally preserve everyone's life certainly generates a duty not to take others' lives or otherwise impair others' efforts to survive, but it also appears to generate a duty to act positively to maintain others' lives. Thus, to the extent that Locke's argument establishes the desired negative rights to life, liberty, and property, it also establishes positive welfare rights to benefits such as a minimal standard of living and life-preserving healthcare, again rendering it unpersuasive as an argument for the classical liberal configuration of rights.

In some ways, it is not unreasonable to view Nozick as rehabilitating Locke's secular argument. By basing his argument on a Kantian foundation, Nozick can be seen as arguing not merely that every human life has equal moral value, as Locke did, but, more specifically, that every human being is equally possessed of a dignity that requires respect for his or her autonomy.[23] This is a much more promising basis for an argument for the existence of Lockean rights. On the one hand it is strong enough to ground not only the right to life, but also broad negative rights to liberty and property. A duty to respect others' autonomy bars not only taking their lives, but also coercing their persons both generally and, more specifically, in order to deprive them of justly acquired possessions. On the other hand, it does not appear to be strong enough to ground positive rights because a duty to respect others'

[23] Nozick can be seen as providing the secular supporting argument for human moral equality that Locke's actual argument based on divine creation lacked. *See supra* note 19.

autonomy does not entail a duty to sustain their lives or benefit them in other ways.

Unfortunately, Nozick's argument has its own set of drawbacks. To begin with, both its moral and metaphysical foundations are far from securely established. To the extent that it is expressly tied to Kantian moral theory, it is subject to the conventional philosophical criticism of this theory and will be convincing only to those who accept Kant's categorical imperative as the fundamental principle of morality.[24] Further, its underlying metaphysical assumptions have been attacked by both feminists and communitarians. Nozick explicitly bases his argument on the contention that human beings are *essentially* separate entities, that rights "reflect the fact of our separate existences." Feminists explicitly reject what they call the "separation thesis,"[25] arguing that "women are 'essentially connected,' not 'essentially separate,' from the rest of human life, both materially, through pregnancy, intercourse, and breastfeeding, and existentially, through the moral and practical life."[26] Communitarians argue that because human identity is socially constructed, because the self is a product of one's social and political roles in one's community that "arises through the common understanding which underlies the practices of our society,"[27] the

[24] In its most familiar version, the categorical imperative enjoins us to "[a]ct so that you treat humanity, whether in your own person or that of another, always as an end and never as a means only." IMMANUEL KANT, THE FOUNDATIONS OF THE METAPHYSICS OF MORALS 9–10 (Lewis White Beck trans., 1959). Some of the more conventional objections to basing ethical theory on the categorical imperative are that it improperly discounts the moral significance of an action's consequences, that it cannot resolve conflicts among duties, e.g., whether one should lie to save an innocent life, and that it provides no ethical guidance in situations in which it is impossible to treat all as ends in themselves, e.g., an overcrowded lifeboat.

[25] The separation thesis consists in "the claim that human beings are, definitionally, distinct from one another, the claim that the referent of 'I' is singular and unambiguous, the claim that the word 'individual' has an uncontested biological meaning, namely that we are each physically individuated from every other, the claim that we are individuals 'first,' and the claim that what separates us is epistemologically and morally prior to what connects us." Robin West, *Jurisprudence and Gender*, 55 U. CHI. L. REV. 1, 2 (1988).

[26] *Id.* at 3.

[27] Charles Taylor, *Atomism*, in POWERS, POSSESSIONS AND FREEDOM 39, 60 (Alkis Kantos ed., 1979).

concept of a pre-social or pre-political separate self is nonsensical. They contend that the very capacities that Nozick identifies as the grounding for his pre-political rights—rationality, free will, moral agency, and the ability to live according to an overarching plan of life (ASU, 49)—are only possible because individuals are formed in an already existing political society, and hence that Nozick's argument is hopelessly circular.

The more serious problem with Nozick's argument, however, is that he does not make it. He supplies no account of the steps in reasoning that lead from either the categorical imperative or the recognition of human beings as essentially separate selves to their inherent possession of Lockean rights.[28] It may appear obvious that respect for individuals as ends in themselves requires a right to life and a right to a significant amount of control over one's existence, but it is not obvious that it requires the broad rights to liberty and property on which Nozick grounds his argument for the minimal state or that it necessarily excludes all positive rights. Unfortunately, all Nozick offers in support of his position is the claim that the possession of Lockean rights is necessary for individuals to have meaningful lives. But Nozick follows his assertion that "[a] person's shaping his life in accordance with some overall plan is his way of giving meaning to his life; only a being with the capacity to so shape his life can have or strive for a meaningful life" (ASU, 50) not with an argument showing why the possession of Lockean rights is necessary for this capacity, but with a list of ten questions that suggest that it may not be, followed by the declaration that he "hope[s]

[28] Judith Jarvis Thomson notes that Nozick's argument that individual rights are inviolable "rests entirely on the supposition that they are," Judith Jarvis Thomson, *Some Ruminations of Rights*, in Reading Nozick 130, 137 (Jeffery Paul ed., 1981), while Thomas Nagel contends that "[t]o present a serious challenge to other views, [Nozick] would have to explore the foundations of individual rights and the reasons for and against different conceptions of the relation between those rights and other values that the state may be in a position to promote, . . . but no such arguments appear in the book." Thomas Nagel, *Libertarianism Without Foundations*, in Reading Nozick 191, 192–193 (Jeffery Paul ed., 1981).

to grapple with these and related issues on another occasion" (ASU, 51). Because it seems obvious that one can have quite a meaningful life without rights that guarantee one remains *entirely* free from coercion by others (else no human being has ever had a meaningful life), Nozick's remarks have little prospect of convincing those who do not already agree with him.[29]

My critique of Locke's and Nozick's arguments does not, of course, suggest that natural rights theorists cannot supply a secure grounding for Lockean natural rights, merely that neither Locke nor Nozick (nor anyone else that I am aware of) has yet done so. But until that grounding is provided, arguments like Locke's and Nozick's, which are profoundly persuasive to those antecedently committed to Lockean natural rights, are likely to remain equally unpersuasive to those who are not.

II. An Alternative Conception of Natural Rights

A. "Empirical" Natural Rights

I make no pretense of being able to offer a satisfactory philosophical grounding for Lockean natural rights. Rather, I would like to sidestep the issue by offering an alternative conception of natural rights that is not beset by the foundational problems discussed in the previous section, but is nevertheless philosophically useful. In

[29] A charge frequently leveled against natural rights theories is that they violate the Humean proscription against deriving a normative conclusion from purely empirical premises. Jeremy Waldron, for example, states that "[t]he idea of *natural* rights is seen as a particularly glaring example of the 'Naturalistic Fallacy,' purporting to derive certain norms or evaluations from descriptive premises about human nature." Jeremy Waldron, *Introduction*, in THEORIES OF RIGHTS 3 (Jeremy Waldron ed., 1984). To the extent that a natural rights theory attempts to derive rights solely from a description of human nature, this charge may be well-founded. However, neither Nozick's argument nor Locke's secular argument falls prey to this critique. Both ground their arguments on genuinely normative premises about moral status of individual human beings. Hence, I have not addressed the Humean objection in this chapter.

place of the traditional conception of natural rights as rights that human beings are inherently *endowed with* in the state of nature, I would like to offer a conception of natural rights as rights that *evolve in* the state of nature. For lack of a better term, I will refer to rights of this type as "empirical natural rights."

In offering this alternative, I am employing a conception of the state of nature that is similar to, but importantly different from, that employed by Locke and Nozick. Like both Locke and Nozick, I am interested in exploring human behavior in the absence of established government, not in the absence of any mechanism of interpersonal governance. Accordingly, my conception of the state of nature is one in which human beings are able to make interpersonal agreements or other private arrangements to ensure their personal security and enjoyment of life—that is, one that is consistent with both antagonistic and highly cooperative behavior. Thus, the conception of the state of nature that I am employing is much more like Locke's than Hobbes's. Unlike Locke and Nozick, however, I am advancing an empirical, rather than an essentially normative, conception of the state of nature.[30]

In the previous section, I described both Locke and Nozick as making genuinely normative arguments, as drawing their normative conclusions from normative premises about the moral status of human beings. Accordingly, their conception of the state of nature is an essentially normative one. Both Locke and Nozick were interested in exploring the human condition in the absence of *morally legitimate* government. Thus, for Locke at least, one subject to a repressive, morally illegitimate regime would still be in the state of nature with respect to that regime.

This normative conception of the state of nature is too broad for my purposes. I am interested in how human beings behave in the absence of any established political authority, morally legitimate or

[30] *See* the discussions of Locke's and Nozick's conception of the state of nature in Section II(A).

not. Thus, the conception of the state of nature that I intend to employ is one defined by the absence of civil government *simpliciter*, that is, of any entity claiming or generally recognized as possessing a monopoly over the legitimate use of force in a geographical area or otherwise vested with the traditional trappings of government such as "finance through taxation, claim of sovereignty, ultimate decision-making authority, and prohibitions on competitive entry."[31] This conception sees the state of nature as an empirical state of affairs rather than a moral condition.

Once the state of nature has been specified, traditional natural rights theorists such as Locke and Nozick ask what moral entitlements human beings possess therein. I intend to ask only what human beings do. This is an empirical question that can be answered only on the basis of empirical evidence. Although there is a wealth of such evidence available both in the form of direct historical accounts of how those who found themselves in this situation behaved and in the form of analogies that can be drawn from situations in which existing governments failed to act with regard to particular avenues of human endeavor, in the present context, I will have to make do with some broad generalizations accompanied by a few illustrative supporting examples.

First, the generalizations.

Historical evidence suggests that life in the state of nature is indeed *originally* beset by the inconveniences Locke identifies. In the absence of civil government, most people engage in productive activity in peaceful cooperation with their fellows. Some do not. A minority engages in predation, attempting to use violence to expropriate the labor or output of others. The existence of this predatory element renders the persons and possessions of those engaged in production insecure. Further, even among the productive portion of the population, disputes arise concerning

[31] Tyler Cowen, *Law as a Public Good: The Economics of Anarchy*, 8 ECON. & PHIL. 249, 250 (1992).

broken agreements, questions of rightful possession, and actions that inadvertently result in personal injuries for which there is no antecedently established mechanism for resolution. In the state of nature, interpersonal conflicts that can lead to violence often arise.

What happens?

The existence of the predatory minority causes those engaged in productive activities to band together to institute measures for their collective security. Various methods of providing for mutual protection and for apprehending or discouraging aggressors are tried. Methods that do not provide adequate levels of security or are too costly are abandoned. More successful methods continue to be used. Eventually, methods that effectively discourage aggression while simultaneously minimizing the amount of retaliatory violence necessary to do so become institutionalized. Simultaneously, nonviolent alternatives for resolving interpersonal disputes among the productive members of the community are sought. Various methods for composing disputes are tried. Those that leave the parties unsatisfied and likely to again resort to violence are abandoned. Those that effectively resolve the disputes with the minimal disturbance to the peace of the community continue to be used and are accompanied by ever-increasing social pressure for disputants to employ them.

Over time, security arrangements and dispute settlement procedures that are well-enough adapted to social and material circumstances to reduce violence to generally acceptable levels become regularized. Members of the community learn what level of participation in or support for the security arrangements is required of them for the system to work and for them to receive its benefits. By rendering that level of participation or support, they come to feel entitled to the level of security the arrangements provide. After a time, they may come to speak in terms of their right to the protection of their persons and possessions against the type of depredation the security arrangements discourage, and eventually even of their rights to personal integrity and property. In addition, as the dispute settlement procedures resolve recurring forms of conflict in similar ways over time, knowledge of these resolutions becomes widely diffused and members of the community come to expect similar conflicts to be resolved in like manner. Accordingly, they alter their behavior toward other members of the community to conform to these expectations. In doing so, people begin to act in accordance with rules that identify when they must act in the interests of others (e.g., they may be required to use care to prevent their livestock from damaging their neighbors' possessions) and when they may act exclusively in their own interests (e.g., they may be free to totally exclude their neighbors from using their possessions). To the extent that these incipient rules entitle individuals to act entirely in their own interests, individuals may come to speak in terms of their right to do so (e.g., of their right to the quiet enjoyment of their property).

In short, the inconveniences of the state of nature represent problems that human beings must overcome to lead happy and meaningful lives. In the absence of an established civil government to resolve these problems for them, human beings must do so for themselves. They do this not through coordinated collective action, but through a process of trial and error in which the members of the community address these problems in any number of ways, unsuccessful attempts to resolve them are discarded, and successful ones are repeated, copied by others, and eventually become widespread practices. As the members of the community conform their behavior to these practices, they begin to behave according to rules that specify the extent of their obligations to others, and, by implication, the extent to which they are free to act at their pleasure. Over time, these rules become invested with normative significance and the members of the community come to regard the ways in which the rules permit them to act at their pleasure as their rights. Thus, in the state of nature, rights evolve out of human beings' efforts to address the inconveniences of that state. In the state of nature, rights are solved problems.

Next, the supporting examples.

Two oft-cited examples of societies in which people lived for extended periods of time without a traditional civil government are ancient Israel in the time of the judges and medieval Iceland.[32] I prefer the example of Anglo-Saxon and early Norman England because I believe it offers a wonderful test case of how human beings behave in the absence of central political authority. As I mentioned in Chapter 1,[33] with the collapse of Roman rule in Britain at the beginning of the fifth century, civil government essentially disappeared from the island. The sudden departure of the Romans, who had provided both law and its enforcement, left the inhabitants of Britain without organized protection against external attack and with no established methods for adjudicating intragroup conflicts. This is a reasonably good approximation of the state of nature.

In such circumstances, people's most urgent need was for a method of deterring violence and theft. This was originally supplied in the form of the blood feud, which consisted in direct reprisal against aggressors. When someone was assaulted, killed, or otherwise wronged, the expected, socially accepted response was for the members of the aggrieved party's household or clan to wage private war against the wrongdoer.[34] Because the prospect of an immediate violent response from a victim's entire family or support group was sufficiently fearful to discourage attack, the blood feud was an effective deterrent. However, the risk to life and limb and the disruption of normal life that it entailed also rendered it highly inconvenient. The violence inherent in the blood feud created strong incentives for people to find alternatives to its prosecution.

[32] For a discussion of the latter, see William Ian Miller, BLOODTAKING AND PEACEMAKING: FEUD, LAW, AND SOCIETY IN SAGA ICELAND (1990) and David Friedman, *Private Creation and Enforcement of Law: A Historical Case*, 8 J. LEGAL STUD. 399 (1979).

[33] *See supra* page 9.

[34] 1 FREDERICK POLLOCK & FREDERIC WILLIAM MAITLAND, THE HISTORY OF ENGLISH LAW 46 (2d ed. 1898).

Hence, the practice developed of holding the feud in abeyance while attempts were made to reach a peaceful settlement through negotiation.

The forum for these negotiations was the moot, a public assembly which served as the chief instrument of social administration.[35] When both parties agreed, they could lay their dispute before the moot, whose members, much like present-day mediators, attempted to facilitate an accommodation that both parties found acceptable. The blood feud would be prosecuted only if no accommodation could be reached. Because such negotiated settlements avoided the strife and physical risk of the blood feud, community pressure gradually transformed the effort to reach them from an optional alternative to the feud to a necessary prerequisite for receiving the help of one's group in prosecuting it.[36]

Unsurprisingly, successful negotiations usually involved some form of compensatory payment. As repetition of this process taught the community what level of compensation would restore peace, a fixed schedule of penalties for various types of injuries evolved. This proved to be an effective deterrent that both punished the wrongdoer and, to the extent that it was possible, made the victim whole.[37] The success of this method of securing peace caused it to spread throughout Britain (and all of Germanic Europe) with the result that "[t]he institution of fixed monetary sanctions payable by the kin of the wrongdoer to the kin of the victim was a prominent feature of the law of all the peoples of Europe prior to the twelfth century."[38]

The process of negotiating settlements of potentially violent conflicts and repeating and eventually institutionalizing successful

[35] When the conflict was between members of households or tribes that did not participate in the same moot, the negotiations took place directly between the clans or tribes.

[36] Pollock & Maitland, *supra* note 34, at 46–47.

[37] Harold Berman, Law and Revolution 54–55 (1983).

[38] *Id* at 55.

resolutions gradually produced a broad body of customary law that served as the basis for the English common law. Having grown out of the resolution of actual conflicts by a process of trial and error, the rules that comprised this law were practical and remarkably subtle and nuanced. For example, no compensatory payment was due if one killed a thief, but only if one immediately publicized the killing[39]—a requirement apparently designed to prevent people from manufacturing evidence of a theft after the fact to legitimize murder. Further, actions that subjected others to humiliation, such as "binding a free man, or shaving his head in derision, or shaving off his beard,"[40] demanded larger compensatory payments than any but the most serious injuries. Why? Apparently because these were precisely the type of actions most likely to evoke a violent response and most in need of discouragement if peace was to be preserved.

By establishing a schedule of payments associated with various types of actions that damaged the interests of others, customary law (which was not distinguished from morality) established the obligations members of the community owed to their fellows. In doing so, it also established the restrictions on the behavior of their fellows that members of the community were entitled to enforce. That is, it established rights. These included, of course, rights not to be murdered, maimed, or physically assaulted that protect one's physical integrity. But they also included rights to be free of certain types of assaults on one's honor that protect one's psychic integrity, to the "peace" of one's home that gave one dominion over one's home and special protection against its invasion, and to the enjoyment of possessions such as cattle when purchased before the proper number of witnesses or land when held by "folk-right."[41] In short, customary law established a set of personal rights that facilitated a peaceful existence in the society of others.

[39] Pollock & Maitland, *supra* note 34, at 53.
[40] *Id.*
[41] *Id.* at 58–62.

A second useful example, although not a territorial one, is supplied by the Law Merchant in medieval Europe. With the revival of long-distance trade in Europe during the eleventh and twelfth centuries, merchants found themselves conducting business across cultural and political boundaries. As foreigners, however, international merchants were vulnerable to expropriation by hostile local merchants and officials. In addition, linguistic and cultural differences, the need to transact business through third-party agents, and the plurality of local customs "gave rise to hostility toward foreign customs and . . . ultimately led to mercantile confrontations"[42] for which there was no antecedently established method of resolution. Thus, *in their capacity as merchants*, medieval traders found themselves without civil government to provide security and resolve conflicts, a reasonable analog for the state of nature.

What happened?

Local merchants wanted the benefits that could be reaped from long-distance trade, but foreign merchants would trade with them only if they had an assurance that their goods would not be expropriated and that they would be treated fairly. Accordingly, merchants sought arrangements that provided the needed assurance. Many such arrangements were tried. Those that worked best were widely copied and eventually institutionalized in the Law Merchant.

> The most viable mercantile practices were enforced in the Law Merchant so that local practices were undermined where they diverged from the Law Merchant. . . . Established custom lay at the foundation of the Law Merchant. The universal system of law thus sought out those customs which were "constant," those practices which were "established" and, in particular, those habits

[42] LEON E. TRAKMAN, THE LAW MERCHANT: THE EVOLUTION OF COMMERCIAL LAW 11 (1983).

which were capable of sustaining a high level of commerce to the satisfaction of merchants, consumers and rulers alike.[43]

As a result, "[i]n twelfth century Europe the transnational character of the law merchant was an important protection against the disabilities of aliens under local laws as well as against other vagaries of local laws and customs."[44]

Medieval merchants also lacked an established system for resolving the disputes that arose among them. The court systems of the various nations and localities were not viable fora for mercantile disputes because they lacked expertise with regard to trade practices and worked too slowly for merchants who could not remain long in one place. In response, merchants began settling disputes among themselves on the basis of informal proceedings and highly streamlined decision-making procedures. To the extent these procedures produced successful and rapid resolutions of mercantile disputes, they became regularized. The merchant courts that evolved in this way eventually grew into a European system of commercial courts in which merchant judges quickly applied the tenets of the Law Merchant to resolve commercial disputes.[45]

The process of applying the principles of the Law Merchant in merchant courts to resolve the actual disputes that arose among merchants established an extremely sophisticated body of customary commercial law that "supplied a great many, if not most of the structural elements of the modern system of commercial law."[46] This law facilitated the creation of bills of exchange and promissory notes and recognized their negotiability, invented the chattel mortgage and other security interests, supported the development

[43] *Id.*

[44] BERMAN, *supra* note 37, at 342.

[45] *See* TRAKMAN, *supra* note 42, at 12–17. For a good synopsis of the development of the Law Merchant and merchant courts, see also BRUCE BENSON, THE ENTERPRISE OF LAW 30–35 (1990).

[46] BERMAN, *supra* note 37, at 350.

of deposit banking and bankruptcy law, and established the limited liability joint venture.[47] In doing so, the Law Merchant established the obligations those engaged in commerce owed to each other, and hence the rights that each enjoyed as a participant in commerce. Thus, good faith purchasers of goods gained the rights of holders in due course and the right to rely on an implied warranty of fitness and merchantability, creditors gained the preferential right to collect property on which they held a security interest, and entrepreneurs gained the right to enjoy limited liability in joint ventures and the protection of trademarks.[48] In short, in the absence of a European civil government, the inconveniences of the "mercantile state of nature" forced merchants to address the problems of security and dispute resolution themselves. The trial-and-error process by which they did so produced the Law Merchant and the system of merchant courts that eventually established a set of commercial rights that facilitated peaceful exchange and the flow of commerce.

Examples of situations in which civil government is entirely lacking will necessarily be rare. Evidence of how human beings behave in the absence of government is not limited to such examples, however, but may also be drawn from situations in which existing governments fail to act. In this respect, the English common law can provide valuable analogical evidence of how rights evolve in the state of nature. For although the English government provided a forum for resolving interpersonal disputes in its common law courts, until fairly recently, it neither directly resolved the disputes nor provided substantive rules for doing so. Instead, the fundamental rules of social order were left to evolve out of the resolution of actual disputes in ways that seemed fair to the ordinary members of the community who served as jurors. And the rules that actually

[47] *See id.* at 349–350.
[48] *Id.*

evolved through this process produced the much vaunted "rights of Englishmen."[49]

For an example of this, we can revisit the discussion of the evolution of the torts of assault and battery in Chapter 2. Recall that the modern law of battery forbids one from intentionally making harmful or offensive contact with another. This prohibits not only direct blows, but insulting or offensive indirect contacts as well. And the law of assault forbids one from intentionally causing another to fear he or she is about to receive such a harmful or offensive contact. These rules invest individuals with a fairly strong set of personal rights. They establish the right to be free not only from physically harmful contact, but from all offensive physical contact as well as from fear that such contact is immediately forthcoming. What accounts for this high level of protection for individuals' bodily and psychic integrity?

As explained in Chapter 2, in past centuries, the most urgent social need was to reduce the level of violence in society, which meant discouraging people from taking the kind of actions that were likely to provoke a violent response. Thus, when disputes arising out of violent clashes were litigated, juries tended to assign liability to parties who had taken such actions. Because both direct physical attacks on one's person and insulting affronts to one's dignity or other attacks on one's honor are likely to provoke violence, the law of battery evolved to forbid not merely harmful contacts, but offensive ones as well. And because an attack that failed was just as likely to provoke violence as one that succeeded, the law of assault evolved to forbid actions that threatened harmful or insulting contact.

[49] The advent of the English common law is usually dated to the realm of Henry II (1154–1189), who provided a nascent form of trial by jury in royal courts. See THEODORE F. T. PLUCKNETT, A CONCISE HISTORY OF THE COMMON LAW 19 (1956). The common law evolution of the rules of private law continued with relatively little interference from the political organs of the English government until well into the nineteenth century.

In the absence of direct government intervention, people faced the problem of how to reduce violence. They dealt with this problem in the entirely natural manner of holding those who took actions likely to provoke it responsible for the injuries that resulted. As more and more cases were decided on this basis, people came to expect that future cases would be as well and adjusted their behavior to that expectation. Over time, these repeated decisions coalesced into the rules specifying what constitutes assault and battery. These rules define individuals' obligations to respect others' personal integrity, and hence their rights to be free from unwanted physical intrusions and threats. The strong personal rights protected by the law of assault and battery are the solution to the past problem of excessive social violence.

For a more contemporary example, it is worth reconsidering the example of the Philippine seahorse fishermen discussed in Chapter 3. Recall that in the village of Handumon in one of the most impoverished regions of the Philippine Islands, the sale of seahorses constituted the only source of income beyond subsistence fishing. Because the waters in this area were open to all, the fishermen went out and harvested as many seahorses as they could. As a result, the population of seahorses in these waters was rapidly declining. As noted in Chapter 3, part of the decline in the seahorse population was due to the practice of harvesting pregnant seahorses, each of whom carried large numbers of young, before they could give birth. No fisherman was willing to forgo harvesting pregnant seahorses because doing so meant another fisherman would take the seahorse and the first would have relinquished an immediate benefit for no resulting gain. The Philippine government had virtually no presence in this impoverished region and took no action to solve the fishermen's problem. In this respect, the fishermen were in the state of nature.

When the fishermen were shown by a marine biologist how to construct netting with mesh small enough to contain adult seahorses, but large enough to allow newly born fish to escape, they built personal floating cages in which they placed the pregnant seahorses that they found. They then allowed the seahorses to give birth before removing them from the water for sale. They also agreed to place a portion of the reef near the village off-limits to all fishing in an attempt to increase the seahorse population. These practices were successful at increasing the seahorse population, but as a result, fishermen from surrounding islands and villages began to "poach" seahorses from the waters around Handumon. In response, the Handumon villagers began patrolling these waters to keep the poachers out. Eventually, fishermen from surrounding areas came to Handumon to learn what the villagers were doing and copied their techniques. As a result, the seahorse population of the entire region began recovering.

In the absence of governmental action, the residents of the Philippines had to address the problem of the declining seahorse population themselves. Handumon developed fishing practices and security arrangements that reversed the decline. Handumon's success stimulated others to inquire into their practices and copy them, thereby transforming them into widespread practices. These practices imposed new obligations on the Philippine fishermen to respect each other's personal cages, to refrain from fishing in the preserve, and to participate in or support the security arrangements. Looked at from the individual fisherman's point of view, these obligations gave them property rights to the contents of their personal cages and to fish within the patrolled waters. The rights of the Philippine seahorse fishermen are the solution to the problem of the declining seahorse population.[50]

These examples are offered to demonstrate that human beings in the state of nature act in ways that ultimately produce individual entitlements. What I am calling empirical natural rights are rights that evolve as a byproduct of human efforts to address the

[50] This example is taken from the PBS science show *Nova*, "The Kingdom of the Seahorse" (broadcast Apr. 15, 1997).

inconveniences of the state of nature. Empirical natural rights are the solutions to the problems the state of nature presents.

B. The Character of Empirical Natural Rights

Are the rights I have labeled empirical natural rights truly natural rights? Traditionally, natural rights have consisted in moral entitlements human beings possess simply by virtue of their humanity—rights that spring directly from human nature or the fundamental principles of morality. Such rights are inherent in, not created by, human beings, and require no human interaction for their existence. The rights I have described clearly do not fit this model. They are not inherent in human beings and do not spring from human nature or fundamental moral principles. They are certainly not natural in the sense of not having been created by human action. Although not consciously created by any human mind, they depend on human interaction for their existence. Thus, although they are "the result of human action, but not the execution of any human design,"[51] they are indeed the creation of human beings.

Empirical natural rights are natural only in the sense that they are the rights which naturally evolve in the state of nature. Nevertheless, I want to claim that this is sufficient for them to be regarded as true natural rights. In my opinion, the essential element of a natural right is its pre-political character. Along with Professor Simmons, I would argue that to qualify as a natural right, a right need only be one that "could be possessed independently of (and logically prior to) civil society, whose binding force is nonconventional"[52]—that is, one that has "natural grounds and could be possessed in the state of nature."[53] Empirical natural rights clearly meet this test. By

[51] Adam Ferguson, An Essay on the History of Civil Society pt. 3, § 2. (1767).
[52] Simmons, *supra* note 16, at 90.
[53] *Id.*

definition, they are rights that human beings possess in the state of nature and that pre-date the formation of civil government. They depend on no conscious human convention (such as a social contract), but merely on the empirical fact (i.e., the natural ground) that human beings tend to act to relieve discomfort. A conception of rights as solved problems depends only upon a conception of human beings as natural problem-solvers.

Although empirical natural rights are true natural rights, they are quite different in character from traditional natural rights. Empirical natural rights are more flexible, more mutable, and less philosophically perfect entities than the rights usually advanced by natural rights theorists. Because traditional natural rights are logically derived from inherent features of human nature or fundamental principles of morality, they are typically seen as vesting individuals with conceptually complete, timeless moral entitlements. For example, the natural right to property is traditionally depicted as the right to the exclusive use and control of an object. In contrast, because empirical natural rights arise out of the uncoordinated efforts of human beings to resolve the problems they encounter in the state of nature, they rarely consist in such philosophically elegant entities. The empirical natural right to property can only be described in extremely inelegant terms as the right to a great amount of use and control of an object most of the time, with exclusive use and control at some times and no use or control at others.

If the natural right to property derives from one's moral entitlement to one's own person, as Locke would have it (STG §27), or from the Kantian injunction to treat all human beings as ends in themselves, as Nozick would have it (ASU, 30–31), then it is perfectly logical to see the right to property as consisting in the exclusive use and control of objects. Because no one can have an ownership interest in another's person and no one is morally entitled to use another merely as a means, there is no ground for seeing individuals as vested with less than full control over their property. In contrast, the empirical natural right to property evolved to help human beings solve the problems of life in the state of nature, the most urgent of which was the need to peacefully resolve conflicts that would otherwise lead to violence. As the burgeoning literature on the evolution of property rights makes clear,[54] the recognition of individual property rights in what would otherwise be a commonly held resource is, in most cases, an excellent mechanism for accomplishing this end. But not in all cases. Consider, for example, the situation in which one person acquires all the real property surrounding the home of another and then denies the homeowner permission to cross his or her land in an effort to force the homeowner to sell at an extortionately low price. In this case, a property right that invests the acquisitive party with the exclusive use and control of property is a prescription not for peace, but for violence. Not surprisingly then, property rights evolved to prevent the employment of this tactic by automatically granting enclosed property owners an easement of necessity that allows them to cross others' property. Consider also cases of emergency in which one person's life may depend on the use of another's property, such as where the captain of a ship caught in a deadly storm lashes the ship to another's dock. Once again, because a right to exclusive use and control that allowed property owners to deny others what they need to save their lives would be a prescription for violent confrontation, property rights evolved to permit the use of others' property in emergencies (although compensation must be paid for any damage done). Thus, in contrast to the more philosophically pleasing conception of the traditional right to property, the empirical right is a highly flexible, exception-laden one that invests individuals with the exclusive use and control of objects only to the extent that doing so facilitates a more peaceful life in society.

The same contrast can also be seen in the context of individuals' personal rights. If natural human equality invests all human beings

[54] *See e.g., supra* Ch. 3 notes 10–12, 15–23.

with the equal right to be free from subjection to the "will or authority" of others, as Locke would have it (STG §54), or if respect for human beings as ends in themselves demands respect for their autonomy, as Nozick would have it, then it is logical to see the natural right to liberty as consisting in the ability to act free from the direct application of coercion or its threat. In contrast, the empirical personal rights that actually evolved are both less and more extensive. As noted in the discussion of assault and battery, they are less extensive because they protect individuals not against the threat of coercion *per se*, but only against the threat of its *immediate* application. Yet they are more extensive because they protect individuals against not only coercion, but offense. The contours of these rights were determined not theoretically, but by what was necessary to reduce social violence to generally acceptable levels. Protection against the threat of future coercion was not necessary to achieve this end, so the rights did not include such protection. Protection against serious affronts to dignity was, so they did. Thus, where the traditional conception of the right to liberty consists in a conceptually neat sphere of protection against interference with one's activities, the empirical right to liberty consists in an oddly shaped, indented, and bulging bubble of personal protection that corresponds to precisely the amount of freedom necessary to solve the problem of excessive social violence.

Individual empirical natural rights, then, are theoretically imperfect, exception-laden, fuzzy-edged entities. Yet taken together, they form a remarkably good approximation of Lockean natural rights. This is not coincidence, but is due to the empirical fact that Locke's set of broad negative rights to life, liberty, and property consists in precisely those rights that are most likely to produce peaceful relationships among human beings in the absence of civil government.[55]

[55] Indeed, it is not unreasonable to view Locke and later natural rights theorists as providing a *post hoc* philosophical justification for a set of rights that had actually evolved, and in doing so, smoothing out their philosophically rough edges.

Consider the right to life. Murder, as the least compensable of all injuries, calls forth the strongest desire for revenge and is more likely than anything else to provoke a violent response. The first priority of any community wishing to live in peace must be to discourage such intentional killings. As a result, the security arrangements that evolve invariably reserve their strongest disincentives for unjustified intentional killings. As these security arrangements give rise to patterns of behavior that become institutionalized into rules, the rules reflect the relatively greater seriousness of murder in comparison to other wrongs. Thus, the rules institutionalize a special level of protection for individuals against having their lives taken that is significant enough to cause the taking of life to be viewed as different in kind from other wrongs. In other words, the rules will provide individuals with a distinct, especially important entitlement not to be unjustly killed by others—a right to life—that is identical to Locke's.

Next, consider the right to liberty. Besides murder, there are many other actions that provoke violent responses. Physical attacks on one's person or the immediate threat of such an attack will do so, as will physical restraints on one's freedom of movement and certain types of serious affronts to one's dignity. As a result, people in the state of nature establish security arrangements that discourage these actions and that eventually evolve into rules prohibiting assault, battery, and false imprisonment. Generally speaking, individuals respond violently only when others interfere with the pursuit of their goals and desires in ways they cannot reasonably avoid. Otherwise, they nonviolently sidestep the interference. But unavoidable interferences are virtually always coercive ones. As a result, the rules that evolve in the state of nature are those that suppress coercion. When the rules prohibiting assault, battery, false imprisonment, and other forms of coercive interaction are taken together and viewed from the perspective of the individual member of the community, they look very much like a general right to be free from coercive interference with their activities—that is, like a broad negative right to liberty. Although, as was noted above, this empirical natural right is not identical to Locke's right to liberty, it does constitute a remarkably close approximation of it.

Now consider the right to property. Murder and the use of force against one's person are not the only actions that provoke violence. Depriving one of his or her possessions or attempting to do so will also elicit a violent response. In addition, violence frequently erupts when different people try to use objects held in common in incompatible ways. As a result, the security arrangements people in the state of nature devise discourage the forcible dispossession of goods. As people conform their behavior to the incentives of these arrangements, rules evolve that protect possession and eventually give rise to a right of continued possession. Simultaneously, the members of the community search for peaceful resolutions to the disputes that arise over the use of common goods. As such successful resolutions are found and repeated, rules governing the use of physical (and intangible) objects emerge. These rules specify procedures by which individuals can acquire control over an object and the extent to which they may exclude others from its use. As a matter of empirical fact, violent conflicts are usually best avoided by allowing those in proper possession of an object to exclude others from using it in most ways most of the time. Therefore, the rules that evolve tend to invest those in possession of an object with almost exclusive control over it.[56] However, because some ways of using objects and some forms of exclusion provoke rather than allay conflict, the rules do not permit those uses or those forms of exclusion. When taken together, the rules that protect possession,

[56] But note that these rules do not result in everything being privately held. In certain cases, holding property in common does not produce conflict and may even facilitate peaceful interaction. This may be the case for road and water ways that aid in commerce. *See* Carol Rose, *The Comedy of the Commons*, *in* Property and Persuasion 105–162 (1994). Where there is no conflict, there are no resolutions, and hence no rules evolve that restrict the use of the commons.

that prescribe the procedures by which individuals may acquire possession of objects, and that specify the ways in which those in proper possession may exclude others from using the objects create a set of individual entitlements that looks very much like a negative right to private property. As previously noted, this empirical right to property is not a perfect match for Locke's right to property, but because the limitations on individuals' control over objects are relatively minor and infrequent, it is a reasonably close approximation of it.

Finally, note that there are no positive empirical rights. There is, of course, no reason why there cannot be. It is logically possible that people in the state of nature would respond to the insecurities and inconveniences of their condition in ways that produced rules that imposed uncompensated obligations on individuals to supply others with particular goods or services. But as a matter of fact, they do not.

Once practices that reduce the threat of violence to manageable levels have evolved, people in the state of nature may then confront the problems posed by the lack of assurance that they will have enough to eat, or receive medical treatment when needed, or receive an education. They may try many different ways to address these problems. The evidence suggests that the arrangements that are most effective in doing so and hence are repeated and become institutionalized are those that involve reciprocal obligations to participate in mutual assurance schemes. That is, people agree to contribute their labor or some of their resources to a common pool in return for the right to draw upon the common pool when needed. In essence, people in the state of nature create self-insurance mechanisms.[57]

[57] And, of course, they encourage purely charitable activities on the basis of religious or cultural beliefs about what God requires or what will make one a good person.
A good source of analogical evidence of how people address these problems when government does not do so for them is historical research into the practices of Jewish communities in Christian Europe, immigrant communities in northern cities of the

I suspect that the reason positive rights do not evolve in the state of nature is that they tend to give rise to rather than resolve interpersonal conflicts. The fundamental problem faced by people in the state of nature is to align individuals' incentives so that they pursue their personal interests in ways that facilitate rather than impede others in the pursuit of their interests. Eliminating the use of violence toward others as a means of pursuing one's interest is a major step in this direction. In contrast, imposing obligations on individuals to provide others with goods or services without compensation places the interests of individuals in conflict. To the extent that individuals are required to serve others' interests, they are not free to serve their own. If individuals are required to give others some of their property or to labor for others without compensation, then they are in the position of those subject to forcible dispossession or coercive restrictions on their freedom of movement. As we have seen, these are situations that tend to provoke rather than resolve conflicts. Voluntary mutual assurance schemes in which everyone who participates receives a personal benefit do a much better job of aligning incentives, and hence would be selected for in the trial-and-error process by which people in the state of nature solve problems.

The absence of the evolution of positive rights in the state of nature can be usefully illustrated by the fact that no duty to rescue

United States in the nineteenth and early twentieth centuries, and black communities in the southern United States during the segregation era. Although these groups existed within states with civil governments and thus were not, strictly speaking, in a state of nature, they were cut off from governmental provision of any welfare services and thus were in a virtual state of nature with regard to such services. (Given the ubiquity of government in the modern world, isolated enclaves within modern states that are denied governmental services are perhaps the best modern proxies for the state of nature. Such enclaves supply real-world situations that allow empirical observation of how people behave in the absence of civil government.) David T. Beito, in his FROM MUTUAL AID TO THE WELFARE STATE: FRATERNAL SOCIETIES AND SOCIAL SERVICES, 1890–1967 (2000), demonstrates how the latter two groups were able to supply such services as poor relief, unemployment compensation, healthcare, old-age annuities, and burial insurance through voluntary mutual assurance arrangements. *See also* CHARLES MURRAY, IN PURSUIT OF HAPPINESS AND GOOD GOVERNMENT ch. 12 (1994).

those in danger ever evolved in either the customary or common law of England. Such a duty would create the fairly minimal positive right to the efforts of others to save one from danger when feasible. If any positive rights were to evolve, this would surely be one of the most likely candidates. The fact that it did not may be due to purely practical difficulties such as the inability to determine the level of risk a rescuer should be required to run, to judge whether the rescue would have succeeded, or to calculate what one owes another for failing to save the other from danger he or she did not create. But it may also be that holding individuals liable for failing to incur personal risks to render aid to others is simply a poor way of resolving disputes and promoting social peace. Indeed, it seems more like a recipe for drawing third parties into dangerous conflicts than for discouraging such conflicts. Whatever the reason, however, even this fairly minimal positive right failed to evolve.

In sum, then, empirical natural rights are true natural rights that evolve out of human interaction in the state of nature. They are theoretically imperfect, exception-laden entities that are the by-product of the efforts of human beings to learn how to live together peacefully in the absence of civil government. And yet when taken together, they form a set of rights that corresponds fairly closely to Locke's negative rights to life, liberty, and property without also including any positive rights to fundamental goods or services. When we recall that the challenge that neither Locke nor Nozick could meet was to establish not only that natural rights exist, but that they consist in all and only the Lockean rights to life, liberty, and property, empirical natural rights begin to look like potentially useful philosophical entities.

C. The Normative Status of Empirical Natural Rights

I have argued that empirical natural rights exist and form a fairly good approximation of the Lockean rights to life, liberty, and property. As yet, however, I have said nothing as to why they are entitled to any respect. Empirical natural rights are merely the rights that evolve in the state of nature. But the fact that they evolve, standing alone, is without normative significance. To argue from their mere existence to the conclusion that individuals are morally entitled to have them respected would be to run afoul of Hume's injunction against deriving normative conclusions from purely empirical premises. What, then, is the normative basis for empirical natural rights?

I can offer no argument that empirical natural rights have any intrinsic moral value. I cannot demonstrate that they capture any principles of justice or embody any moral principles. I certainly cannot claim to know which underlying moral theory is correct, or even whether to take a deontological, consequentialist, or Aristotlean approach to ethics. I can, however, argue that empirical natural rights have instrumental moral value regardless of the moral theory and general approach to ethics one adopts. This is because empirical natural rights facilitate peaceful human interaction and peace is an important, if not pre-eminent, moral value in virtually all moral theories.

To make this point, I would like to offer an analog of the Rawlsian concept of a primary good that might be called a "primary value." Rawls defines primary goods as "things that every rational man is presumed to want [because t]hese goods normally have a use whatever a person's rational plan of life."[58] Primary goods have universal instrumental value because "whatever one's system of ends, primary goods are necessary means."[59] Thus, goods such as health, intelligence, liberty, and wealth are all primary goods. Analogously, I would define a primary value as something that every moral theory regards as valuable because it normally advances the realization of the ultimate end of the (consequentialist or Aristotlean)

[58] John Rawls, A Theory of Justice (1971), 62.
[59] *Id.* at 93.

theory or is entailed by the fundamental principles of the (deontological) theory. Primary values have universal instrumental moral value because whatever a moral theory's ultimate goals or requirements, primary values are means to their fulfillment.

Peace, I would argue, is a primary value. Whatever the end or ends of a consequentialist moral theory, peace makes its realization more likely. Whether the theory requires the maximization of one or the optimal increase in each of many human goods such as pleasure, happiness, the satisfaction of rational desires, social wealth, knowledge, friendship, etc., peace is a necessary prerequisite to the achievement of the theory's goal. Further, whatever an Aristotlean moral theorist may mean by human flourishing, a peaceful social environment is necessary for its realization. It is much more difficult for one to live well or reach one's potential when surrounded by strife. Finally, it is difficult to imagine a deontological moral standard that does not either explicitly prescribe peaceful behavior or implicitly require a peaceful environment for human beings to behave as it does prescribe.

Peace, then, is morally valuable because it is a prerequisite for or facilitates the realization of all other moral values. Empirical natural rights are rights that exist precisely because they facilitate peaceful interaction among human beings. Hence, empirical natural rights are entitled to respect because they are instrumental in promoting the primary value of social peace. They are entitled to respect not merely because they *evolve* in the state of nature, but because they *are productive of peace* in the state of nature. Therefore, empirical natural rights have genuine, if instrumental, moral value.

D. The Philosophical Value of Empirical Natural Rights

In Section I, I argued that the weakness of natural rights political philosophy lies not in its derivation of limited government from the existence of Lockean natural rights, but in its inability to supply a firm normative foundation for Lockean natural rights. I now want to suggest that empirical natural rights can supply such a foundation.

Let me begin by reviewing the essential role that natural rights play in political philosophy. Natural rights serve as a basis on which to determine whether political authority is morally justified. To be morally legitimate, political authority must come into existence in ways that are consistent with the natural rights of those subject to it. To retain its legitimacy, political authority must not be exercised in ways that violate those natural rights. Thus, the essential philosophical purpose of natural rights is to serve as a ground upon which to morally evaluate both the existence and actions of civil government. To serve this purpose, natural rights must be morally well-grounded entities whose existence in no way depends upon civil government. That is, natural rights must be morally legitimate, logically pre-political entities; they must be rights that can exist in the state of nature.

As previously discussed, empirical natural rights are neither direct grants from God, logically deducible from inherent features of human nature, nor directly entailed by fundamental moral principles. Further, they are artificial entities in the sense that they are the creation of human action. They are natural only in the sense that they naturally evolve in the state of nature and are logically independent of the existence of civil government. Yet if they are normatively well-grounded, this is all that is required for them to perform philosophically as natural rights. For, as long as they supply a ground outside of the political realm on which to base evaluative judgments about political arrangements—a sort of normative Archimedean point from which to move the political world—they need possess no particular ontological, metaphysical, or normative pedigree to function as true natural rights.

Further, empirical natural rights are normatively well-grounded. They exist only because they have been proven to facilitate peaceful social relationships among human beings. Empirical natural rights are, by their nature, productive of peace. And peace is a primary value, one that is morally valuable if not in itself, then instrumentally because it facilitates the realization of virtually all other moral values. Empirical natural rights help produce the good or help ensure that human beings act rightly regardless of how the good and the right are defined. They therefore possess genuine moral value.

Finally, when taken together, empirical natural rights comprise a set of rights that corresponds closely, although not perfectly, to Locke's negative rights to life, liberty, and property. Because murder, coercive interference with others' persons and freedom of movement, forcible dispossession of goods, and conflicts over the use of resources are the activities most likely to produce violence in the state of nature, these are the activities that people in the state of nature most urgently seek to discourage. Hence, the rules that evolve out of these efforts vest individuals with rights that protect their lives, persons, freedom, and goods against invasion by others. These rights may be conveniently and reasonably grouped together under the rubric of the rights to life, liberty, and property to produce a set of rights almost as extensive as Locke's. However, because giving some people claims over the labor or possessions of others tends to promote rather than reduce interpersonal conflict, no positive rights evolve. As a result, empirical natural rights consist in almost everything that constitutes Lockean rights and nothing else.

Once natural rights theorists such as Locke and Nozick complete their demonstrations that Lockean natural rights entail that only limited government can be morally justified, they face the skeptical question of why one should believe that Lockean natural rights and only Lockean natural rights exist and should be respected. The philosophical value of the concept of empirical natural rights is that it can supply an answer to this question. Lockean natural rights and only Lockean natural rights exist because Lockean rights and only Lockean rights evolve in the state of nature. And Lockean natural rights should be respected because doing so promotes social peace, which is necessary to realize any and all other moral values.

The fact that Lockean empirical natural rights exist and are normatively well-grounded tells us nothing, in itself, about the contours of a morally justified civil government. This is determined by the method by which individuals delegate the power conferred by these rights to the government and the amount of power so delegated. Thus, empirical natural rights will not by themselves settle any of the substantive questions concerning the morally proper extent of government power. They will, however, get the natural rights project off the ground by providing the normative grounding for natural rights that Locke and Nozick could not.

Grounding one's argument for limited government on empirical rather than traditional natural rights has both advantages and disadvantages. The main advantage is the potentially greater persuasive force of arguments grounded on empirical natural rights. Because accepting the existence and normative force of empirical natural rights requires no prior theological, metaphysical, or normative commitments, arguments based on them can have a very broad appeal. One need not believe in the existence of God or that certain substantive propositions are self-evident or that human beings are essentially equal or essentially separate or have any essential non-socially-constructed nature at all to believe that empirical natural rights exist. One need only observe the behavior of people in the state of nature.[60] Therefore, arguments based on empirical natural rights should have the power to persuade not only those who do not subscribe to a Lockean or Nozickian theological or metaphysical position, but also those who do not engage in theological or metaphysical reflection at all. Answering the question of why one should believe that natural rights exist by pointing at the way the world works is a much more promising way of persuading those of primarily empirical intellectual

[60] Or, more accurately, one need only review the available historical evidence of how people who lived either in societies without civil government or in situations in which extant governments did not provide basic security or welfare services behaved.

orientation than is presenting a complex theological or metaphysical disquisition. Further, one need not subscribe to any particular moral theory to recognize the normative force of empirical natural rights. One need only appreciate that empirical natural rights are productive of peace and that peace is a primary value. Therefore, arguments based on empirical natural rights should have the power to persuade not only those who do not subscribe to Kantian moral theory, but all those who perceive the normative value of peace. Thus, empirical natural rights can allow natural rights–based arguments for limited government to avoid the metaphysical and normative cul-de-sacs in which they have become trapped in the past.

The main disadvantage of basing arguments for limited government on empirical natural rights is that the grounding is less certain than that aspired to by those who base their arguments on traditional natural rights. God's commands, the essential features of human nature, and the inviolability of individuals all represent morally fundamental considerations. If natural rights really derive from one of these sources, then they have an absolute moral force that is not subject to being overridden or abridged for the sake of other moral concerns. There really can be no stronger grounds upon which natural rights can rest. The normative force of empirical natural rights, on the other hand, derives from their capacity to promote social peace. But peace is an instrumental moral value and, as such, retains its value only so long as it promotes more ultimate moral values. This implies that empirical natural rights may be overridden or abridged when doing so would better promote such ultimate moral values. And this apparently opens the door to arguments that there are conditions under which civil government may legitimately abridge empirical natural rights.

I believe, however, that this does not constitute as serious a drawback as may initially appear. In the first place, peace is a primary value. Therefore, although peace may possess only instrumental value, it is a particularly strong form of instrumental value. Because peace facilitates the realization of all other moral values, it is an exceptionally rare case in which social peace must be sacrificed to attain a more ultimate moral value.[61] Indeed, it is difficult to imagine a situation in which sacrificing a peaceful social environment would truly help realize a more significant moral end. This suggests that the conditions under which civil government would be justified in abridging an empirical natural right would be equally rare. But secondly and more significantly, there is, at present, no alternative to employing empirical natural rights. It would indeed be better to ground arguments for limited government on natural rights derived from morally fundamental values that cannot be overridden. But as we saw in Section I, neither Locke nor Nozick was able to provide an effective argument demonstrating that Lockean natural rights can be derived from such values. This, of course, does not mean that such arguments may not be found, and, indeed, such arguments constitute the holy grail of natural rights theory. But while the quest for them continues, empirical natural rights represent the best available ground for natural rights–based arguments for limited government. The fact that arguments based on empirical natural rights cannot provide a guarantee that there are no situations in which one's natural rights can be legitimately overridden is no reason not to make such arguments if empirical natural rights are the only well-grounded natural rights one has. I conclude, therefore, that the advantages of empirical natural rights outweigh their disadvantages sufficiently to render them a philosophically promising foundation for arguments for limited government.

[61] This claim must be read in context. It is, of course, true that nations are often forced to go to war to realize values more important than maintaining international peace. But this is not the sense in which the term "peace" is being used at present. The peace protected by empirical natural rights is social peace, i.e., the peace internal to a society that consists in the maintenance of nonviolent relationships among the members of a community.

III. Conclusion

Shorn of all metaphysical and normative presuppositions and viewed from a purely empirical perspective, rights are solved problems. When human beings with their various and often incompatible personal interests live together in a world of scarcity, conflicts invariably arise. Given all that human beings have in common, certain types of conflicts regularly and widely recur. The discomfort and disruption these conflicts produce give rise to a widely shared desire to resolve or avoid them.

In a society with civil government, this desire frequently expresses itself in a call for action by government to address the problem. For example, in a society beset by racial antipathy, citizens may exert sufficient pressure to cause the government to enact a law prohibiting employers from making any employment-related decisions on the basis of race. Imposing such an obligation on employers simultaneously vests citizens with a right to be free from racial discrimination in the workplace. Thus, the right to be free from discrimination is the solution to the problem of widespread racial antipathy. In a society with civil government, rights are often the solutions to social problems *that are produced by politically effective forces.*

In the state of nature, there is no civil government for people to call on to resolve widely recurring conflicts for them. Hence, they must find ways to resolve such conflicts for themselves. They could do this through explicit collective action. The members of the community could meet in congress to create a set of rules to regulate their future behavior toward one another. They do not. Rather, they pursue many uncoordinated efforts to address the problems caused by the conflicts, repeat successful resolutions and discard unsuccessful ones, and observe, learn from, and copy the successful resolutions of others. In doing so, they create widespread practices to which the members of the community conform their behavior—practices that eventually evolve into rules imposing obligations on community members and hence simultaneously endowing them with rights. For example, the need to reduce public brawling causes members of the community to bring pressure on their fellows not to engage in the actions most likely to give rise to it. This evolves into the obligation to refrain from making harmful or offensive physical contact with others, which vests each member of the community with the right not to be battered. Thus, the right not to be battered is the solution to the problem of excessive public violence. In the state of nature, rights are the solutions to social problems *that have been proven by experience to produce a predominantly peaceful social environment.*

From a purely empirical standpoint, the difference between the rights one enjoys due to membership in a society with civil government and one's natural rights is the problem-solving mechanism employed in their creation. To the extent that societies with civil government employ the political process to resolve social problems, citizens' rights reflect, for good or ill, the dominant political influences within their society. In contrast, because people in the state of nature are forced to employ a trial-and-error process of learning through experience to resolve their social problems, their rights reflect the practical demands of maintaining life in society with others. Accordingly, what I have been calling empirical natural rights encapsulate the wisdom of centuries of human experience concerning how human beings can best live with each other in peace. Because a peaceful social environment is a prerequisite to the attainment of almost everything that makes life worthwhile, this is a wisdom that should not be lightly disregarded. I believe that it is also a good basis from which to make moral judgments about the quality of civil government and its actions. Accordingly, I offer empirical natural rights as an alternative foundation for the classical liberal arguments for limited government advanced by John Locke and Robert Nozick.

5

Freedom of Speech and the Return of the Invisible Gorilla

The proper scope of freedom of speech is a perennial controversy in the United States. Why? Perhaps it is because of the way the debate is framed, which is usually as follows.

> The First Amendment to the United States Constitution states that "Congress shall make no law . . . abridging the freedom of speech, or of the press."[1] But everyone knows that the word "no" cannot be taken literally in this context. For doing so would mean that individuals could falsely shout "Fire" in a crowded theater and cause a panic, or make an incendiary speech to a hungry crowd urging it to burst into the nearby house of a grain dealer and kill him, or utter fighting words designed to provoke an immediate violent response, or commit fraud, or publish obscene materials with no redeeming social value, or publish the private intimate details of another's life, or falsely accuse others of despicable sexual practices. Because unregulated speech poses many dangers and can do much harm, the government must step in somewhere to prevent the most dangerous and harmful speech. The debate is over where to draw the line. Should it be only when the speech poses a clear and present danger of serious harm? Only when it can result in physical harm? Why not serious psychic harm? On which side of the line is speech that tends to undermine democratic government, or hateful speech that has

[1] U.S. Const. amend. I.

Common Law Liberalism. John Hasnas, Oxford University Press. © Oxford University Press 2024.
DOI: 10.1093/9780197784631.003.0006

a disproportionately damaging impact on members of socially subordinated groups, or disinformation that tends to undermine support for necessary public health measures? Advocates stake out positions at various points along the spectrum from greater to lesser restrictions on speech and offer principled arguments as to why they have identified the proper place to draw the line.

What's wrong with this way of addressing the issue? To answer this question, I suggest re-reading Chapter 2 because this line of reasoning is based on the same inaccurate worldview that undergirds the market failure argument.

Recall that in Chapter 2, I discussed the "academic model" of the relationship between the law and the market. This model, reproduced in Figure 5.1, views the free market as the realm of unregulated voluntary action by individuals and law as consciously created legislation designed to regulate the actions of individuals for the public good.

I argued there that this is an inaccurate view of both the law and the market—that in the real world, the law consists of both

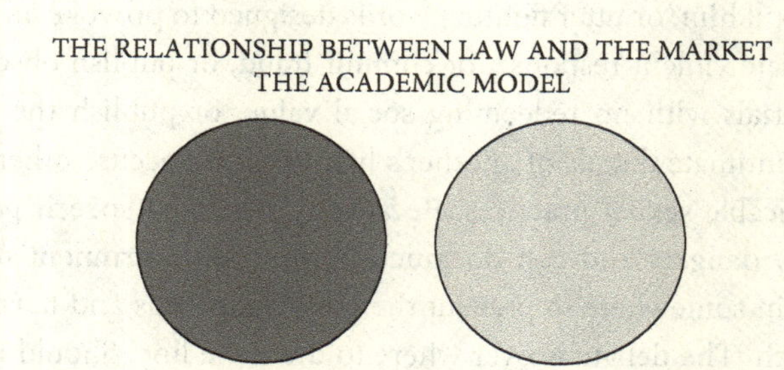

Figure 5.1 The academic model of the relationship between the law and the market, demonstrating the law and market as entirely separate.

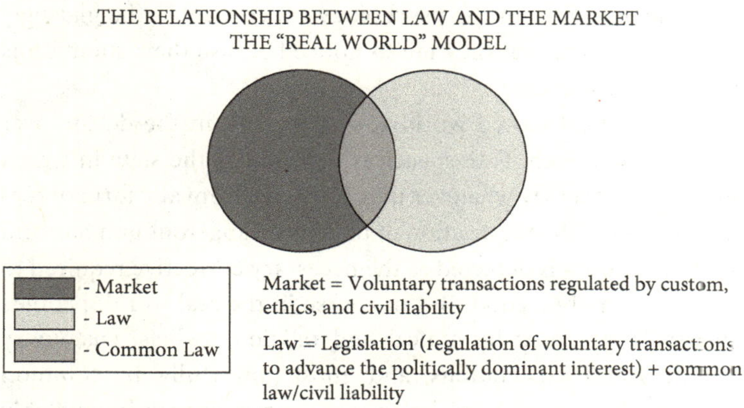

Figure 5.2 The real-world model of the relationship between the law and market, demonstrating the law and market as overlapping, with their shared area being common law.

consciously created legislation, which is law designed to serve the politically dominant interest, and spontaneously evolved rules of common law; and that the market is the realm of individual action regulated by the forces of ethics, custom, and common law civil liability free from political regulation by the state. This is represented in Figure 5.2.

I further argued that the persistence of the academic model could be explained by inattentional blindness—the psychological phenomenon of failing "to notice a fully-visible, but unexpected object because attention was engaged on another task, event, or object."[2] My suggestion was that political and economic theorists become so fixated on their academic models that they fail to notice the nonpolitical regulatory forces at work in the world, especially that of civil liability. As I pointed out in that context, to mainstream political and economic theorists, civil liability is the analog of the

[2] Daniel J. Simons, *Inattentional Blindness*, 2(5) SCHOLARPEDIA 3244 (2007), http://www.scholarpedia.org/article/inattentional_blindness.

invisible gorilla from the psychology experiments—the glaringly obvious element that they fail to notice because their attention is focused elsewhere.

The identical flawed worldview is at work in the debate over freedom of speech. Free speech is depicted as the state in which individuals may say whatever they want free from any form of regulation. Legislative restriction of the more dangerous and harmful forms of speech is depicted as the necessary corrective required to protect the public good. But of course in the real world, people's speech is regulated by ethical and religious beliefs, customary practices and expectations, and, most powerfully, by common law civil liability; and legislation that restricts speech is inevitably designed to advance the politically dominant viewpoint whether or not this corresponds with the public good.

There is no value in freedom of speech per se. The value being pursued is free *and responsible* speech—speech subject to regulation that ensures it does not impose unacceptable harm on others. An advocate of freedom of speech is not arguing for speech free of all regulation but for speech free from political regulation by the state—for speech regulated by ethics, custom, and common law civil liability.

The problem with the conventional approach to freedom of speech described above—the problem with the academic model of the relationship between law and the market—is that it overlooks the existence of civil liability as a regulatory mechanism. It frames politically regulated speech as the only alternative to completely unregulated speech and sets advocates off on a perennial quest to find the proper scope of the state's power to restrict speech. In the context of the debate over freedom of speech, just as much as in the context of the market failure argument, civil liability is an invisible gorilla.

This is unfortunate because, as explained in Chapter 2, civil liability is a powerful tool for linking freedom with responsibility. And, just as was the case with the market failure argument, if the common law provides the regulation needed to discourage unacceptably harmful speech, there is no need to empower politicians to create legislation to do the same thing. And, once again, this is indeed the case.

I. Constitutional Common Sense

There is no way to discuss freedom of speech in the United States without talking about the Constitution and the First Amendment. So let's begin with a little common sense constitutional analysis.[3]

The Constitution of the United States was adopted in 1787 to create a strong national government to replace the Articles of Confederation. In 1791, the first ten amendments to the Constitution were enacted to place explicit limitations on the power of this strong new government. The First Amendment, in relevant part, states that "Congress shall make no law . . . abridging

[3] An important disclaimer: Nothing in this chapter (or in the entire book, for that matter) addresses or is relevant to the debate among legal scholars over how the text of the Constitution should be interpreted. Many people find the study of constitutional law fascinating. I do not. I am unable to generate any enthusiasm for arguing over the content of oxymorons such as "substantive due process," finding new constitutional rights in the penumbras and emanations of a subset of the Bill of Rights, *see* Griswold v. Connecticut, 381 U.S. 479, 484 (1965), attempting to determine which rights are "deeply rooted in the Nation's history and traditions," *see* Washington v. Glucksberg, 521 U.S. 702, 721 (1997), or explaining how the power to regulate interstate commerce permits the federal government to limit the amount of wheat a farmer can grow on his own farm to feed to his cattle, *see* Wickard v. Filburn, 317 U.S. 111, 118–130 (1942). The knowledge that the vast majority of Supreme Court constitutional decisions interpret a total of four words—"due process" and "equal protection"—leads me to regard constitutional law as a species of Felix Cohen's transcendental nonsense—the practice of resolving legal questions by the manipulation of abstract concepts that are not explicitly connected to matters of empirical fact or ethical value—that is, by "legal magic and word-jugglery," *see* Felix Cohen, *Transcendental Nonsense and the Functional Approach*, 35 Colum. L. Rev. 809, 821 (1935).

The Constitution identifies the powers possessed by the federal government of the United States and the limitations on those powers. Originalists favor an interpretation of the Constitution that tends to restrain these powers. Living Constitutionalists favor an interpretation that permits the expansion of these powers. This is an argument about political philosophy dressed up to look like a legal dispute. To my mind, it would be better to cut out the middleman and engage in the philosophical debate directly.

the freedom of speech, or of the press."[4] The adoption of this amendment did not guarantee citizens freedom of speech. It simply stated that the *federal* government did not have the power to pass legislation restricting the speech of the citizens of the United States.

State constitutions had similar, more expansive provisions restraining the state governments' power to legislatively suppress the speech of their citizens. For example, the Virginia constitution proclaims

> that the freedoms of speech and of the press are among the great bulwarks of liberty, and can never be restrained except by despotic governments; that any citizen may freely speak, write, and publish his sentiments on all subjects, being responsible for the abuse of that right; that the General Assembly shall not pass any law abridging the freedom of speech or of the press, nor the right of the people peaceably to assemble, and to petition the government for the redress of grievances.[5]

Similarly, Pennsylvania's constitution states:

> The printing press shall be free to every person who may undertake to examine the proceedings of the Legislature or any branch of government, and no law shall ever be made to restrain the right thereof. The free communication of thoughts and opinions is one of the invaluable rights of man, and every citizen may freely speak, write and print on any subject, being responsible for the abuse of that liberty.[6]

And New York's constitution declares that "[e]very citizen may freely speak, write and publish his sentiments on all subjects, being

[4] U.S. Const. amend. I.
[5] Va. Const. art. I, § 12.
[6] Pa. Const. art. I, § 7.

responsible for the abuse of that right; and no law shall be passed to restrain or abridge the liberty of speech or of the press."[7]

There is an interesting distinction between the First Amendment and the state constitutions' free speech clauses. The First Amendment simply says that Congress shall make no law abridging freedom of speech. The state provisions all contain a responsibility clause, a clause indicating that although the state government cannot infringe on the right to speak, the speaker bears responsibility for his or her expression. Thus, the Virginia constitution states "that any citizen may freely speak, write, and publish his sentiments on all subjects, *being responsible for the abuse of that right*"; the Pennsylvania constitution states that "every citizen may freely speak, write and print on any subject, *being responsible for the abuse of that liberty*"; and the New York constitution states that "[e]very citizen may freely speak, write and publish his sentiments on all subjects, *being responsible for the abuse of that right.*"

There is a fairly straightforward explanation for this distinction. Each state had inherited the common law of England on its separation from the mother country. Hence, each had a developed body of law designed to discourage unacceptably harmful speech. Lawsuits for libel, slander, fraudulent misrepresentation, breach of contract, tortious interference with business relationships, and even breach of a promise to marry could be brought to hold individuals responsible for the harmful effect of their speech on others. The state constitutional provisions were clearly designed to prohibit only legislative restrictions on speech—to guarantee individuals freedom from governmental efforts to suppress their speech—while preserving the private common law actions designed to

[7] N.Y. Const. art. I, § 8. Similar provisions exist in the constitutions of the states that joined the union after the adoption of the Constitution. *See, e.g.*, Cal. Const. art. I, § 2 ("Every person may freely speak, write and publish his or her sentiments on all subjects, being responsible for the abuse of this right. A law may not restrain or abridge liberty of speech or press"); Fla. Const. art. I, § 4 ("Every person may speak, write and publish sentiments on all subjects but shall be responsible for the abuse of that right. No law shall be passed to restrain or abridge the liberty of speech or of the press").

ensure that citizens did not exercise this freedom harmfully and irresponsibly.

The federal government, in contrast, was entirely a creation of the Constitution, and had no prior existence and no preexisting body of common law. The First Amendment contained no responsibility clause because none was needed. There was no underlying federal common law to be preserved.

The power to regulate speech is part of what is known as the police power—the power to enact legislation designed to protect or improve the health, safety, morals, and general welfare of the populace. The state governments possess the police power. The federal government is endowed only with the powers enumerated in Article I, § 8, which do not include the police power.[8]

In the debates over the ratification of the Constitution, the supporters of the Constitution argued that the new national government posed no danger to citizens' civil liberties because it was a government of limited enumerated powers that did not include the police power. Hence, the federal government was not empowered to pass legislation restricting citizens' freedom of speech or other civil liberties. Opponents of the Constitution countered that this implicit limitation on the power of the federal government was insufficient to protect citizens' liberty—that political incentives and the temptations of power will inevitably cause the federal government to exceed its designated authority. The Bill of Rights was added to the Constitution to meet this criticism by making the implicit limitations on federal power explicit.

The purpose of the First Amendment was to provide an explicit statement that the Congress of the United States could not legislate restrictions on speech. The state constitutions prohibited the state legislatures from enacting laws that restrained or punished speech.

[8] Many political theorists argue that the police power derives from the social contract that is the basis of and justifies the existence of the state governments. No such argument is available for the federal government, however, because the federal government was not created by a social contract. It was consciously created by the Constitution.

The First Amendment was designed to make it clear that in creating a national legislature, the states were not investing it with a power that they had denied themselves.

This understanding makes it perfectly sensible to treat the First Amendment as an *absolute* bar on federal legislation restricting speech. The states had the power to regulate speech. Their constitutions barred the state legislatures from restricting speech, leaving all regulation to the state's underlying common law. The First Amendment made it clear that the federal legislature was subject to the same prohibition as the state legislatures. Speech in the United States was to be regulated by common law, not by politicians.

II. The Great Non Sequitur

As it turns out, the opponents of the Constitution were correct to be skeptical of the limitations on federal power, as was proven by the adoption of the Sedition Act in 1798. This act, which punished "written, printed, uttered or published" opposition to the federal government and its policies,[9] demonstrated not only that the federal government would not be bound by the implicit limitation of its enumerated powers, but that it would disregard the First Amendment as well. The act, which expired in 1801, was never challenged in court—probably because *Marbury v. Madison*, the case that established the power of judicial review, was not decided until 1803.[10]

For the next 118 years, there was virtually no judicial history of the First Amendment because the federal government did not

[9] Sedition Act of 1798, ch. 74, § 2, 1 Stat. 596.

[10] 5 U.S. 137 (1803). This is not technically correct. In United States v. Callender, 25 F. Cas. 239 (C.C.D. Va. 1800), a seditious libel case brought under the act, defense council argued that the petit jury was entitled to disregard the law if it believed it to be repugnant to the Constitution. However, this was not a direct challenge to the legal validity of the act and was not based on the First Amendment.

attempt to restrict speech. Then, in 1919, the Court decided the case of *Schenck v. United States.*[11] In this case, the defendant was convicted of violating the Espionage Act of 1917 for opposing military conscription during World War I by distributing leaflets that quoted the Thirteenth Amendment, identified conscription with involuntary servitude, and advocated that citizens assert their right to oppose the draft.[12] In upholding Schenck's conviction, Oliver Wendell Holmes offered the greatest non sequitur in the history of the Supreme Court. After admitting that "in ordinary times the defendants in saying all that was said in the circular would have been within their constitutional rights," he stated,

> [b]ut the character of every act depends upon the circumstances in which it is done. The most stringent protection of free speech would not protect a man in falsely shouting fire in a theatre and causing a panic. It does not even protect a man from an injunction against uttering words that may have all the effect of force.[13]

This assertion is perfectly true and utterly irrelevant. Indeed, one is not legally free to falsely shout fire in a crowded theater and cause a panic or utter words that have the effect of force because one would be subject to civil liability for doing so. Such speech is subject to regulation at the state level under common law. But the relevant question in *Schenck* is not whether speech is subject to regulation, but whether it is subject to legislative regulation by the federal government. The fact that individuals are not free to falsely shout fire in a crowded theater tells us exactly nothing about whether *the federal government* should have the power to suppress citizens' ability to express opposition to the military draft in times of war.

[11] 249 U.S. 47 (1919).
[12] *Id.* at 49.
[13] *Id.* at 52.

This line of reasoning makes sense only under the assumption that the only alternatives are totally unregulated speech and speech regulated by federal legislation—that is, only if one does not notice the existence of the regulatory effect of civil liability. Apparently, the invisibility of the common law is not a contemporary phenomenon.

The First Amendment states that *Congress* may not infringe on freedom of speech, not that nothing may. This implies that regulation of speech must occur at the state level. The state constitutions, in turn, state that the regulation must come via common law, not state legislation.

There is a good reason for this. It is difficult to suppress speech through common law. To recover damages, there must be a plaintiff who can prove by a preponderance of the evidence that the speech in question caused him or her legally cognizable harm. And to impose a prior restraint on speech—to get an injunction—the plaintiff must demonstrate that the speech presents a high probability of irreparable harm. The requirement to establish both harm and causation significantly limits the power to suppress speech through the common law.

Neither limitation applies to legislation. Legislation can suppress speech purely on the basis of speculation as to what might happen—e.g., prohibiting publication of leaflets opposing the draft because it might undermine the war effort—and what constitutes harm can be defined in any way the politically dominant party wants—e.g., prohibiting expression that appeals to the prurient interest and lacks serious literary, artistic, political, or scientific value.

Schenck gave us the "clear and present danger" test for when the federal government may legislatively restrict speech.[14] This is often hailed as a great protection for freedom of speech. It is not. *Schenck* is the case that turned the word "no" in the First Amendment into the word "some," and turned an impermeable barrier into a

[14] *Id.* ("The question in every case is whether the words used are used in such circumstances and are of such a nature as to create a clear and present danger that they will bring about the substantive evils that Congress has a right to prevent").

porous sieve permitting an ever-increasing number of legislative restrictions on speech to seep through it.

Holmes himself quickly came to regret his statement when later in the same year, the Court heard the case of *Abrams v. United States*.[15] In this case, the defendant was convicted of violating the Espionage Act by distributing leaflets opposing American intervention in Russia and calling for proletarian revolution to overthrow capitalism.[16] When the Court upheld the conviction, Holmes dissented on the ground that the majority was misapplying the clear and present danger test—that "nobody can suppose that the surreptitious publishing of a silly leaflet by an unknown man, without more, would present any immediate danger that its opinions would hinder the success of the government arms or have any appreciable tendency to do so."[17]

But Holmes was quite wrong. The majority of the Court could and did make that supposition. By removing the prophylactic of the First Amendment as an absolute bar on the legislative restriction on speech, Holmes had opened a Pandora's box of political regulation that could not be limited to "attempts to check the expression of opinions that . . . so imminently threaten immediate interference with the lawful and pressing purposes of the law that an immediate check is required to save the country,"[18] as he desired.

Six years later, in *Gitlow v. New York*,[19] the Court decided that the Due Process Clause of the Fourteenth Amendment meant that the First Amendment applied to the state governments as well as the federal government.[20] This, too, is typically hailed as a bulwark for

[15] 250 U.S. 616 (1919).

[16] *Id.* at 617.

[17] *Id.* at 628.

[18] *Id.* at 630.

[19] 268 U.S. 652 (1925).

[20] *Id.* at 666 ("For present purposes we may and do assume that freedom of speech and of the press—which are protected by the First Amendment from abridgment by Congress—are among the fundamental personal rights and 'liberties' protected by the due process clause of the Fourteenth Amendment from impairment by the States").

freedom of speech. Once again, it was not. The state constitutions already contained their own clauses prohibiting legislative restriction on speech and preserving its regulation by common law. Applying the First Amendment to the states added no additional protection for speech but brought along the clear and present danger test (and other subsequently developed exceptions) that taught the states how to evade the constitutional limitations on their legislative power.

Having opened the door to the legislative regulation of speech, the Court spent the next century distinguishing speech that is protected by the First Amendment from speech that is not. Political speech is protected unless it creates "a clear and present danger that [it] will bring about the substantive evils that Congress has a right to prevent." Then it is not.[21] Are fighting words—words "which by their very utterance inflict injury or tend to incite an immediate breach of peace" protected? No.[22] Speech advocating the violent overthrow of the federal government? No.[23] Movies? Yes.[24] Obscenity? No.[25] Symbolic speech? Sometimes,[26] unless it's cross-burning; then, no.[27] Students' speech in schools? Yes,[28] unless it encourages drug use; then no.[29] Spending money to promote a political candidate? Yes.[30] Contributing money to a political candidate? No.[31] Commercial speech? No,[32] then yes,[33] then

[21] Schenck v. United States, 249 U.S. 47, 52 (1919).
[22] Chaplinsky v. New Hampshire, 315 U.S. 568, 572 (1942).
[23] Dennis v. United States, 341 U.S. 494 (1951).
[24] Joseph Burstyn, Inc. v. Wilson, 343 U.S. 495 (1952).
[25] Roth v. United States, 354 U.S. 476 (1957).
[26] United States v. O'Brien, 391 U.S. 367 (1968).
[27] Virginia v. Black, 538 U.S. 343 (2003).
[28] Tinker v. Des Moines Indep. Cmty. Sch. Dist., 393 U.S. 503 (1969).
[29] Morse v. Frederick, 551 U.S. 393 (2007).
[30] Buckley v. Valeo, 424 U.S. 1 (1976).
[31] *Id.*
[32] Valentine v. Chrestensen, 316 U.S. 52 (1942).
[33] Virginia State Bd. of Pharmacy v. Virginia Citizens Consumer Council, Inc., 425 U.S. 748 (1976).

sometimes.[34] Pornography? Yes.[35] Child pornography? No.[36] Hate speech, yes.[37] Video games, yes.[38]

What basis does the Court have for making such distinctions? One would think that it would look at the purpose of the First Amendment—the reason that it was added to the Constitution. But that cannot help. The original purpose of the First Amendment was to maintain the separation of powers between the state and federal governments by denying the federal government the power to regulate speech. But the Court abandoned that purpose in *Schenck*, when it permitted federal regulation of speech, and *Gitlow*, when it held that the First Amendment applied to the state governments.[39]

This forced the Court to seek a normative grounding for the First Amendment by asking what value it serves. Its initial answer was that the First Amendment was designed to preserve a well-functioning representative democracy. As the Court explained in *Terminiello v. Chicago*,[40]

> The vitality of civil and political institutions in our society depends on free discussion. . . . [I]t is only through free debate and free exchange of ideas that government remains responsive to the will of the people and peaceful change is effected. The right

[34] Cent. Hudson Gas and Elec. Corp. v. Pub. Serv. Comm'n, 447 U.S. 557 (1980).
[35] Ashcroft v. Free Speech Coalition, 535 U.S. 234 (2002).
[36] New York v. Ferber, 458 U.S. 747 (1982).
[37] R.A.V. v. City of St. Paul, 505 U.S. 377 (1992).
[38] Brown v. Ent. Merchs. Ass'n, 564 U.S. 786 (2011).
[39] *See* New York Times v. Sullivan, 376 U.S. 254, 276–77 (1964) ("It is true that the First Amendment was originally addressed only to action by the Federal Government, and that Jefferson, for one, while denying the power of Congress 'to controul the freedom of the press,' recognized such a power in the States. But this distinction was eliminated with the adoption of the Fourteenth Amendment and the application to the States of the First Amendment's restrictions"); Gitlow v. New York, 268 U.S. 652 (1925); Schenck v. United States, 249 U.S. 47 (1919).
[40] 337 U.S. 1 (1949).

> to speak freely and to promote diversity of ideas and programs is therefore one of the chief distinctions that sets us apart from totalitarian regimes.[41]

This could explain why the realm of protected speech included an expansive conception of political speech—including symbolic speech, hate speech, and campaign expenditures—but excluded incitement of violence, obscenity, and commercial speech.

In the 1960s, the Court expanded its concept of the value undergirding the First Amendment beyond merely the preservation of representative government to the facilitation of the exchange of ideas and personal expression. Thus, in *New York Times v. Sullivan*,[42] the Court limited the ability of public officials to sue for defamation—requiring them to demonstrate actual malice to recover—on the ground that the First Amendment embodied "a profound national commitment to the principle that debate on public issues should be uninhibited, robust, and wide-open, and that it may well include vehement, caustic, and sometimes

[41] *Id.* at 4. This is an illustrative example of a point the Court reiterated over the course of decades. *See, e.g.*, Stromberg v. California, 283 U.S. 359, 369 (1931) ("The maintenance of the opportunity for free political discussion to the end that government may be responsive to the will of the people and that changes may be obtained by lawful means, an opportunity essential to the security of the Republic, is a fundamental principle of our constitutional system"); De Jonge v. Oregon, 299 U.S. 353, 365 (1937) ("The greater the importance of safeguarding the community from incitements to the overthrow of our institutions by force and violence, the more imperative is the need to preserve inviolate the constitutional rights of free speech, free press and free assembly in order to maintain the opportunity for free political discussion, to the end that government may be responsive to the will of the people and that changes, if desired, may be obtained by peaceful means. Therein lies the security of the Republic, the very foundation of constitutional government"); United States v. United Auto Workers, 352 U.S. 567, 593 (1957) (Douglas, J., dissenting) ("Under our Constitution it is We The People who are sovereign. The people have the final say. The legislators are their spokesmen. The people determine through their votes the destiny of the nation. It is therefore important—vitally important—that all channels of communication be open to them during every election, that no point of view be restrained or barred, and that the people have access to the views of every group in the community").

[42] 376 U.S. 254 (1964).

unpleasantly sharp attacks on government and public officials."[43] And in *Curtis Publishing Co. v. Butts*,[44] the Court similarly limited the ability of all public figures to recover for defamation, declaring that the First Amendment

> is as much a guarantee to individuals of their personal right to make their thoughts public and put them before the community, as it is a social necessity required for the "maintenance of our political system and an open society. . . . The dissemination of the individual's opinions on matters of public interest is for us, in the historic words of the Declaration of Independence, an 'unalienable right' that 'governments are instituted among men to secure.'"[45]

This could explain the Court's inclusion of student speech, movies, pornography, and video games in the realm of protected speech. But note that by limiting individuals' ability to recover for defamation, the Court treated the First Amendment as a restraint not only on the legislative regulation of speech, but also on the regulation of speech by state common law.

Thus, over the course of a century, Holmes's non sequitur transformed the First Amendment from an absolute ban on the regulation of speech by the federal government into an exception-laden bar to the regulation of speech by both the federal and state legislatures and state common law. By opening the door to the political regulation of speech, it turned the scope of freedom of speech into a political football that theorists would struggle to move up or down the ideological field, resulting in the conventional way of addressing the issue described at the beginning of this chapter.

[43] *Id.* at 270.
[44] 388 U.S. 130 (1967).
[45] *Id.* at 149–150.

III. A Comparative Assessment

How does the common law regulate speech? The first thing to note is that under common law, there is no need to make a conceptual distinction between speech and conduct. As explained in Chapter 2, the common law evolved to discourage individuals from intentionally or carelessly harming others. Liability attached to conduct that caused harm, regardless of whether it was speech or physical conduct.

Consider intentional torts first. A false statement intended to cause others to rely on it and suffer a loss gives rise to liability for misrepresentation. False statements intended to damage another's reputation and standing in the community give rise to liability for defamation. Publicly disclosing certain types of private information gives rise to liability for invasion of privacy. Extreme forms of offensive speech intended to cause another severe emotional distress give rise to liability for the intentional infliction of emotional distress. Disclosure of confidential information one is contractually bound not to reveal gives rise to liability for breach of contract. And, of course, falsely shouting fire in a crowded theater with the intent to cause others to be injured in a panic gives rise to liability for battery.[46]

Speech is also regulated by the tort of negligence. Negligence requires us to exercise reasonable care—the amount of care a reasonably prudent person would use—to avoid causing harm to others. This requires us to be careful about what we say as well as what we do. A personal trainer who causes an injury by carelessly instructing a client to lift much too much weight is liable for negligence. So is a financial advisor who causes a financial loss by telling a client to buy a stock without doing proper research, or a doctor

[46] *See* Restatement (Second) of Torts § 13 (Am. L. Inst. 1965) ("An actor is subject to liability to another for battery if a) he acts intending to cause a harmful or offensive contact with the person of the other of a third person, . . . and b) a harmful contact with the person of the other directly or *indirectly* results" (emphasis added)).

who tells a patient having a heart attack to ignore the chest pain without doing a proper medical examination.

The common law also permits the prior restraint of speech in exceptional circumstances. A plaintiff who can show that there is a high probability that he or she will suffer irreparable harm if another is permitted to speak can obtain an injunction barring that speech. Although rare, such circumstances sometimes exist. For example, an author of a book deemed sacrilegious and under a fatwa of death could obtain an injunction barring the disclosure of his location, as could the proverbial grain dealer with a hungry crowd outside his or her home who needed to prevent an incendiary speech. As Holmes pointed out in *Schenck*, "[t]he most stringent protection of free speech would not protect a man . . . from an injunction against uttering words that may have all the effect of force."[47]

Under the common law, would a neo-Nazi organization be permitted to hold a march in Skokie, Illinois, a community with a large Jewish population that included many survivors of the Holocaust?[48] Yes, if none of the residents can demonstrate that there is a high probability that they will suffer irreparable harm. No, if they cannot.

In sum, under common law, people would be able to speak freely, but would be required to speak responsibly, using reasonable care not to harm others by what they say.

Note that under common law, there are many forms of unpleasant speech that are not subject to regulation. Offensive speech that does not cause the type of harm that can give rise to a lawsuit will not be suppressed. This would include the publication of obscene and pornographic materials, advocacy of "blasphemous" religious doctrines or extreme political positions, insulting racial or ethnic stereotypes, and any other assertions that most people

[47] Schenck v. United States, 249 U.S. 47, 52 (1919).
[48] *See* Collin v. Smith, 578 F.2d 1197 (7th Cir. 1978).

do not want to hear.[49] In addition, in many cases, speech that may influence others to do bad things will not be suppressed. This is because absent a special relationship that makes one responsible for the actions of another (e.g., the employer/employee relationship) or gives him or her the ability and duty to control the other, the common law will not trace causation through the voluntary action of a third party—that is, one who tells another to do something harmful will not be held liable if the other party does it of his or her own free will.[50]

Common law regulation of speech will never be perfect because the common law is never perfect. A feature of the common law is that it is always wrong in the present but is self-correcting. At any point in time, one can identify ways in which the rules of common law are not doing an adequate job of resolving human conflicts. But in such cases, the litigation load increases until a new rule evolves that does a better job resolving the conflict. This trial-and-error learning process keeps the common law responsive to changing cultural and social mores that are expressed through jury decisions. But the adjustment takes time. As the technology of communication advances, there will be cases in which the common law rules have not yet evolved sufficiently to provide effective regulation of its new use. As a result, there may well be cases of socially damaging speech where no individual has been sufficiently harmed to bring suit or is in a position to obtain an injunction. Can this situation be improved by permitting the legislative regulation of speech?

[49] The parameters of what the common law will recognize as harm are constantly changing. At one point in time, the common law permitted recovery for physical, but not psychic harm. But over the course of the twentieth century, the tort of the intentional infliction of emotional distress and the ability to recover damages for negligently inflicted emotional distress evolved as juries came to recognize psychic harm as worthy of legal protection. Many people currently advocate that derogatory racial, ethnic, and sexual assertions cause a type of harm that the law should protect. If juries come to agree with this, then the line between offensive and harmful speech will shift once again.

[50] There are exceptions to this principle, notably the incendiary speaker who sets the crowd on the hypothetical grain dealer.

Theoretically, yes. Academics can always describe an omniscient, beneficent government that only legislates restrictions designed to achieve the public good. But as pointed out in Chapter 2, we do not live in the world of academic models. In the real world, legislation is not correctly understood as regulation of individual behavior for the public good, but as regulation of individual behavior to advance the politically dominant interest whether that interest corresponds with the public good or not. So the relevant question is whether politicians functioning in the real world of rough-and-tumble politics can improve upon the common law.

There is good reason to believe that the answer is no. Under common law, there can be no legal action without either a party who has been harmed or one who can demonstrate a high probability of irreparable harm. This limits the scope of speech subject to suppression. But as noted in Section II, legislators are not bound by this limitation. They are free to envision speculative connections between speech and harm to society, and to legislate restrictions on such speech. And because politicians tend to identify the policies they support with the public good, dangerous speech invariably turns out to be speech that opposes their policies. Recognition of this tendency was the reason that the First Amendment was added to the Constitution in the first place.

Consider the results of Oliver Wendell Holmes's opening the door to the legislative regulation of speech just a crack to permit the suppression of words that are "used in such circumstances and are of such a nature as to create a clear and present danger that they will bring about the substantive evils that Congress has a right to prevent."[51] That crack permitted legislation that suppressed leaflets quoting the Thirteenth Amendment and encouraging citizens to oppose military conscription,[52] leaflets opposing American intervention in Russia and calling for the overthrow of capitalism,[53] the

[51] Schenck v. United States, 249 U.S. 47, 52 (1919).
[52] *Id.*
[53] Abrams v. United States, 250 U.S. 616 (1919).

advocacy of communism,[54] and membership in the Communist Party.[55] It permitted legislation that invested the state with the power to punish "utterances inimical to the public welfare, tending to incite to crime, disturb the public peace, or endanger the foundations of organized government and threaten its overthrow by unlawful means."[56] It gave the state the power to punish speech not because it *did* cause harm or *would* cause harm, but because it *might* cause harm. Whatever Holmes's intention, for the first half of the twentieth century, the clear and present danger test served as an authorization for the punishment of dissident speech.

Note also that having opened the door to the legislative regulation of speech, the Court had to determine where to place the doorstop. The initial stopping point was political speech. The Court viewed the purpose of the First Amendment as the maintenance of "the opportunity for free political discussion, to the end that government may be responsive to the will of the people and that changes, if desired, may be obtained by peaceful means."[57] Hence, political speech was at the core of the First Amendment's protection.

But placing political speech at the core meant that other forms of speech were at the periphery. Highly offensive, nonpolitical speech that can undermine public and private morality—obscene speech[58]—is not required to maintain a well-functioning representative government. Neither is commercial speech—speech used to advertise and sell products. So neither obscenity[59] nor commercial speech (at first)[60] received First Amendment protection.

[54] Dennis v. United States, 341 U.S. 494 (1951).

[55] Scales v. United States, 367 U.S. 203 (1961).

[56] Whitney v. California, 274 U.S. 357, 371 (1927), *overruled by* Brandenburg v. Ohio, 395 U.S. 444 (1969).

[57] De Jonge v. Oregon, 299 U.S. 353, 365 (1937).

[58] *See* Louis Henkin, *Morals and the Constitution: The Sin of Obscenity*, 63 Colum. L. Rev. 391 (1963).

[59] *See* Alberts v. California, 354 U.S. 476 (1957); Roth v. United States, 354 U.S. 476 (1957).

[60] *See* Valentine v. Chrestensen, 316 U.S. 52 (1942). The Court changed this holding, giving commercial speech partial First Amendment protection in 1976. *See* Virginia

Over the course of the twentieth century there are many Supreme Court decisions that strike down state and federal statutes restricting speech with ringing endorsements of the importance of freedom of speech to the American form of government.[61] Legal scholars exalt these decisions as embodiments of the Court's commitment to protect freedom of speech. Are they? The reason there are so many of them is because the Court authorized legislators to pass restrictions on dangerous and obscene and commercial speech in the first place—something the legislators did with gusto. And invariably, the speech politicians found to be dangerous or obscene or commercially objectionable was the speech of disfavored ideological and cultural minorities. Having narrowed the range of speech it would protect, I am not sure the Court deserves laurels for vigorously protecting the part that remains.

Interestingly, the Court's ultimate construction of the scope of First Amendment protection was not only too narrow, but also too broad. As noted in Section II, in the 1960s, the Court held that the First Amendment restrained not only the federal Congress and state legislatures, but also state common law. In *New York Times*

State Bd. of Pharmacy v. Virginia Citizens Consumer Council, Inc., 425 U.S. 748 (1976); Cent. Hudson Gas and Elec. Corp. v. Pub. Serv. Comm'n, 447 U.S. 557 (1980).

[61] Although some of the most illustrious endorsements came in dissents. A good example is Justice Douglas's opinion in *United States v. United Auto Workers*:

> Under our Constitution it is We the People who are sovereign. The people have the final say. The legislators are their spokesmen. The people determine through their votes the destiny of the nation. It is therefore important—vitally important—that all channels of communication be open to them during every election, that no point of view be restrained or barred, and that the people have access to the views of every group in the community. . . . Some may think that one group or another should not express its views in an election because it is too powerful, because it advocates unpopular ideas, or because it has a record of lawless action. But these are not justifications for withholding First Amendment rights from any group—labor or corporate. First Amendment rights are part of the heritage of all persons and groups in this country. They are not to be dispensed or withheld merely because we or the Congress thinks the person or group is worthy or unworthy.
>
> United States v. United Auto Workers, 352 U.S. 567, 593–97 (1957) (Douglas, J., dissenting).

v. Sullivan and *Curtis Publishing Co. v. Butts*, the Court ruled that public officials and public figures could not recover for defamation unless the defendant acted with actual malice, which required knowledge of the falsity of the defamatory statement or reckless disregard for its truth.[62] This was essentially a judicially created constitutional tort reform measure. It freed individuals and media from the requirement to exercise reasonable care not to harm the reputation of others in their public statements.

The language the Court used in these decisions suggests it suffered from the same inattentional blindness that I have been ascribing to political theorists—the inability to see the regulatory effect of civil liability. For example, in *Sullivan,* the Court justified its holding by claiming that there is "a profound national commitment to the principle that debate on public issues should be uninhibited, robust, and wide-open, and that it may well include vehement, caustic, and sometimes unpleasantly sharp attacks on government and public officials."[63] But this is clearly wrong. There may be a profound national commitment to robust and wide-open debate on public issues, but there is not one to uninhibited debate. The common law of defamation, invasion of privacy, nondisclosure contracts, and the intentional infliction of emotional distress is designed to place inhibitions on the way debate is conducted.

Boxing matches encourage the robust, wide-open exchange of physical rather than rhetorical blows that include vehement and unpleasantly sharp attacks on the fighters, but there are still many blows that are barred by the rules of the sport. The common law of speech provides the rules of responsible political debate.

Similarly in *Curtis Publishing*, the Court justified limiting the ability of public figures to recover for defamation on the ground that the First Amendment is

62 New York Times Co. v. Sullivan, 376 U.S. 254 (1964).
63 *Id.* at 270.

> a guarantee to individuals of their personal right to make their thoughts public and put them before the community . . . The dissemination of the individual's opinions on matters of public interest is for us, in the historic words of the Declaration of Independence, an "unalienable right" that "governments are instituted among men to secure."[64]

This is one of the Court's ringing endorsements for limiting the government's power to restrict speech. The Declaration of Independence is an inspiring affirmation of the limitation individual rights place on government power. But it is a non sequitur in the context of civil liability, which is about resolving conflicts between the individual members of society, not protecting individuals from government.

In *Sullivan*, the Commissioner of Public Affairs of Montgomery, Alabama, recovered a $500,000 libel judgment against the New York Times and several individuals for publishing an advertisement accusing the Montgomery police force of several abusive practices against Martin Luther King and African American demonstrators.[65] This lawsuit may be the world's most famous example of an abusive SLAPP (strategic lawsuit against public participation) suit. There is good reason to believe that it is an unjust result deriving from a biased jury pool in Alabama, and something that needed correction on appeal. But the solution to problems like this cannot be to free individuals and the media from the duty to exercise due care not to damage others' reputation in their public statements.

The *Sullivan* and *Curtis Publishing* cases may have had little initial effect on the New York Times and other mainstream media organizations that practiced responsible journalism. But it opened the door to publications like the National Enquirer to cut corners

[64] Curtis Pub. Co. v. Butts, 388 U.S. 130, 149–50 (1967).
[65] *Sullivan*, 376 U.S. at 256.

on their reporting standards. The growth of similar tabloids over the last decades of the twentieth century may be due in part to these decisions. It cannot be surprising that relieving people of the duty to use reasonable care in reporting results in less careful reporting. And to some extent, the explosion of irresponsible journalism that accompanied the advent of the internet and social media in the twenty-first century may be a second-order consequence of these decisions. There is some reason to believe that this instance of judicial tort reform is, at least in part, responsible for the transition from the time in which CBS news anchor Walter Cronkite was the most trusted man in America to the present, in which only 42 percent of people say they trust most news most of the time.[66]

As it does with the market, the common law provides good but imperfect regulation of speech. It suppresses most truly harmful speech, but only truly harmful speech. It is not perfect because there will always be new forms of harmful speech for which effective common law regulation has not yet evolved. And political theorists will always be able to imagine emergency situations that the common law would not address.

They will also be able to imagine legislation that would cure these ills. But to attempt to address the flaws in the common law by empowering politicians to regulate speech is to make the perfect the enemy of the good.

As explained in Chapter 2, politicians are necessarily driven by political considerations, and almost never anticipate new dangers in advance. Legislation is almost always a response to harm that has already occurred. And even when a future danger is perceived, the political process ensures that it will not be addressed in a timely manner. It is not news that the Social Security fund is running out of money or that greenhouse gases are affecting the climate. More

[66] Helen Coster, *More People Are Avoiding the News, and Trusting it Less, Report Says*, Reuters, June 14, 2022, https://www.reuters.com/business/media-telecom/more-people-are-avoiding-news-trusting-it-less-report-says-2022-06-14/.

significantly, politicians tend to identify the public good with the policies they support, which causes them to identify dangerous speech with dissident speech that opposes those policies. The prospects of any government composed of human beings who must be responsive to political considerations to obtain and retain power legislating only beneficial corrections to the flaws of the common law of speech are vanishingly small.

The Supreme Court tried this experiment with *Schenck*'s clear and present danger test. Opening the door to the political regulation of speech just a crack gave us not only a century of legislation aimed at suppressing dissident political, cultural, and sexual speech, but also judicial tort reform relieving individuals and media from their common law duty to use reasonable care not to harm others by their speech. The fact that, despite the obvious parallel with George Orwell's Ministry of Truth from *1984*,[67] the United States government just created the Disinformation Governance Board in the Department of Homeland Security[68] suggests that it is better to keep this door shut and locked and be satisfied with the good but imperfect regulation of the common law.

IV. Conclusion

In Chapter 2, I argued that political theorists suffered from inattentional blindness—that they were so focused on their academic model of the relationship between law and the market that

[67] George Orwell, 1984 3 (1992).

[68] Amanda Seitz, *Disinformation Board to Tackle Russia, Migrant Smugglers*, Associated Press, April 28, 2022, https://apnews.com/article/russia-ukraine-immigration-media-europe-misinformation-4e873389889bb1d9e2ad8659d9975e9d. Within weeks of the announcement and amid outcry from across the political spectrum, the board was paused; a subsequent review by Homeland Security Department advisors deemed there was "no need" for the board. Kanishka Singh, *U.S. Advisers Say No Need for Disinformation Governance Board*, Reuters, July 18, 2022, https://www.reuters.com/world/us/us-advisers-say-no-need-disinformation-governance-board-2022-07-19/.

they could not perceive the regulatory effect of common law civil liability. In this chapter, I have argued that legal theorists and the justices of the Supreme Court suffer from the same malady.

From Holmes's great non sequitur in *Schenck*, which ignored the difference between common law and legislative regulation of speech, through *Sullivan* and *Curtis Publishing*, which similarly failed to distinguish regulation by the common law of defamation from political regulation, the justices wrote as though the only two options were no regulation at all or political regulation by legislators. They wrote as though they were unfamiliar with the original constitutional relationship in which the federal and state constitutions prohibited legislative regulation of speech, but the state constitutions contained responsibility clauses specifically endorsing common law regulation. They wrote as though they had fully assimilated the academic model of the market and law, which viewed free speech as the complete absence of regulation and legislation as regulation of speech for the public good—as though they were blind to the fact that in the real world, speech is regulated by ethics, custom, and common law and free speech is correctly understood as speech free from *political* regulation.

It appears that in jurisprudence, as much as in political theory, common law civil liability is the invisible gorilla.

PART III
ANARCHY

The first two parts of this book argued that proper public policy analysis requires a comparative assessment of the effectiveness of legislative and common law regulation of human behavior. But what if these assessments invariably demonstrated the superiority of common law regulation? Wouldn't that be an argument for anarchy?

This part of the book makes such an argument. Chapter 6 distinguishes *political* law from *nonpolitical* law and shows that because nonpolitical law is not made by the state, it can serve as the legal system of anarchy. Chapter 7 argues that there can be a moral duty to obey the law of anarchy—that the law of anarchy is binding even though not derived from individual consent. Finally, Chapter 8 argues that none of the services necessary for a peaceful and prosperous life in society must be provided by the state, and in fact, are better provided nonpolitically.

6
The Law of Anarchy

Libertarian philosophers of law often write as though law is morally legitimate only if grounded in individual consent. They assume that unless law springs from some act of agreement, some express or implicit social contract by which individuals consent to be bound, it is nothing more than force. On this view, law is either a legitimate mechanism of social ordering that is consistent with respect for individual autonomy or an illegitimate mechanism of coercion by which some human beings are subjected to the will of others.

This is a false dilemma. Law is rarely, if ever, grounded in consent. That does not imply, however, that law necessarily gives some individuals command over others. As we saw in previous chapters, there is a third possibility. Law can arise through a process of unplanned evolution. It can be a product of "human action, but not the execution of any human design."[1] When this is the case, those subject to law are indeed bound, but not by the will of any identifiable human beings. Although law is inherently coercive, it is not inherently a vehicle for domination. In this chapter, I argue that this law—law that evolves from human interaction without the conscious guidance of any particular human intelligence—is the law of anarchy.

[1] Adam Ferguson, An Essay on the History of Civil Society, pt. 3, § 2 (1767).

Common Law Liberalism. John Hasnas, Oxford University Press. © Oxford University Press 2024.
DOI: 10.1093/9780197784631.003.0007

I. Four Types of Law

A. Customary Law

Customary law is often identified with the archaic rules of primitive and rudimentary legal systems. This is perhaps understandable because "primitive" legal systems are those associated with societies that lacked a highly organized central authority in which most law was customary law. Additionally, common law courts recognize only "ancient"[2] customs of "immemorial usage"[3] as having the force of law. Although this identification may be understandable, it is nevertheless unfortunate because it suggests that customary law is an obsolete legal form that is irrelevant to contemporary concerns. This is to mistake a part for the whole. The fact that primitive legal systems consist predominantly in customary law does not imply that customary law exists *only* in primitive legal systems, and the fact that common law courts recognized only ancient customs does not imply customary law consists *only* in ancient customs. Customary law still exists and continues to play a significant role in the modern world, as illustrated by the fact that much of international law is customary law and the Uniform Commercial Code has explicitly incorporated custom into the commercial law of the United States.[4]

The essence of customary law is not its antiquity, but its origin. Customary law is law that arises out of human interaction—law that "is not the product of official enactment, but owes its force to the fact that it has found direct expression in the conduct of men toward one another."[5] Customary law arises because of the limitations

[2] Arthur R. Hogue, Origins of the Common Law 195.

[3] William Blackstone, Commentaries on the Laws of England (9th ed.) (1783) 46.

[4] *See, e.g.,* UCC §§ 1-205, 2-202, 2-208.

[5] Lon L. Fuller, *Human Interaction and the Law, in* The principles of Social Order: Selected Essays of Lon L. Fuller 212.

of human knowledge—because human beings are unable to specify in advance the rules that will facilitate cooperative behavior in a complex society. Friedrich Hayek famously compared the price mechanism to "a system of telecommunications"[6] that enables human beings to coordinate their economic activities. Customary law is similarly a system of communication that enables humans to coordinate their social interaction so as to avoid violence and facilitate joint pursuits:

> [C]ustomary law can best be described as a language of interaction. To interact meaningfully men require a social setting in which the moves of the participating players will fall generally within some predictable pattern. To engage in effective social behavior men need the support of intermeshing anticipations that will let them know what their opposite numbers will do, or that will at least enable them to gauge the general scope of the repertory from which responses to their actions will be drawn. We sometimes speak of customary law as offering an unwritten code of conduct. The word code is appropriate here because what is involved is not simply a negation, a prohibition of certain disapproved actions, but also the obverse side of this negation, the meaning it confers on foreseeable and approved actions, which then furnish a point of orientation for ongoing interactive responses.[7]

Understanding customary law as a system of communication focuses our attention on its essential characteristic, which is not that it arises through repetition, but that it exists when and to the extent that members of the community have adapted their behavior to it. This occurs when members of the relevant community have had sufficient interaction to be able to predict how others will react to their behavior and to incorporate this prediction into their

[6] Friedrich A. Hayek, Individualism and Economic Order 87 (1948).
[7] Fuller, *supra* note 5, at 213–214.

decisions about how to behave. As Lon Fuller puts it, customary law is law that arises from the formation of "interactional expectancies."

> Instead, therefore, of speaking vaguely of an obligation arising through mere custom or repetition, it would be better to say that a sense of obligation will arise when a stabilization of interactional expectancies has occurred so that the parties have come to guide their conduct toward one another by these expectancies.[8]

In describing customary law as arising from the formation of interactional expectancies, one must be careful not to read any intentionality into its creation. The mutual expectations that develop typically are not formed on the basis of conscious reflection about the nature of others' behavior or the best way to react to it. Rather, human beings learn to adjust their behavior toward one another gradually over the course of repeated dealings and typically without being conscious that they are beginning to conform their conduct to a rule. As Fuller explains,

> The term interactional expectancy is itself, however, capable of producing difficulties. We shall be misled, for example, if we suppose that the relevant expectancy or anticipation must enter actively into consciousness. In fact the anticipations which most unequivocally shape our behavior and attitudes toward others are often precisely those that are operative without our being aware of their presence. To take an example from a somewhat trivial context, experiments have shown that the distance people stand from one another in carrying on ordinary conversations varies predictably among cultures and between individuals. At the same time most people would not be able to state, without some preliminary testing, what they themselves regard as a normal conversational distance. My inability to define offhand a proper

[8] *Id.* at 219–220.

distance would not prevent me, however, from finding offensive the action of someone who projected his face uncomfortably close to mine, nor would it relieve my puzzlement and distress at the conduct of someone who kept retreating when I approached what seemed to me a normal speaking distance. Our conduct toward others, and our interpretations of their behavior toward us, are, in other words, constantly shaped by standards that do not enter consciously into our thought processes. The analogy of language is once again useful; often we only become aware of rules of grammar when they are broken, and it is sometimes their breach that leads us to articulate for the first time rules we had previously acted on without knowing it.[9]

Furthermore, customary law is not rational in any mean-ends sense of rationality. The rules that evolve are not necessarily those that produce the most logical solution to the problem they address, but those that facilitate the peaceful interaction of the members of the community with regard to it:

> Generally, we may say that where A and B have become familiar with a practice obtaining between C and D, A is likely to adopt this pattern in his actions toward B, not simply or necessarily because it has any special aptness for their situation, but because he knows B will understand the meaning of his behavior and will know how to react to it.[10]

On this point, consider the example of US-Soviet relations that Fuller used in 1969 as an illustration of customary law:

> To illustrate the points I have been making with regard ... to the communicative function of customary practices, I should like

[9] *Id.* at 220.
[10] *Id.* at 228.

> to refer briefly to a development that appears to be occurring in the diplomatic relations of Russia and the United States. Here we may be witnessing something like customary law in the making. Between these two countries there seems to have arisen a kind of reciprocity with respect to the forced withdrawal of diplomatic representatives. The American government, for example, believes that a member of the Russian embassy is engaged in espionage, or, perhaps I should say, it believes him to be *over*engaged in espionage; it declares him *persona non grata* and requires his departure from this country. The expected response, based on past experience, is that Russia will acquiesce in this demand, but will at once counter with a demand for the withdrawal from Russia of an American diplomatic agent of equal rank. Conversely, if the Russians expel an American emissary, the United States will react by shipping back one of Russia's envoys.
>
> Here we have, for the time being at least, a quite stable set of interactional expectancies; within the field covered by this practice each country is able to anticipate with considerable confidence the reactions of its opposite number. This means that its decisions can be guided by a tolerably accurate advance estimate of costs. We know that if we throw one of their men out, they will throw out one of ours.[11]

We know that since Fuller wrote, the practice he described continued and hardened into a rule that was consistently followed by the United States and Soviet Union and, following the collapse of the Soviet Union, by Russia. Further, we know that after observing this behavior by the United States and the Soviet Union/Russia, other nations adopted it in their dealings with not only the United States and the Soviet Union/Russia, but with each other. Now, even in the context of superpower relations in which it arose, few

[11] *Id.* at 218.

would argue that a rule calling for the calibrated reciprocal expulsion of diplomats is the most logical solution to the problem of diplomatic espionage, or even that it is moderately well-adapted to its end. And there is still less reason to believe it is a logical way to deal with diplomatic espionage between superpowers and lesser powers or among the lesser powers that adopted the rule by imitation. The rule does, however, have the virtue of allowing nations to continue peaceful interaction in the face of events that could otherwise raise the specter of the termination of relations, if not war.

What this shows is that customary law is a solution to coordination problems. The rules evolve not to resolve the particular problem their content addresses, but to facilitate peaceful human interaction. The solutions they provide to substantive problems are a byproduct of this essential function. There is every reason to believe that a political theorist charged with the task of resolving a particular social problem could devise a theoretically superior and more elegant rule than any produced by customary law. But customary law develops precisely because no such legislator exists. In this sense, customary law truly is grown law, a set of rules that develop without a guiding intelligence.

Although I have been at pains to argue that customary law should not be identified with ancient law, it is worth devoting some attention to the customary law that developed in Britain during the Dark Ages. As detailed in Chapter 4, the collapse of Roman rule at the beginning of the fifth century produced an extended period during which the inhabitants lived without centralized legislative authority. Hence, the law that arose during this period was necessarily customary law. Because the process by which this law arose is instructive, a reprise of the account provided in Chapter 4 will be helpful.

As recounted there, the departure of Roman law and law enforcement left the British exposed to violent attack upon their persons and property without pre-established procedures for dealing with such aggression. Initially, the response to acts of assault, murder, and theft was for the members of a victims' household or clan to directly retaliate against the wrongdoer[12]—to prosecute the blood feud. But the risk to life and limb and disruption of normal life inherent in the blood feud created strong incentives for people to escape from the necessity of combating violence with violence.

Interestingly, they initially did this through agreement; that is, the practice developed of delaying the prosecution of the feud while efforts were made to negotiate a peaceful settlement of the dispute.[13] At the time, the chief instrument of social administration was the public assembly, the *moot*. When a dispute arose between two members of the community, the parties could agree to present their case to the *moot*, whose members, acting like present-day mediators, would help the parties find a settlement that both could accept.[14] When reached, such settlements resolved the dispute in a way that preserved the peace of the community.

Dispute settlement by such publicly mediated negotiations was popular because it avoided the strife of the blood feud. As a result, recourse to the *moot* was gradually transformed from an optional alternative to self-redress to a necessary prerequisite for receiving the help of one's support group and retaining one's good standing in the community.[15] What once had been voluntary became mandatory upon pain of outlawry, that is, upon pain of being put outside the protection, the "law," of one's group.

The virtue of settling disputes before the *moot* was that the *moot* had an institutional memory. When parties brought a dispute

[12] *See* Frederick Pollock and Frederic William Maitland, The History of English Law 46 (2d ed. 1898).

[13] *See* Julius Goebel, Jr., Felony and Misdemeanor: A Study in the History of Criminal Law 28–33.

[14] When the conflict was between members of households or tribes that did not participate in the same moot, the negotiations took place directly between the clans or tribes.

[15] *See* Pollock and Maitland, *supra* note 12, at 47–48. *See also* Bruce Benson, The Enterprise of Law 23 (1990).

before the *moot* that was similar to ones that had been resolved in the past, someone would remember the previous efforts at composition. Accommodations that had failed in the past would not be suggested; those that had succeeded would be repeated. Because the *moot* was a public forum, the repetition of successful methods of composing disputes gave rise to expectations in the community as to what the *moot* would recommend, which in turn gave the members of the community advance notice of how they must behave in order to avoid the feud. As the members of the community conformed their behavior to these expectations and took them into consideration in the process of composing subsequent disputes, rules of behavior gradually evolved. This, in turn, allowed for the transformation of the dispute settlement procedure from one dominated by bargaining to one consisting primarily in the application of rules.

As noted in Chapter 4, successful negotiations usually involved some form of compensatory payment. Over time, the community learned what level of compensation would effectively discourage violence and, as bargaining gave way to the application of rules, an "extraordinarily detailed schedules of tariffs . . . for various injuries"[16] developed. The same repeated process also produced a set of rules governing the conditions under which compensatory payments were due. Indeed, over the course of the centuries between the departure of the Romans and the coming of the Normans, the process described above produced an extensive body of customary law that served as the basis of English common law and to a large extent still resides within contemporary common law.[17]

[16] Harold Berman, Law and Revolution 54 (1983).

[17] *See* Hogue, *supra* note 2, at 190–192. Although for purposes of brevity I have limited my discussion to matters concerning what today would be called either tort or criminal law, the customary law that developed in Anglo-Saxon England was much broader than this. Precisely the same process that gave rise to the basic rules of order and personal security gave rise to property rules governing the descent of land and for determining when one was wrongfully dispossessed of chattels. For example, cattle theft was apparently a significant enough problem that one would have to purchase cattle before a required number of reliable witnesses to establish a right to continued possession.

Note the nature of the process. Human beings live together without fixed, known rules of behavior. No central authority exists with the power to establish and enforce such rules. Conflicts inevitably arise, often resulting in violence that disrupts normal life in the community and undermines cooperative activities. This creates strong social incentives to find an alternative method of resolving the conflicts. At first, the members of the community encourage disputants to voluntarily negotiate settlements and facilitate such negotiations by acting as mediators. As this process reduces social strife, publicly mediated negotiations become mandatory and, thus, more frequent. As certain types of negotiated settlements prove successful and are repeated, the members of the community come to expect that similar disputes will be resolved similarly. They begin to base their behavior on these expectations. They also take them into consideration when mediating subsequent disputes, basing their judgment of what constitutes a fair accommodation at least in part on what they believe the parties should have expected given the resolution of past disputes. This makes it more likely that subsequent disputes will be resolved in the same way as previous ones, further reinforcing the emerging expectations. Eventually, there develops a sufficient "stabilization of interactional expectancies" for the members of the community "to guide their conduct toward one another by these expectancies."[18] The continued iteration of the dispute settlement process then gradually transforms these interactional expectancies into recognized rules of behavior. This, in turn, allows the process itself to evolve from one of mediated bargaining into one of the enforcement of rules. And this transforms the question at issue from what constitutes a fair composition of a dispute to what constitutes the fair application of rules to a particular case.

See Pollock and Maitland, *supra* note 11, at 58–59. Further, much of contemporary commercial law is derived directly from the customary law of the Law Merchant of the eleventh and twelfth centuries. *See* Benson, *supra* note 14, at 30–35.

[18] Fuller *supra*, note 5, at 219–220.

Note also the basic normative features of this process. In the early stages of development, in which disputes are resolved through negotiation, settlements must be regarded as fair by both parties to command mutual assent. The purpose of community involvement is to help discover such "fair" compositions. But as successful compositions are repeated, people come to expect future cases to be resolved in the same way and feel unfairly treated if their expectations are violated. To be accepted as fair, proposed settlements must now conform to the evolving public expectations. This requires that new disputes be resolved in the same way as past similar ones, i.e., that like cases be treated alike. And the operation of this principle over time gives rise to identifiable and definite rules of behavior. In this way, an entire body of customary law arises purely from a commitment to fairness that is operationalized in the form of the principle that like cases should be treated alike.[19]

Customary law, then, is the law that arises from the repeated process of settling disputes on the basis of conventional notions of fairness—a process that is entirely backward-looking in orientation. Past resolutions matter because they establish expectations that are themselves an element in determining what constitutes a fair resolution to a present dispute. But in each individual case, the issue is always what constitutes a resolution that is fair to the parties to the instant dispute—not how the outcome of the case will affect the interests of other parties in the future. Cases are never decided on the basis of their precedential value, that is, on the basis of how the rules they instantiate will operate in future cases. Although the rules of customary law *derive from* considerations of fairness, they are not created *for the purpose of* ensuring fairness or any other social value.

It is precisely this backward-looking orientation that distinguishes customary law from both legislation, which consists in rules consciously designed to guide future behavior, and

19 *See* BERMAN, *supra* note 16, at 479–480.

modern common law, which, as we shall see presently,[20] explicitly considers the prospective effects of its decisions in resolving present controversies. With its inherent focus on settling actual disputes fairly rather than on the realization of any abstract ideal of justice, customary law provides fundamental rules of order that allow human beings to coordinate their activities without a guiding intelligence. By facilitating cooperative human interaction, these rules enable the individual members of society to better achieve their separate ends without necessarily advancing any particular collective end.

Each individual decision in a system of customary law is made on the basis of its own merits (e.g., what is the fair resolution of the dispute or the fair application of a rule given each party's conduct, any particular mitigating or aggravating conditions, and any legitimate expectations that could be drawn from past decisions), usually without explicit conceptual analysis. Yet the sum total of these individual decisions produces a body of law that is reasonably efficient at facilitating cooperative human interaction.

B. The Old Common Law

"Customary law" is a phrase of abstract and universal significance, referring to a form of law that can and does exist wherever people live in society. "Common law" is not. "Common law" has a distinct and parochial referent. The common law is the law that emerged from the royal courts of England.[21]

[20] *See infra* text accompanying notes 45–52.

[21] *See e.g.*, Hogue, *supra* note 17, at 5 (Common law "is simply the body of rules prescribing social conduct and justiciable in the royal courts of England"); John Hudson, The Formation of the English Common Law 18 (Common law is "the normal law of England, enforced by the king's court, above local custom"); Berman, *supra* note 16, at 480 (Common law is "the rules applicable in the central royal courts at Westminster").

This simple fact is typically obscured by the many metaphorical and otherwise indistinct and poorly discriminated uses to which the phrase is put. "Common law" can be used to refer generally to the legal systems of the British Commonwealth countries or to any in which precedent has binding legal authority, or more specifically to nonstatutory law, to "judge-made" law, or to the undifferentiated mass of procedural and substantive rules that comprise Anglo-American law. However, if we are interested in identifying the essential nature of the common law, none of these metaphorical uses are helpful. We must focus on the more precise, parochial definition of the term.

Until the nineteenth century, there would have been little harm in identifying the common law with the customary law of England. This is because the common law was simply the customary law as it was applied in the king's courts. During the formative period of the common law, the royal courts constituted only one among many fora in which the English could settle their disputes.[22] The royal courts operated alongside and in competition with ecclesiastic, manorial, urban, mercantile, and local courts.[23] Because the various courts collected their fees from the litigants,[24] they competed with each other for business, often creating elaborate legal fictions to extend their jurisdictions to include newer and more types of

[22] *See* Hogue, *supra* note 2, at 5:

> We should remember that the law enforced in royal courts, and common to all the realm of England, was in competition with concurrent rules enforced in other courts. Save when a matter of freehold was at issue, Englishmen were not compelled to present their causes before the king's courts. Men were free to take their cases into the local courts of the counties, which administered local, customary law; men might seek justice from the church courts administering rules of canon law, which touched many matters, especially those related to wills and testaments, marriage and divorce, and contracts involving a pledge of faith; feudal barons might accept jurisdiction of a baronial overlord whose court applied rules of feudal custom; townsmen might bring their causes before the court of a borough, which would judge them by rules of the law merchant.

[23] *See* Berman, *supra* note 16, at 10.

[24] *See* Adam Smith, An Inquiry into the Nature and Causes of the Wealth of Nations 720 (R. H. Campbell & A. S. Skinner eds. 1976) (1776).

disputes.[25] In this market for dispute settlement services, the main competitive advantage of the royal courts was not the substance of the rules being applied but the procedural innovation of the inquest—the fact-finding procedure that was the basis for trial by jury. The king attracted business to his courts by offering what was regarded as a more rational method of resolving disputes than was available in the other fora.[26]

Although litigants came to the royal courts for their superior dispute settlement procedure, the disputes they brought for settlement were those that arose under the customary law. Thus, the substantive law of the royal courts was the customary law:

> [T]he common law of England is usually said to be itself a customary law. It is not easy to know what this means. The English common law is usually traced back to the Assize of Clarendon and other twelfth-century royal enactments; these constitute enacted law, which is the opposite of customary law. What is meant, no doubt, is that the royal enactments established procedures in the royal courts for the enforcement of rules and principles and standards and concepts that took their meaning from custom and usage. The rules and principles and standards and concepts to be enforced . . . were derived from informal, unwritten, unenacted norms and patterns of behavior. These norms and patterns of behavior existed in the minds of people, in the consciousness of the community.[27]

[25] For an excellent discussion of the competition among the various courts prior to the nineteenth century, see Todd Zywicki, *The Rise and Fall of Efficiency in the Common Law: A Supply-Side Analysis*, 97 Nw. U. L. Rev. 1551, 1582–1589 (2003).

[26] *See* J. H. Baker, An Introduction to English Legal History 72–74 (4th ed. 2002). *See also* John Hudson, The Formation of the English Common Law 19 (1996) ("With regards to land law, there was not so much a chance of substantive rules as a transfer of jurisdiction from local to royal courts, the latter offered swifter and more rational justice").

[27] Berman, *supra* note 16, at 480–481.

As late as 1765, Blackstone could still identify the common law with "general customs; which are the universal rule of the whole kingdom, and form the common law, in its stricter and more usual signification."[28]

That the common law retained its customary nature for so long is not surprising given that for most of its history, the essential machinery of the common law was procedural. Almost all of the issues of concern to the lawyers and judges of the king's courts related to matters of jurisdiction or pleading. Given the competition among legal fora, and later among the different benches within the king's courts (i.e., exchequer, common pleas, king's bench, and chancery), the most important question to be decided was often whether the matter was properly before the court at all.[29] When it was, the job of the lawyers and judges was to ensure that the pleadings properly specified the issues to be submitted to the jury.[30] Once that was done, the matter was simply handed to the jury, "who were expected to do substantial justice."[31] Thus, the substantive decisions in the common law courts were made on the same basis as they were under customary law; the jury, who were members of the community, decided what was fair to the parties given the expectations that could be drawn from custom.

In addition, prior to the nineteenth century, the common law courts did not apply the doctrine of *stare decisis*; that is, they did not treat previous judicial decisions as binding legal authority for the decision of present cases.[32] Cases were mentioned, if at all, only

[28] WILLIAM BLACKSTONE, COMMENTARIES ON THE LAWS OF ENGLAND 67 (1765). *See also* FREDERICK POLLOCK, FIRST BOOK OF JURISPRUDENCE 254 (6th ed. 1929) ("[T]he common law is a customary law if, in the course of about six centuries, the undoubting belief and uniform language of everybody who had occasion to consider the matter were able to make it so").

[29] *See* Zywicki, *supra* note 25, at 1584–1587.

[30] *See* BAKER, *supra* note 26, at 76–81.

[31] *Id.* at 80.

[32] The most obvious reason for this is that before the printing press, the state of the written records of cases rendered such a practice utterly impracticable. *See* POLLOCK & MAITLAND, *supra* note 12, at 183 ("By some piece of good fortune Bracton, a royal justice, obtained possession of a large number of rolls. But the ordinary litigant or his

as evidence of the existence of a custom. A long line of cases decided in the same way could provide a strong reason to believe that a valid rule of customary law existed, but a single precedent did not constitute a statement of the law:

> [C]ases are used only as evidence of the existence of a custom of the court. It is the custom which governs the decision, not the case or cases cited as proof of the custom. Nor does it appear that a court would follow a case where it felt the result would be mischievous. The distinction is clearly seen when mediaeval practice is contrasted with that of our own day; at the present time it is possible for a judge to explain that his decision works substantial injustice, and is questionable on principle but he is bound by a particular case. This is a typical example of the working of the principle of precedent. Such things are not to be found in the Year Books, however. A single case was not a binding authority, but a well-established custom (proved by a more or less casual citing of cases) was undoubtedly regarded as strongly persuasive.[33]

Further, in keeping with the essentially procedural superstructure of the common law, when cases were referred to, it was usually to illustrate a matter of pleading. Indeed, Plucknett points out that the early Year Books themselves "are mainly concerned with the details of process and pleading."[34] When private reports

advocate would have had no opportunity of searching the rolls, and those who know what these records are like will feel safe in saying that even the king's justices can not have made a habit of searching them for principles of law"). *See also* Theodore F. T. Plucknett, A Concise History of the Common Law 343 (5th ed. 1956). Further, even in the sixteenth and seventeenth centuries, when written records were becoming somewhat more accessible, past cases were cited primarily on matters of pleading and procedure, not for authoritative statements of substantive law. *See* Harold J. Berman, *The Origins of Historical Jurisprudence: Coke, Selden, Hale,* 103 Yale L. J. 1651, 1732 (1994).

[33] Plucknett, *supra* note 32, at 347. For an excellent discussion of the weakness of precedent before the nineteenth century, see Zywicki, *supra* note 25, at 1565–1578.

[34] Plucknett, *supra* note 32, at 269.

of cases became available in the late sixteenth and early seventeenth centuries, cases were mentioned more frequently, but even then only

> to reinforce a newly emerging principle that in matters of procedure and pleading the common law courts would adhere to their custom—and, in that sense, their precedents. . . . Moreover, the principle was largely confined to procedural matters, including matters of competence, and was probably related to the necessity of maintaining lines of separation between the jurisdiction of the common law courts and that of the other types of courts.[35]

Therefore, for most of the common law's history, its substantive rules were free to develop along with the community's sense of fairness as expressed by the jury. Other than procedurally, common law was not "judge-made" law. Despite the ridicule it was subjected to by the legal realists, the image of the common law judge as the discoverer of the law is really quite appropriate. The judge did not make law, but discovered the law by discovering what constituted the customs of the country. Hence, through the eighteenth century, the substantive common law could be accurately described as a case-generated, customary law.

C. The Modern Common Law

By the beginning of the nineteenth century, the common law courts had absorbed most of the business of their nonroyal competitors, although there was still internal competition among the different common law courts themselves. During the nineteenth century, legal reform movements in both England and the United States

[35] Harold J. Berman and Charles J. Reid, Jr., *The Transformation of English Legal Science: from Hale to Blackstone*, 45 Emory L. J. 437, 446 (1996).

brought this to an end as well by merging the various common law courts into a unified system of courts with a formal hierarchical structure.[36] This and the advent of reliable private case reporters made adherence to the doctrine of *stare decisis* practical, and the practice soon evolved of holding judges to be bound by the decisions of courts of superior or equal status in their jurisdiction.[37]

This development was followed closely by the "knowledge revolution of the late nineteenth century," in which "a mode of conveying information that stressed the recapitulation and memorization of a finite body of knowledge was replaced with a mode—widely labeled 'scientific'—that assumed knowledge to be complex and infinite but capable of orderly classification and analysis through the use of proper methodological techniques."[38] This revolution manifested itself in the legal world in the form of the "law as science" movement spearheaded by Christopher Columbus Langdell at Harvard Law School. Langdell reconceived legal education as an inductive process in which general substantive principles of law were abstracted from appellate judicial decisions—the data points of "legal science."[39] Langdell's "case method," which was adopted by virtually all American law schools and thereby influenced the outlook of almost all twentieth-century lawyers and judges, manifested a "distrust of ancient maxims" and "an enthusiasm for the appellate case as a training device, since cases, being

[36] In England this was effected by the Judicature Act of 1873 and the Appellate Jurisdiction Act of 1876. In the United States, hostility to the chancery courts, which were identified with the hated royal prerogative courts, stimulated the legal reform movements in many states.

[37] Zywicki argues persuasively that the same legal reforms that made the doctrine of *stare decisis* practical also made it necessary by ending competition among the courts. Without the check that the existence of alternative fora put on the discretion of judges, some mechanism was needed to ensure that judges did not legislate from the bench. He contends that *stare decisis* was adopted to supply the needed constraint. *See* Zywicki, *supra* note 25, at 1631.

[38] G. Edward White, Tort Law in America 20–21 (1980).

[39] Actually, from a limited set of appellate decisions selected for the purpose by Langdell and his Harvard colleagues—a fact exploited by later realist critics of Langdell's method as patently undermining any claim it may have to scientific objectivity.

concrete manifestations of abstract principles, embodied 'both the scientific and the practical side of the law.'"[40]

In pursuit of their new scientific method, the legal academicians of the late nineteenth and early twentieth centuries mined the reported appellate decisions for substantive legal doctrines that would bring intellectual coherence to various areas of law.[41] For example, Oliver Wendell Holmes and other tort scholars developed the fault theory that organized tort law around the concept of a universal duty of care limited by the requirement that the defendant be at fault to incur liability.[42] This represented a sharp break with earlier legal thought in that "to the extent that American law had an intellectual organization in the early nineteenth century, that organization had been procedural rather than doctrinal. Jurisprudential rules . . . were linked more to the writ system than to any substantive grouping of 'fields' of law.'"[43] To continue the tort example, not only was there no substantive tort doctrine, "[t]here was no 'field' of 'Torts' at all prior to 1870; the 'tort' writs (trespass and case) had their own separate rules."[44]

These twin developments radically changed the nature of the common law process. By causing lawyers and judges to seek the rules of the common law in individual past decisions, the doctrine of *stare decisis* changed the putative source of the common law from custom to the opinions of appellate judges. And by mining these opinions for substantive principles of law, the legal scientists transformed the content of the common law from a body of essentially procedural rules to one containing the substantive rules of

[40] White, *supra* note 38, at 31 (quoting William Keener, *The Inductive Method in Legal Education*, 17 Report of the American Bar Association 473, 488–489 (1894)).

[41] *See id.* at 40–41 ("In its formative years, the late nineteenth-century academic-judicial symbiosis placed a high value on the achievement of order and coherence in fields of law. A successful law review article or treatise was one that 'illuminated' a field by propounding doctrines capable of continuing to organize an increasing number of cases in an intelligible fashion").

[42] *See id.* at 38–41.

[43] *Id.* at 40.

[44] *Id.*

tort, contract, property, and criminal law. By the end of the nineteenth century, the operation of these forces had transformed the common law process from one designed to properly prepare a dispute for submission to a jury, who would do justice according to custom, to one designed to ensure that courts of inferior jurisdiction were applying both procedural and substantive rules of law consistently with the rules announced in prior judicial decisions. Significantly, the focus of the process had shifted from the just resolution of particular disputes to the maintenance of a consistent and coherent body of rules. At this point, the common law had lost its character as customary law.

The transformation of the common law was far from complete, however. The convergence of *stare decisis* and the law-as-science movement had placed the focus on the past decisions of appellate judges. The legal scientists sought to extrapolate a coherent body of rules from these decisions to which the doctrine of *stare decisis* would demand adherence. Like the customary law, this conception of the common law was essentially backward-looking in that present cases were to be decided exclusively on the basis of past holdings. Unlike the customary law, however, it was without a firm normative foundation. Where the rules of customary law were derived from the ordinary person's sense of what was fair in particular circumstances, under the legal scientists' conception, the rules of common law were derived from appellate judges' opinions as to which precedents governed the instant case and how broadly or narrowly they should be construed. Critics promptly pointed out that such judgments were not objective, but were necessarily based on the judges' personal values and beliefs about what was right.[45] Why were rules derived from such a source entitled to respect? Why should anyone believe that rules reflecting the moral

[45] I have discussed this matter in depth elsewhere. If you are interested in pursuing the matter, *see* John Hasnas, *Back to the Future: From Critical Legal Studies Forward to Legal Realism, or How Not to Miss the Point of the Indeterminacy Argument*, 45 DUKE L. J. 84, 86–98 (1995).

and political presuppositions of the mostly dead, propertied, white, Anglo-Saxon, Protestant males who made up the judiciary were either just or appropriate to the rapidly changing conditions of modern life at the beginning of the twentieth century?

The legal realists argued that it was pointless to attempt to decide cases strictly on the basis of their logical relationship to past precedents. Not only was this impossible,[46] but even if it could be done, there was no reason why the dead hand of the past should control the present. The purpose of the law cannot be merely to maintain a consistent and coherent body of rules regardless of their content, but must be to maintain as consistent and coherent a body of rules as can be made to serve progressive social ends. This, however, requires an at least partially forward-looking decision-making process. Legal decisions must be rendered not solely in terms of their coherence with past decisions, but also in terms of their real-world effects.[47] In deciding cases, therefore, judges must explicitly consider both the social ends the law is supposed to serve and whether a particular ruling will advance or retard the achievement of those ends. Thus, the common law required Janus-faced decision-making—backward-looking in that judges had to ensure sufficient consistency and stability over time for the law to be intelligible to the public whose behavior it was to govern, and forward-looking in that they also had to ensure that the actual effects of the decision advanced the law's normative ends.

Within a generation, the realist critique of the formalistic legal science approach had incorporated itself into legal and judicial practice in the form of public policy arguments.[48] Attorneys

[46] *See id.* at 88–89.

[47] *See, e.g.,* Karl Llewellyn, *Some Realism About Realism—Responding to Dean Pound*, 44 HARV. L. REV. 1222, 1237 (1931); LAURA KALMAN, LEGAL REALISM AT YALE 3 (1986); Oliver Wendell Holmes, *The Path of the Law*, 10 HARV. L. REV. 457, 467 (1897); Felix Cohen, *Transcendental Nonsense and the Functional Approach*, 35 COLUM. L. REV 809, 822–826 (1935).

[48] The realists actually called for the explicit use of empirical social science in judicial decision-making, but such a radical change in judicial practice was not to be.

regularly presented and judges frequently based their decisions on arguments detailing the anticipated empirical effects of those decisions. This practice was most famously exemplified by Louis Brandeis's Supreme Court brief in the 1908 case of *Muller v. Oregon*,[49] which contained two pages of legal argument and over a hundred pages of sociological data and analysis.[50] As this forward-looking aspect of judicial decision-making became an integral part of the common law process, the concept of the common law judge as the discoverer of the law was discarded. The common law was no longer purely case-generated law embodying the practical wisdom and normative sentiments of the community. It was now truly judge-made law.

Consider, then, the nature of the modern common law. It still contains within it the rules that evolved from custom and were recognized by the king's courts as well as those from other fora that the common law absorbed over the course of its development. The content of many of these rules has been modified, however, and the corpus as a whole both pared and supplemented—first, in order to fit the conceptual structures of the legal scientists, and then, by the iterated process of judicial decision-making governed by the demands of both *stare decisis* and public policy. Rather than a set of uncoordinated rules, each of which facilitates peaceful human interaction without the whole advancing any particular normative end, the modern common law consists in an integrated body of rules designed to achieve valuable social ends and help create a more just society. The common law judge no longer acts merely as a referee overseeing the adversarial process to ensure that the disputed issues are properly framed for submission to the jury, but also as the arbiter of the substance of the law. No longer merely a discoverer of customs, the judge is now

[49] 208 U.S. 412 (1908).

[50] *See* Edward A. Purcell, Jr., The Crisis of Democratic Theory 76 (1973). This brief was so remarked upon that subsequent briefs containing empirical public policy arguments became known as "Brandeis briefs."

an intellectual craftsman, charged with sculpting the rules into a consistent and coherent body of law while ensuring that the whole does not lose touch with the normative ends it is designed to serve. In every appellate decision, the judge must consider not merely what is fair to the parties to the dispute, but how the decision will impact the law's twin goals of maintaining a reasonable consistency with past rulings and advancing good public policy. Hence, the modern common law is case-*generated*, but judge-*made* law.

Now consider the essential normative features of modern common law. Like customary law and the older common law, it retains a commitment to fair treatment for the parties, although in a somewhat attenuated form. Where this commitment previously resided in the jury's or other decision-maker's power to directly decide what is fair based on the parties' custom-derived expectations, in the modern common law, it resides in the doctrine of *stare decisis*. By providing assurance that future cases will be decided in the same way as factually similar precedents, *stare decisis* ensures that those who make good faith efforts to conform their behavior to the law will not have their expectations unfairly thwarted. The commitment is attenuated, however, because *stare decisis* actually protects only those who are not only familiar with past decisions, but are able to correctly predict both which precedent the judge will apply to his or her case and how broadly the precedent will be construed.

Unlike the customary law and the old common law, however, the modern common law makes normative commitments to society at large as well as to the parties to the dispute. These commitments are to shape the law into a doctrinally coherent corpus and to ensure that the law advances normatively valuable social ends. Honoring these commitments requires more than a purely retrospective adherence to the demands of procedural justice; it requires substantive conceptions of social value and justice. Judges cannot bring coherence to a body of law without a substantive conception of the law's purpose.[51] To determine which rules are essential to the law's mission and which are aberrations or mistakes that should be discarded, a judge must have some conception of the end the law is designed to serve. A judge that believes the purpose of contract law is to maximize free exchange and individual control of resources will come up with a very different set of rules than one who believes the purpose of contract law is to ensure that all parties receive fair bargains. Just as obviously, judges cannot base their decisions on considerations of public policy without a substantive conception of justice. To determine whether a decision advances public policy, a judge must have some conception of what makes society better. A judge that believes that a good society is one that maximizes social wealth will have a very different idea of public policy than one who believes that a good society is one in which opportunities and wealth are distributed equally or democratically or for the benefit of the least well-off.

Modern common law, then, is the law that arises from the interplay between the effort to afford procedural justice to litigants and the effort to advance the normatively valuable substantive ends of society at large. This interplay requires the common law judge to look both forward and back—forward, to ensure that his or her decisions are advancing the relevant collective end, and back, to ensure that in doing so, he or she is not unduly trammeling the individual interests of litigants who relied on past decisions in good faith. It is immaterial whether the process by which the modern common law evolves is described as one in which the concern for fairness to the parties constrains the pursuit of the collective good or one in which the attempt to provide perfect justice to the parties must be tempered by the needs of the greater society. The difference is one of emphasis only. The fact is that the rules of modern

[51] For a famous defense of this point, *see* Lon L. Fuller, *Positivism and Fidelity to Law—A Reply to Professor Hart*, 71 Harv. L. Rev. 630, 661–669 (1958).

common law derive from both considerations of individual fairness and the explicit effort to advance valuable collective ends.

It is the Janus-faced nature of modern common law that distinguishes it from both legislation and customary law. Legislation is entirely forward-looking. Legislators are free to consciously design rules to influence future behavior unrestrained by either the interests of particular parties or the previous state of the law. Common law judges, in contrast, are never free to ignore the past. They may base their decisions on future-oriented, public policy considerations only to the extent that doing so is neither wildly inconsistent with the body of existing law nor works an unacceptable injustice on litigants who relied on past decisions in good faith.[52] Yet it is precisely this limited ability to take future-oriented considerations into account that distinguishes modern common law from customary law. With no guiding intelligence, customary law evolves strictly in response to past conflicts. Compositions or decisions are always attempts to restore harmony to the community, which requires resolutions to be seen as fair by all parties. Thus, only the past behavior, entitlements, and legitimate expectations of the parties play a role in deciding cases under customary law. On the other hand, although common law judges are partially bound by the preexisting law and the expectations of the parties, they are always free to consider the future in deciding whether to expand a precedent by applying it to the instant case, to terminate its growth by distinguishing its facts, or, when the litigation is in a court of at least equal status, to kill it off entirely by overruling it.

It is true that common law judges can decide only the cases that are brought before them. But in each of these cases, they may make future-oriented normative judgments that work minor alterations in the law. Although no individual judge has the power to remake

[52] Even when overruling a precedent, common law judges are bound to show how the new or altered rule is more consistent with the general body of law and better serves its normative purpose than the rule it is replacing.

the law by himself or herself, as a group, common law judges can make interstitial changes in the law that, over time, significantly alter its substance. One might say that common law judges are empowered to legislate at the margins.

D. Legislation

In Chapter 2, I described legislation as the law that is consciously created by those who exercise political power. In the present context, I am using the term expansively to include not only the direct product of the legislative branch of government, but also the administrative regulations created by the executive agencies that have been endowed with rule-making authority by the legislature. Thus, legislation encompasses the output of the state legislatures and the federal Congress as well as the regulations issued by agencies such as the Environmental Protection Agency, the Food and Drug Administration, or the Federal Communications Commission.

II. Political vs. Nonpolitical Law

Customary law and the old common law share an important characteristic—the rules of law evolve without a guiding human intelligence. Legislation and the modern common law share the opposite characteristic—the rules of law are consciously created either in full—legislation—or in part—the modern common law—by the agents invested with political power. Thus, the four species of law can be easily grouped into two genuses—political and nonpolitical law.

Political law is law that is generated by political forces—law that is consciously created by an agent or agency of the state. Political law consists of legislation, administrative regulations, and the modern common law. Nonpolitical law is law that evolves without a guiding intelligence—law that develops independently of any intentional action by an agent of the state. Nonpolitical law consists of customary law and the old common law.

III. The Incompatibility of Political Law with the Rule of Law

Little need be said to show that political law is incompatible with the rule of law *when the rule of law is understood to refer to a system in which citizens are governed by neutral rules and not the will of others.* In fact, there is little that I can add to the observations of the public choice scholars in economics and the legal realists and critical legal studies scholars in law to help establish this point. Consider legislation first.

Legislation is law that is consciously created by political agents. Even in an ideal democracy, legislation is supposed to embody the *will* of the majority. In the real world, public choice economics has demonstrated *ad nauseam* how politically adept rent-seekers shape legislation to effectively impose their will on their fellow citizens. Western liberal democracies may have tamed the more objectionable aspects of personal rule. Rather than being subject to the arbitrary will of one ruler or clique, the citizens of such regimes are subject to the will of more diversified political coalitions that can effectively manipulate the cumbersome machinery of the democratic state. But the essence of legislation remains what it always was—the imposition of some people's will upon others. Casting legislation in neutral terminology may obscure this fact from the citizens being subjected to the will of those who control the machinery of government, but it does not change the character of the subjection. A rose by any other name would smell as sweet. The same is true of pork.

Despite the reflexive obeisance paid to the conception of "a government of laws and not of men," no one believes or acts like legislation produces it. From time immemorial, good-government reformers have been on a quest to find just the right set of restrictions to place on legislators to prevent them from favoring their parochial interests over the common good. The never-ending search for the right set of parliamentary or congressional "ethics" rules, the proper restrictions on campaign contributions and political speech, and the correct configuration of anti-corruption criminal statutes indicates the widespread belief that legislation improperly imposes the will of "special interests" on the rest of society. It is true that the never-ending nature of the search also indicates the belief that this situation can be changed—that there exists some configuration of rules that can counteract human nature and cause those motivated enough to engage in the struggle for political power, and skillful and ruthless enough to triumph in that struggle, to use that power solely to enact impersonal legislation of equal benefit to all members of society. Of course, human beings spent a considerable amount of time attempting to square the circle as well.

The situation is no different when we consider administrative regulations, which, like legislation, are consciously created by political agents. Administrative agencies are run by political appointees. It can hardly be surprising that the nature of the regulations tends to change as the party affiliation of the executive making the appointments changes. Further, administrative agencies are famously subject to being "captured" by the industries they are designed to regulate, privileging the interests of the entrenched firms over that of society as a whole.[53] Other public choice explanations of what skews the functioning of regulatory agencies from the neutral pursuit of the public interest[54] need not be canvassed to recognize that the quest for regulatory reform, like that for the proper constraints upon legislators, is a never-ending

[53] George Stigler, *The Theory of Economic Regulation*, 2 BELL J. ECON., 3 (1971). A good example of regulatory capture was provided in the account in Chapter 2 of the BP oil disaster in the Gulf of Mexico.

[54] *See, e.g.*, WILLIAM A. NISKANEN, JR., BUREAUCRACY AND REPRESENTATIVE GOVERNMENT (1971).

one. No less than legislation, in the real world, regulation is a mechanism by which those able to manipulate the machinery of government impose their will on society.

Finally, the legal realists and the critical legal scholars have spent decades demonstrating that the modern common law is similarly a vehicle for politically dominant parties to impose their values on society. The now century-old indeterminacy argument of the legal realists established that the rules of law do not bind common law judges to decide controversial appellate cases one way rather than another. The existence of contradictory rules of law and construction and the open-textured nature of legal language always permits the judge sufficient leeway to arrive at the legal conclusion that he or she believes to be correct—something that is determined by his or her preexisting moral and ideological commitments.[55] More recently, the critical legal theorists added the "mystification thesis" that demonstrates how the contrary belief that judges impersonally and objectively decide cases according to neutral criteria merely masks the imposition of the ideological preferences of the judges (and those who select them) on the entire community.[56] But there is little need to rehearse the arguments of the realists and critical legal scholars to make this point. It should be clear that when judges can rule that the words "Congress shall make no law abridging the freedom of speech" permits Congress to make laws prohibiting speech that creates a clear and present danger or advocates the election of a federal candidate within sixty days of an election—thereby interpreting the word "no" to mean "some"—but prohibits Congress from making laws banning topless dancing or flag burning—thereby interpreting the word "speech" to mean

[55] *See, e.g.*, Felix Cohen, *Transcendental Nonsense and the Functional Approach*, 35 Colum. L. Rev. 809 (1935).

[56] *See* Lawrence B. Solum, *On the Indeterminacy Crisis: Critiquing Critical Dogma*, 54 U. Chi. L. Rev. 462, 463–470 (1987). For a more detailed account of both the realists' indeterminacy argument and the critical scholars' mystification thesis, *see* John Hasnas, *Back to the Future: From Critical Legal Studies Forward to Legal Realism, or How Not to Miss the Point of the Indeterminacy Argument*, 45 Duke L. J. 84, 86–98 (1995).

"expressive conduct"—it is the judges' moral values and ideological beliefs, rather than the legal language, that determines what the law is. The titanic political struggles that accompany each vacancy on the United States Supreme Court would not ensue were there not a clear public awareness that the substance of the law varies with the Court's personnel. Thus, to the extent that judges are "legislating at the margins," it is they (and derivatively, those who select them) and not the rules of law that govern. Like legislation and regulation, the modern common law necessarily involves the imposition of one party's or faction's will upon the entire citizenry.

IV. Nonpolitical Law and the Rule of Law

A. Compatibility

Political legal systems do not produce what Friedrich Hayek referred to as rules of just conduct—general rules of universal application that do not favor the interests of any particular group.[57] Recognition of this has led many libertarian scholars to conclude law is inherently a coercive mechanism for subjecting some people to the will of others. But this move is too fast. What has been ignored is the possibility of nonpolitical law.

Nonpolitical law is law. Hence, it is coercive. The duty to obey has not been voluntarily assumed, and compliance is not optional. However, nonpolitical law is not the conscious creation of any identifiable person or group of persons. It evolves out of the effort of human beings to resolve interpersonal disputes in the absence of a centralized authority. The slow accretion of successful resolutions of individual disputes eventually produces recognizable rules of law of binding effect. Such rules do not represent the command of any identifiable person and are not an embodiment of anyone's

[57] Friedrich A. Hayek, Law, Legislation and Liberty ch. 4 (1973).

will. Therefore, one can be bound by nonpolitical law without thereby being rendered subject to the will of another. In a system of nonpolitical law, it really is the law and not men or women that rule.

This, of course, does not imply that all systems of nonpolitical law are just or will, in fact, produce general rules of just conduct. Social forces and governmental influences can skew the evolution of customary law to privilege the interests of some groups over others. In general, there is little reason to believe that rules that emerge from systems of case-by-case decision-making will be normatively superior to those that emerge from legislative processes. Nevertheless, when the proper institutions and incentive structures are in place—institutions and incentive structures such as the weak commitment to precedent and the competitive legal environment that rendered the old common law an extremely poor mechanism for rent-seeking[58] or the absence of well-organized central authority and the communal/mediational dispute settlement procedures that gave rise to the antecedent customary law—the evolutionary processes of legal development can be channeled toward the production of neutral rules of general application. Under appropriate conditions, nonpolitical legal systems can be very likely to produce the type of rules required by the ideal of the rule of law.

For a good illustration of how evolutionary forces can yield rules of just conduct simply recall the evolution of the torts of assault and battery described in Chapter 2. Citizens of England and the British Commonwealth countries are bound by the law of assault and battery. Yet this law is not the expression of any human will. Indeed, this law consists of general, neutral rules that do not favor the interests of any particular group. And, of course, this characteristic is not limited to the law of assault and battery. Similar stories may be told for wide swathes of the customary/old common law of England.[59]

[58] *See* Zywicki, *supra* note 25, at 1564–1565.

[59] This is clearly true for the rules of tort; contract, which evolved in the ecclesiastical courts and chancery; and commercial law, which evolved independently as the Law Merchant; and, to a perhaps more limited extent, the rules of property law as well.

When we limit our focus to that portion of our law that originated through these nonpolitical, evolutionary processes, the concept of the rule of law becomes a real possibility. In the case of nonpolitical law, there really can be a government of law and not of men.

B. Relevance

This observation will be a matter of purely academic interest unless a system of nonpolitical law can function in the contemporary world. However, I see no reason to believe that it cannot. Common law processes were effective at producing a complex network of general, neutral rules prior to the nineteenth-century reorganization of the courts into a hierarchical structure, which, when combined with the doctrine of *stare decisis*, invested judges with legislative power. All that would be required to return to a nonpolitical system would be to remove this power from the judge. And this can be done fairly easily.

To show that this is the case, let me ask you to imagine a significantly reformed common law legal system. In this reformed system, trial judges would function much as they presently do. They would rule on whether cases are properly before the court by addressing matters such as whether the litigants had standing to sue and whether the court is a convenient and fair forum. They would supervise trial procedures to ensure a fair trial by ruling on motions and enforcing the rules of evidence. They would not, however, issue instructions to the jury or other decision-maker. After both sides had presented their cases, judges would simply charge the decision-maker to do justice to the parties.

The role of appellate judges would be greatly altered in the reformed system. They would still review the procedural decisions of their trial court brethren to ensure that both sides had received a fair trial. They would not, however, review the substantive decisions of the jury or other decision-maker for consistency with the established rules of law. They would not reverse verdicts in favor of plaintiffs for failure to establish all the currently required elements of a cause of action nor those in favor of defendants by announcing new rules or expanding the range of application of old ones to encompass the plaintiff's complaint. And although the facts of cases and their outcomes would be reported, appellate judges would not issue judicial opinions in which they commented on, contracted, expanded, announced new, or overruled old rules of substantive law.

Academics or other legal scholars could, of course, analyze the reported cases to abstract rules of law much as the legal scientists of the late nineteenth and early twentieth century did. They could publish the results of their analyses in casebooks to help students learn the law, in articles and treatises to help attorneys prepare cases more effectively, and in more popular works to help the members of public understand both what to expect if they become involved in litigation and how to conform their behavior to the law. Further, these rules could play a role in litigation in that the rules of evidence would permit a litigant to introduce them to show that he or she acted reasonably in light of past legal decisions—something the decision-maker would be allowed to consider in reaching its verdict. But no judge would directly apply, create, or amend such rules. Trial judges would not dismiss complaints that did not conform to their requirements, and appellate judges would have no role in their articulation.

In this hypothetical legal system, rules arise from decisions in individual cases based upon the jury's or other decision-maker's judgment of what is fair to the parties. These decisions would, in turn, be based in part on what it was reasonable for the parties to expect given the decisions in past cases. Judges function solely as referees and have no direct role in making the law. By encapsulating past practice, the existing rules of law help determine the outcome of cases by suggesting to the jury or other decision-maker what constitutes a fair resolution of the instant case, but no party is called upon to consider how the rule that can be abstracted from the decision will function prospectively.

In this system, the law evolves without a guiding human intelligence. As new decisions that address changing social or technological conditions or that are based on evolving moral sentiments or notions of fairness are assimilated into the mass of previously decided cases, the range of application of many of the existing rules of law will either contract or expand. As juries or other decision-makers come to believe that something that was previously regarded as proper is, in fact, unjust, old rules will be discarded and overruled. And as juries or other decision-makers are called on to decide novel cases unlike those that have previously arisen, new rules will be added to the system. But these changes to the body of law will derive from the jury's or other decision-maker's judgments as to what is fair to particular parties in particular cases, not from any conscious consideration of what the rules of law should be.

There is good reason to believe that such a system would, in the main, produce general, neutral rules that do not favor the interests of any particular group.[60] There is no forward-looking element in the system's decision process—no cases are decided on the basis of their prospective effect as a rule of law. There is no doctrine of *stare decisis* by which present decision-makers can bind future ones. No intentional law-making is taking place. Rules of law simply evolve out of the jury's or other decision-maker's intuitive sense of what is

[60] It is important to realize that in making this claim, I am not comparing the output of some idealized system of customary/common law with that of the flawed, real-world legislative process. The fanciful thought experiment being offered is not intended to suggest that such a system would operate perfectly. At best, it will function as well as the old system of customary and common law on which it was modeled. The comparison being made in this article is always between the real and the real—between the output of the flawed, real-world customary/common law process, which produced the fundamental rules of contract, tort, property, and commercial law that undergird the legal systems of the British Commonwealth countries, and that of the flawed, real-world legislative process. For an excellent account of the reasons that the old common law did a better job of producing general, neutral rules than the modern common law and the legislative state, *see* Zywicki, *supra* note 25.

just in particular, concrete situations. Such rules, which reflect conventional notions of fairness, are precisely the ones most likely to facilitate peaceful interaction among citizens. Thus, the structure and incentives of the hypothetical legal system favor the creation of reasonably neutral rules that help individuals peacefully coordinate their activities, rather than rules that elevate the interests of one group of citizens over those of others.

The nonpolitical processes inherent in the customary and old common law of England produced an impressive body of general, neutral rules that forms the infrastructure of the modern commercial society. These processes can function perfectly well in contemporary circumstances and may still be harnessed. Hence, there is every reason to believe that a system of nonpolitical law is both feasible and compatible with the ideal of a government of law and not of men.

V. The Law of Anarchy

The holy grail of libertarian legal theory is "free market law." Several libertarian scholars have undertaken a quest to show how market forces can generate the rules of law necessary for a peaceful and orderly society. These scholars have made their task unnecessarily difficult, however, by adopting economists' definition of the ideal market and by limiting their analysis to the effect of competitive forces. Whether competition alone can produce a viable, liberal legal regime in an unregulated environment is undoubtedly an interesting theoretical question. But it is not one that must be answered to determine whether free market law can exist. For, when we turn our attention from flights of economic fancy to the real world, it becomes apparent that nonpolitical law *is* free market law.

As noted in Chapter 2, in the real world, human action is always subject to some form of regulation. There can be a free market in the real world only in the sense that human beings are permitted to transact their business free from *political* regulation. This means that the free market is correctly understood as the realm of human activity regulated by ethical beliefs, customary practices, and spontaneously evolved law. But spontaneously evolved law is nonpolitical law. When we are not blinded by ideal economic types, we can see that nonpolitical law is an integral part of the free market.

In my judgment, the quest for an account of how purely competitive forces can produce a functioning system of consent-based law is a red herring. As intriguing as this speculation may be, it is tangential to the central question of libertarian theory, which is how human beings organize themselves in the absence of a centralized coercive authority. The answer to this question is not merely that they buy, sell, and trade with each other in a manner that increases aggregate welfare, but also that they resolve interpersonal disputes in a way that gives rise to general rules that enhance the ability of individuals to pursue their ends free from violent interference by their fellows. The spontaneous generation of such nonpolitical law is part and parcel of the market process. Nonpolitical law is as much a product of the market as cars, coal, and tangerines. In economic terminology, nonpolitical law is endogenous to the market.

In my opinion, libertarians can call off the quest. The grail has been found. Just as in the movie *Indiana Jones and the Last Crusade*, it was hidden in plain sight.[61] Free market law is the nonpolitical law that has been with us for centuries and that forms the infrastructure of the British Commonwealth's legal system. Nonpolitical law—law that does not depend on the intentional actions of any agent of the state[62]—is the law of anarchy.

[61] Although not in Petra.

[62] Nonpolitical law does not require state-supplied courts for its formation. This will be discussed in the next chapter.

Afterword

The hypothetical reformed legal system described in Section IV(B) is offered as an example of how a nonpolitical system could function under contemporary conditions, not as prescription for what should be adopted. Indeed, it was chosen because it is the least unconventional example—that is, the one most resembling the present legal system—not because it is necessarily the optimal one. For example, it assumes that incentives adequate to generate general rules can function within a monopolistic legal system in which courts do not have to compete for litigants. This is in defiance of historical experience indicating that the competitive legal environment was an important factor in preventing the common law from becoming a vehicle for rent-seeking. Hence, it should be considered for illustrative purposes only, and not regarded as a proposal for reform.

7

Can an Anarchist Have a Moral Duty to Obey the Law?

"Can an anarchist have a moral duty to obey the law?" seems like an absurd question. The answer must be "No." I believe that the answer is "Yes." It might be absurd to claim that an anarchist has a moral duty to obey the state. It is not absurd to claim that an anarchist has a moral duty to obey the law.

In this chapter, I present an argument for this conclusion. I begin by establishing what a duty to obey the law entails and distinguishing the duty to obey the law from political obligation. I then provide a natural duty argument that shows that, although there is no duty to obey the law in general, there can be a duty to obey the law generated by a customary/common law evolutionary process.

I. Definitions and Distinctions

A. Definition: The Duty to Obey the Law

Precisely what does the duty to obey the law entail? Matthew Kramer provides a concise answer by noting that "[f]or centuries, political and legal theorists have pondered whether each person is under a general obligation of obedience to the legal norms of the society wherein he or she lives. The obligation at issue in those theorists' discussions is usually taken to be prima-facie,

Common Law Liberalism. John Hasnas, Oxford University Press. © Oxford University Press 2024.
DOI: 10.1093/9780197784631.003.0008

comprehensively applicable, universally borne, and content independent."[1]

This definition highlights the four essential characteristics of the duty to obey the law. The first is that the duty to obey the law is a prima facie duty—one which, although binding under ordinary circumstances, can be overridden when more important moral considerations are at stake. This means that despite the moral duty to obey the law, there can be circumstances in which an individual acts morally by violating it, such as running a red light to rush a heart attack victim to the hospital. The second characteristic, that the duty is comprehensively applicable, means that those subject to the law are obligated to obey the law in its entirety—they may not pick and choose among the laws they are required to obey. The third characteristic, that the duty is universally borne, means that the duty applies to all parties within the law's jurisdiction. Finally, the fourth and most important characteristic of the duty to obey the law is that it is content independent. This means that one is obligated to obey the law simply because it is the law, and not because of the content of the legal rules. As explained by William Edmundson, "[a] content-independent duty effectively preempts the subject's individual assessment of the merits of the action required by law and is categorical in the sense that it is not contingent upon any motivating end or goal of the subject."[2]

B. Distinction: The Duty to Obey the Law and Political Obligation

The duty to obey the law is not the same thing as political obligation. The duty to obey the law is a duty to conform one's behavior

[1] Matthew H. Kramer, *Moral and Legal Obligation*, *in* The Blackwell Guide to the Philosophy of Law and Legal Theory 179, 179 (Martin P. Golding & William A. Edmundson eds., 2005).

[2] William A. Edmundson, *State of the Art: The Duty to Obey the Law*, 10 Legal Theory 215, 218 (2004).

to the rules of a particular legal system. Political obligation is the duty to obey (and perhaps support and defend) the state in which one holds citizenship. Legal systems can and do exist that are not associated with any particular government or centralized political structure. A legal system may exist independently of any state. Therefore, it is possible to have a duty to obey the law without a duty to obey, support, or defend a state.

Nevertheless, the duty to obey the law is routinely conflated with political obligation. Because the state almost always administers the legal system—because state officials routinely speak with the voice of the law—this is understandable. Further, the conflation usually causes no confusion. Most theorists who consider the duty to obey the law are actually seeking the basis for political obligation. Such theorists are interested in the duty to obey the law only because they view it as a necessary condition for the existence of political obligation. As William Edmundson points out, "[t]he question: Is there a duty to obey the law? seems particularly urgent insofar as a No answer calls into question the very possibility of a legitimate state."[3] Because these theorists consider the duty to obey the law only in the context of a state-administered legal system, they have no reason to distinguish the duty to obey the law from political obligation. Hence, they do not.[4]

For my purposes, however, it is essential to avoid conflating the duty to obey the law with political obligation. This is because I intend to present an argument that provides a moral justification for

[3] *Id.* at 215.

[4] *See, e.g.*, David Lefkowitz, *The Duty to Obey the Law*, 1 PHILOSOPHY COMPASS 571, 571 (2006), where, after explicitly recognizing that "there is more to the modern state than its legal order, and not every legal order exists within a state," Lefkowitz nevertheless ignores the distinction stating, "the terms 'law,' 'legal,' and 'state' will be used interchangeably; for instance, by referring in some cases to a duty to obey the law, and in other to a duty to obey the state (or the state's directives)"; and Edmundson, *supra* note 2, at 217, where, after recognizing that "[r]ecent usage has tended also to conflate the duty (or obligation) to obey the law with what is referred to as 'political obligation,'" Edmundson nevertheless recommends that "the term 'political obligation' . . . should be understood to refer preeminently to the duty to obey." *Id.*

the duty to obey the law, *but not for political obligation.* Indeed, I intend to suggest that there is a duty to obey the law even though there is no duty to obey the state—that the recognition of a duty to obey the law is perfectly consistent with philosophical anarchism.[5] It is therefore necessary to maintain a clear distinction between the duty to obey the law and political obligation.

C. Definition: Natural Duty Argument

The quest for the moral grounding for state authority is an ancient one. At least since Plato's *Crito*, philosophers have been seeking the argument that will establish that citizens have a moral obligation to obey the state. As a result, many different types of arguments have been offered in support of political obligation, and, hence, for the duty to obey the law that political obligation entails. It has become conventional to categorize these arguments into three basic types: (i) associative—arguments "that appeal to the alleged normative importance of the fact that an agent occupies . . . the role of member in the political community to justify the duty to obey its laws,"[6] (ii) transactional—arguments that "ground our duty (or obligation) to obey in our morally significant interactions with our states or fellow citizens,"[7] and (iii) natural duty—arguments that "are predicated upon nothing more than the personhood of the duty-bearer."[8]

[5] Philosophical anarchism is the position that holds that although states are morally illegitimate, there does not exist a "a strong moral imperative to oppose or eliminate states; rather [philosophical anarchists] typically take state illegitimacy simply to remove any strong moral presumption in favor of obedience to, compliance with, or support for our own or other existing states." A. John Simmons, Justification and Legitimacy: Essays on Rights and Obligations 104 (2001).

[6] Lefkowitz, *supra* note 4, at 572.

[7] A. John Simmons, *The Duty to Obey and Our Natural Moral Duties*, *in* Is There a Duty to Obey the Law? 93, 102 (2005).

[8] Edmundson, *supra* note 2, at 229.

The argument being advanced in this chapter is a natural duty argument—one that derives the duty to obey the law directly from the moral obligations we are clothed with as human beings. It makes no appeal to duties that arise from one's role in a particular community and is not based on a claim that individuals have either implicitly consented to obey the law or otherwise interacted with others so as to give rise to such a duty. Rather, in what follows, I argue that the duty to obey the law arises directly out of the combination of the epistemic limitations inherent in the human condition and the moral value of social peace.

II. The Challenges Facing a "Natural Duty" Argument

Many theorists have attempted to provide a natural duty argument for political obligation.[9] These attempts have given rise to a set of objections that beset any effort to demonstrate that human beings have a natural moral obligation to submit to the authority of a state. Although I will argue that human beings have a duty to obey the law, not the state, my argument will nevertheless have to overcome these hurdles. Hence, it is worth taking a moment to examine the most serious of them. These are the problems of identifying the morally compelling end the duty serves, the problem of particularity, the problem of legitimacy, and the problem of harmless disobedience.

[9] *See, e.g.*, JOHN RAWLS, A THEORY OF JUSTICE (1971); Jeremy Waldron, *Special Ties and Natural Duties*, 22 PHIL. & PUB. AFF. 3, 3–30 (1993); David Lefkowitz, *A Contractualist Defense of Democratic Authority*, 18 RATIO JURIS 346, 346–364 (2005); John Finnis, *The Authority of Law in the Predicament of Contemporary Social Theory*, 1 NOTRE DAME J. L., ETHICS, & PUB. POL'Y 115, 115–137 (1984–1985); Christopher Heath Wellman, *Samaritanism and the Duty to Obey the Law*, *in* IS THERE A DUTY TO OBEY THE LAW? 3–89 (2005).

A. The Problem of the Morally Compelling End

No one, myself included, argues that the duty to obey the law is a fundamental moral duty—one that is worth complying with for its own sake or is somehow constitutive of the good. Making a natural duty argument for the duty to obey the law does not require one to claim that the duty to obey the law is itself a natural duty, but merely that its existence is essential for human beings to satisfy one of their natural duties—that compliance with the law is necessary for human beings to realize a more ultimate, compelling moral end.

William Edmundson represents the general form of a natural duty argument for the duty to obey the law as "(P1) whatever is typically a necessary means to a morally compelling end is at least a pro tanto duty; (P2) law-abidingness is typically a necessary means to a morally compelling end; therefore (C) law-abidingness is at least a pro tanto duty."[10] Edmundson notes that "[o]ne point of contention invited by such [arguments] is the specification of morally compelling ends."[11] Another is the claim that the existence of a duty to obey the law is necessary for the realization of the specified end. To succeed, a natural duty argument must both identify a morally compelling end and demonstrate that without a duty to obey the law that end cannot be realized.

Theorists who make natural duty arguments have proposed several candidates for the morally compelling end that can be realized only if individuals have a duty to obey the law. For example, John Finnis argues that a duty to obey the law is necessary to resolve the coordination problems that would otherwise prevent the attainment of the common good.[12] Similarly, John Rawls

[10] Edmundson, *supra* note 2, at 235.

[11] *Id.*

[12] John Finnis, *Law as Co-ordination*, 2 Ratio Juris 97, 102 (1989) ("[T]he existence of the legal order creates a shared interest which gives everyone moral reason to collaborate with the law's co-ordination solutions, i.e., moral reason to regard the law as (morally) authoritative").

and Jeremy Waldron argue that, when the law is a product of reasonably just political institutions, the duty to obey it is necessary to fulfill one's obligation to support just institutions.[13] Christopher Heath Wellman argues that fulfilling one's duty to obey the law is the only way to meet one's Samaritan duty to rescue the members of one's society from the dangers inherent in the Hobbesian state of nature.[14] Another example is supplied by David Lefkowitz, who argues that a duty to obey the law is necessary to secure respect for human beings' basic moral rights, which requires "the creation and maintenance of political institutions that publicly enact, apply, and enforce laws."[15]

The stumbling block for natural duty arguments is usually establishing the required connection between the duty to obey the law and the morally compelling end. The main difficulty lies in demonstrating that individual *as opposed to general* compliance with the law is required to achieve the common good, maintain just institutions, escape the ravages of the state of nature, or secure basic rights. For example, Joseph Raz points out that although government may be necessary to resolve the coordination problems that impede the attainment of the common good, a comprehensively applicable, universally borne duty to obey the law is not required for it to do so. Raz notes that although Finnis "properly explains why the law is a way of achieving coordination, . . . he never even attempts to show that coordination requires general obedience to law."[16] Similar difficulties plague the effort to derive a duty to obey the law from the natural duty to support just institutions. As A. John Simmons points out,

[13] *See* RAWLS, *supra* note 9, at 333–355; Waldron, *supra* note 9, at 3–30.

[14] *See* Christopher Heath Wellman, *Toward a Liberal Theory of Political Obligation*, 111 ETHICS 735, 745 (2001).

[15] Lefkowitz, *supra* note 4, at 590.

[16] Joseph Raz, *The Obligation to Obey: Revision and Tradition*, 1 NOTRE DAME J. L. ETHICS, & PUB. POL'Y 139, 152 (1984–1985).

> actual governments have taken on many functions that have nothing obvious to do with the task of administering justice. So the scope of any authority they might wield . . . would appear to be far more limited than the authority actually claimed by modern states; and our duties to obey would seem to be correspondingly limited.[17]

And the matter is no better for claims that the duty to obey the law is necessary to rescue one's fellows from the Hobbesian state of nature or maintain a governmental structure sufficient to secure individual rights since any individual violation of the law can almost never lead to the collapse of the state, or for that matter, even have a noticeable effect on the state's ability to provide security or protect rights.

Hence, the first major challenge for a natural duty argument for the duty to obey the law is to show that the individual duty really is necessary for human beings to attain a genuine morally compelling end.

B. The Problem of Particularity

A second problem besetting all natural duty arguments for the duty to obey the law is what has been called the particularity problem. A natural moral duty is one that all persons possess in their capacity as human beings. How, then, can such a general duty bind individuals to any specific set of political institutions or code of laws?

As A. John Simmons explains this problem,

> Natural duties, remember, bind those who have them not because of anything those persons have done, or because of the special

[17] Simmons, *supra* note 7, at 174.

> positions those persons occupy, but because of the moral character of the required acts . . . This means that natural moral duties will bind me as strongly with respect to persons or institutions that are not close to me (or my own) as they will with respect to those that are . . . [B]ecause this is true, it is difficult to see how a natural moral duty could ever bind citizens specifically to their own particular laws or domestic institutions. It is easy to see why Socrates should promote justice. It is much harder to see why Socrates should specially support Athens or regard himself as specially bound by Athenian law if it really is after all the importance of *justice* that explains his duty.[18]

I am a human being who lives in the state of Virginia in the United States of America. As a human being, I am invested with several fundamental moral duties with which I must comply if I am to behave in a morally proper way. But as noted above, the duty to obey the law is not itself one of these fundamental duties—it is not a duty worth complying with for its own sake. The duty to obey the law, if it exists, is a derivative duty—one which must be derived from one of our fundamental moral duties. But how can any general moral duty bind me to obey the law of Virginia rather than that of Maryland or the District of Columbia? I may have a duty to comply with a set of laws that maximizes the good, or promotes individual human flourishing, or embodies the ideal of justice, or perhaps, is merely the closest approximation of the ideal of justice that exists in the real world. But how can that give rise to a duty to obey the law

[18] Simmons, *supra* note 7, at 166. *See also*, Lefkowitz, *supra* note 4, at 592 ("A second objection leveled against all natural duty accounts involves their inability to justify the particularity of the duty to obey the law. Granting for the sake of argument that an agent's fulfilling her natural duties requires support for just political institutions, and that such support must take the form of obedience to law, critics argue that natural duty theorists cannot demonstrate why agents must obey the law of the state that claims jurisdiction over them, rather than, at least in some cases, the law of some other state"); Waldron, *supra* note 9, at 5 ("The first objection is that a theory basing the requirement of obedience simply on the quality of legal and political institutions is unable to explain the special character of a person's allegiance to the particular society in which he lives").

of the jurisdiction in which I reside unless its law happens to be the one that possess the essential characteristic?

Answering this question is the second major challenge for a natural duty argument. To succeed, such an argument must explain how complying with the underlying natural duty requires obeying the law of the particular legal system governing one's community.

C. The Problem of Legitimacy

A third challenge for any natural duty argument for the duty to obey the law is to establish that the relevant legal institutions have legitimate authority over those subject to it. Meeting this challenge requires something more than merely showing that those institutions can be morally justified. This is because there is a significant conceptual distinction between the justification of an institutional arrangement and its legitimacy with respect to individuals subject to it. Once again, A. John Simmons provides a useful explanation of this distinction.

> We can justify arrangements simply by demonstrating that their existence is a good thing, that we have good reason to create or refrain from destroying such things. We justify them by showing that arrangements have value, that their benefits outweigh their costs, that they possess interesting virtues. By contrast, legitimating an arrangement that involves some claiming the authority to control others involves showing that a special arrangement of a morally weighty kind exists between those persons, such that those persons should have authority and those particular others should have a duty to respect that authority. This kind of legitimation simply cannot be demonstrated by merely pointing to the justifying virtues of an arrangement, . . . Only a legitimating special relationship, not a justifying virtue or benefit, can ground claims of authority and subjection. Control of

> some by others is personal; so must be its legitimation. The impersonal virtues of arrangements involving control simply do not entail personal legitimations of control.[19]

This distinction between justification and legitimacy indicates that showing that a body of law serves a morally compelling end is not in itself sufficient to establish that citizens have a moral obligation to obey it. To the extent that the law invests some human beings with the authority to control the behavior of others, a showing that there is a moral basis for the exercise of that authority—that the authority is legitimate—is required as well. This is the third major challenge facing a natural duty argument for the duty to obey the law.

D. The Problem of Harmless Disobedience

Finally, there is the problem of harmless disobedience, sometimes referred to as the problem of the stop sign in the desert. One of the defining characteristics of the duty to obey the law is that it is comprehensively applicable. This means that those subject to the law have a prima facie obligation to obey all laws simply because they are laws. The problem is that "there is nothing even pro tanto wrong with disobeying the law when there is a vanishingly low chance of harm and a palpable benefit to be gained."[20] Or, as Christopher Morris points out, "[t]here are numerous laws that it seems reasonable not to obey on some occasions—for example, coming to a *full* stop at a stop sign on a deserted road where there is good visibility."[21]

[19] Simmons, *supra* note 7, at 148–149. *See also* Robert Ladenson, *Legitimate Authority*, 9 AM. PHIL. Q. 335, 335–341 (1972); Edmundson, *supra* note 2, at 223.
[20] Edmundson, *supra* note 2, at 235.
[21] CHRISTOPHER MORRIS, AN ESSAY ON THE MODERN STATE 214 (1998).

Natural duty arguments for the duty to obey the law are instrumental arguments. They contend that the duty to obey the law is necessary to achieve some more fundamental moral end. But, "[a] specific individual's failure in a particular case to obey certain traffic laws, tax laws, environmental regulations, and many other types of laws, will often have no discernable effect, or even any effect at all, on the ability of the state to provide its subjects with secure enjoyment of their basic moral rights."[22] This suggests that a duty to obey the law that requires "universal obedience is as a matter of fact not necessary to achieve plausible social ends—such as order, harmony, or substantive justice."[23] Hence, the fourth major challenge for a natural duty argument is to explain why the underlying morally compelling end cannot be realized unless individuals have a duty to comply with *all* the laws of a jurisdiction, even those whose disobedience appears to be harmless.

III. An Epistemic Argument for the Duty to Obey the Law

For most of my life I have believed that there is no moral duty to obey the law. As I saw it, our actions are either morally obligatory, morally prohibited, or morally permissible. When the law embodies our moral obligations, adding a duty to obey the law is redundant and adds nothing of significance to our underlying obligations. When the law conflicts with our moral obligations—when it imposes a legal duty to act in a way that violates our underlying moral obligations—the existence of a moral duty to obey the law is both pernicious—it instructs us to act immorally—and paradoxical—it creates a *moral* obligation to act *immorally*. And

[22] Lefkowitz, *supra* note 4, at 590.
[23] Edmundson, *supra* note 2, at 235.

when the law enjoins us to take one morally permissible action rather than another, a duty to obey the law requires us to relinquish our autonomy and conform our behavior to the will of others with no assurance that their moral judgment is superior to ours. In essence, a duty to obey the law creates an obligation to alienate our own moral judgment—an obligation to "just follow orders" even when we believe that that is not the right thing to do. And this, I believed, could not be right.

Recent reflection has led me to conclude that this line of thinking is flawed in at least two respects. First, by naively assuming that one can always know whether a particular action is morally obligatory, morally prohibited, or morally permissible, it fails to consider the limitations on human beings' intelligence and ability to gather knowledge. Yet these limitations imply that there are instances in which one *can* have a moral obligation to alienate one's personal moral judgment. Second, by assuming that the duty to obey the law requires individuals to submit to the will of others, it, like the traditional arguments on the subject, improperly conflates the duty to obey the law with political obligation.

I now believe that there may indeed be a duty to obey the law. Specifically, when the law arises through an evolutionary process of settling interpersonal disputes—when the law is created by a process productive of social peace—there can be a moral obligation to conform one's behavior to the law. To show that this is the case, I will present an argument that proceeds in three steps. First, I will show that, due to epistemic limitations, human beings are sometimes morally obligated to alienate their personal moral judgment, or, at least, to refrain from acting upon it. Second, I will show that living in a society governed by a customary/common law legal system comprises such a situation and gives rise to a duty to obey the law. Finally, I will show that the duty to obey the law of a customary/common law legal system is well-grounded because compliance with it is necessary for human beings to fulfill one of their natural moral duties.

A. Step 1: The Professional Obligation of Attorneys

Although human beings are generally required to act in accordance with their best moral judgment, there are specific situations in which not only are they not required to act on their own judgment, but it would be wrong for them to do so.

Professionals often find themselves in such situations. For example, trustees have a duty to use their best judgment to advance the specified interests of beneficiaries, even when they personally believe that the beneficiaries do not deserve the benefits and that the resources would be better employed by others. Similarly, clergymen have a duty to keep their parishioners' communications confidential, even when they believe that disclosure is necessary to protect third parties from harm or would be fairer to all parties concerned. Physicians have a duty to refrain from acting without their patients' informed consent, even when they personally believe that treatment represents the ethical course of action. And attorneys have a duty to serve the interests of their clients, even when they personally believe that justice demands that their clients' interests be thwarted. In each case, the duty to refrain from acting on one's own moral judgment is justified by the need to attain an important moral end served by the professional system as a whole.

To see what bearing this has on the duty to obey the law, let us examine attorneys' professional obligations more closely. Attorneys are subject to the Model Rules of Professional Conduct, which require attorneys to assume a fiduciary obligation to their clients. Under the Model Rules, attorneys are required to keep their clients' communications confidential[24] and to zealously represent their clients' interests[25] to the exclusion of the interests of both other individuals and society as a whole. Attorneys may depart from this

[24] Model Rules of Pro. Conduct r. 1.6 (Am. Bar Ass'n 1983).
[25] Model Rules of Pro. Conduct pmbl. (Am. Bar Ass'n 1983).

fiduciary relationship only in a small and definitely identified class of exceptional cases.

These requirements mean that attorneys are often called upon to act in ways that conflict with their personal moral judgment. They must argue for the enforcement of contracts whose terms they regard as overly harsh or inequitable. They must provide the best defense they can to individuals and corporations in tort actions despite their personal belief that fairness requires their client to compensate those they have injured. They must attempt to uphold property rights even in cases in which they believe it would be better for society if the property were redistributed. They must protect the civil liberties of parties that they believe should be locked away such as terrorists, rapists, child molesters, or racists. And they must refrain from disclosing the contents of confidential client communications even when they believe that disclosure would prevent serious suffering by others and otherwise better serve the interests of justice. Under the Canon of Ethics, attorneys have a moral obligation to act in ways that they would otherwise regard as morally wrong.

What justifies such an obligation? In the Anglo-American legal system, it is the recognition of the epistemic limitations of human beings. Attorneys' fiduciary obligation to their clients is justified on the ground that it is a necessary feature of an adversarial system of justice. And an adversarial system of justice is justified on the ground that it is the most effective way to address the limitations on human beings' ability to discover the truth.

Law is concerned with interpersonal human conflict. Human beings have both limited knowledge and limited ability to distance themselves from their own goals. Hence, we are aware that we do not have direct access to objective truth. As illustrated by the famous Akira Kurosawa movie *Rashomon*, we know that our perceptions of reality are affected by our interests.

The foundation of the adversarial system of justice is the belief that letting each party tell his or her story to an impartial decision-maker will get as close to the truth as is humanly possible—that the clash of opposing stories will burn away falsehood and biased judgment to reveal the truth and produce a just result. This belief is justified, however, only if all parties are able to tell their story effectively. This implies that for an adversarial system of justice to work, all parties to a legal dispute need access to a skilled advocate who can make sure that their side of the story is adequately presented. For such an advocate to be able to perform his or her function effectively, the advocate needs the client's full confidence—the client's willingness to relate all the details of the case no matter how unfavorable, embarrassing, or threatening to the client's future interests they may be. Only one who undertakes a fiduciary obligation to the client—an obligation to preserve the client's confidential communications and to employ the information gained exclusively for the client's benefit—can generate this level of confidence. Supplying each potential litigant with an expert representative who has undertaken the obligations described in the Canon of Ethics is necessary to maintain the likelihood that the justice system actually produces a just result.

The adversarial system of justice is a discovery device. It is designed to overcome human beings' epistemic weaknesses and provide a more accurate account of the demands of justice than individuals can obtain by directly employing their partial and somewhat biased knowledge. A useful analog for the adversarial system may be found in contemporary prediction markets. By allowing numerous parties with different information and viewpoints to back their predictions of future events with financial investments, these markets frequently provide more accurate information about such events than do the most well-informed individual experts.[26] Similarly, an adversarial system of justice provides a forum for the interaction of parties with different information and viewpoints that frequently produces a closer approximation of

[26] *See* James Surowiecki, The Wisdom of Crowds 3–22 (2004).

justice than can be obtained by consulting the opinion of even the most experienced jurist.

We can now see that the justification for the attorney's professional obligation is that it is a component part of a social institution that helps human beings achieve justice. The social institution itself is a learning system by which human beings seek to overcome the epistemic limitations that prevent them from perceiving justice directly.

This does not mean that attorneys always act wrongly by failing to comply with their obligations under the Canon. There will be cases in which attorneys can have a high degree of certainty that adhering to the Canon will produce morally pernicious results. In such cases, the morally proper course of action for an attorney may be to violate his or her professional obligation. But this shows only that the attorney's professional obligation is prima facie rather than absolute. Given human beings' epistemic weaknesses, it is rational to doubt individuals' ability to accurately determine which cases are the exceptional ones in which violating one's professional duty is the proper course of action. For this reason, the claim that attorneys have a prima facie duty to conform their behavior to the requirements of the Canon of Ethics—one which can be overcome only by extremely strong evidence that violating the duty serves a more important moral end—is well grounded.

Note also that attorneys' professional obligations require them to conform to the provisions of the Canon, not the conscious instructions of other human beings. Attorneys are morally bound to act in certain ways, not to submit to the will any other human authority. Although attorneys are bound, they are not bound to a master.

In sum, attorneys have a prima facie duty to conform their behavior to a code of rules even when doing so conflicts with their personal moral judgment. Yet this duty does not require them to submit to the conscious authority of any human agency or commit them to comply with commands to engage in immoral action.

Indeed, its very purpose is to help human beings better serve the interests of justice.

The duty to obey the law similarly requires individuals to conform to a code of rules even when doing so conflicts with their personal moral judgment. Could this duty have a similar character to that of the attorney's professional obligation?

B. Step 2: The Nature of the Duty to Obey the Law

I will argue that the answer to this question is "yes" *when the law is the product of a customary/common law evolutionary process rather than the product of conscious legislation.* Notice that the italicized clause places a significant limit on the range of application of my conclusion. Although I am arguing that the duty to obey the law is analogous to the professional obligation of attorneys, I am also arguing that the analogy holds only when the duty is associated with customary and common law legal systems. This excludes almost all the legal systems of contemporary states in which designated agents of the government are empowered to consciously create law through legislation. Hence, although this analogy may support an argument for a duty to obey the law, it cannot support an argument for a duty to obey the state. This analogy cannot provide a grounding for political obligation.

The nature of the customary and common law was described in detail in Chapter 6. We saw there that customary law is law that evolves to solve coordination problems. Its rules, which are "the result of human action, but not the execution of any human design,"[27] serve no overriding moral purpose other than to facilitate peaceful human interaction. Customary law is essentially a discovery device that teaches human beings what forms of behavior most effectively discourage violence and promote cooperative activities. It is a

[27] Adam Ferguson, An Essay on the History of Civil Society pt. 3, § 2 (1767).

mechanism human beings employ to overcome the epistemic limitations that make it impossible for them to specify the rules that best facilitate these ends in advance of experience.

We also saw that the old common law was originally nothing more than the customary law that was administered by the royal courts of England. But we also saw that over the last century and a half the Anglo-American common law has come to be identified with the rules of law that arise from appellate judicial decisions issued within a hierarchical system of courts that are bound by the doctrine of precedent. I noted in Chapter 6 that because the modern common law is a system in which rules are often consciously created by judges, it is but a dim shadow of the traditional, customary common law. Nevertheless, it retains sufficient ability to learn and grow for me to include it within the ambit of the analogy I am currently attempting to draw.[28] This is because of both the limited scope for judicial legislation and the inherent trial-and-error method of legal evolution that common law systems permit.

The ability of contemporary judges to create law is severely limited by the context in which they function. Judges act only when there is a case before them. This means that there has to be an actual conflict between members of the community for judges to be involved. Appellate judges issue rulings only when there is an unresolved question of law—only when the currently operative rules of law do not clearly and adequately resolve conflicts of the type that gave rise to the case. Thus, in deciding the appellate cases that create new law, common law judges are always seeking rules that will fairly resolve such conflicts—rules that will convert contentious situations into cooperative ones.[29]

[28] In this context, please banish from your mind any association of this discussion with the high-profile constitutional decisions made by the Supreme Court of the United States. The current discussion applies only to judicial behavior in common law cases, not cases in which judges interpret constitutions or statutes, which are the type of consciously created state law that I am excluding.

[29] Common law judges are never in a position to make up rules out of whole cloth or create rules as a mechanism of social control as legislators are. The need for a plaintiff to bring a case means that there must always be harm to some individual's interest before

Of course, as human beings, judges are subject to the same epistemic limitations as everyone else. Judges are no better at anticipating future consequences and overcoming their personal biases than legislators. Common law judges may be trying to find a rule that facilitates peaceful cooperation, but there is no reason to think that they will always succeed. The fact that common law judges often "make errors" is not problematic, however, because the common law is a trial-and-error learning system.

When judges make rules that are not effective at reducing social strife, interpersonal disputes continue to arise, which causes the issue to be relitigated. Eventually, a judge hearing a subsequent case proposes a different rule. If this rule is no better, the process repeats itself. When a rule that facilitates cooperative interaction is tried, conflicts subside, the issue is not relitigated, and the rule persists. It is through this built in trial-and-error process that the common law overcomes the epistemic limitations of the judges who comprise it and discovers the rules that tend to promote peaceful and productive social interaction.

We can now see that the essential feature that both customary and common law legal systems share is that they are legal systems in which the rules of law evolve without a guiding human intelligence. The judicial body is stimulated into action by the irritant of interpersonal conflicts that give rise to lawsuits. That body keeps working until it finds the proper unguent to relieve the irritation—until it finds the rules that are acceptable enough to all parties to

judges can get involved. There are no victimless torts. No harm to an individual means no plaintiff. No plaintiff means no lawsuit. No lawsuit means no judicial ruling. No judicial ruling means no rule of law.

Note also that the evolution of rules takes place at the appellate level. That is, when there is either no rule governing a type of conflict or the currently operative rule is unclear, archaic, or produces putatively unjust results, appeals from jury verdicts allow judges to attempt new resolutions that can create new or reshape old rules of law. Such evolution is not stimulated by any and all violations of law. For when an effective rule of law exists, violations of it are easily resolved at the trial level and do not give rise to appeals. The law of battery has been stable for centuries. The fact that individuals continue to commit batteries does not produce change because the assignment of liability for battery does not raise any controversial questions of law that can generate controversial appeals.

promote peaceful cooperation, at which point the conflicts that stimulate change subside.

Is the duty to obey the law produced by a customary/common law legal system analogous to the attorney's professional obligation?

Like the attorney's professional obligation, the duty to obey the law requires individuals to conform their behavior to a code of rules even when doing so conflicts with their personal moral judgment. Yet also like the attorney's professional obligation, the duty to obey the law does not require individuals to submit to the conscious authority of any human agency or commit them to follow commands to engage in immoral action.

Like the attorney's professional obligation, the justification for the duty to obey the law produced by a customary/common law legal system is that it is a component part of a social institution that helps human beings overcome their inherent epistemic limitations. The professional obligation of attorneys is a component of the adversarial system of justice that teaches human beings what justice requires in particular cases. The duty to obey the law is a component of the customary/common law legal system that teaches human beings what rules are productive of peaceful interaction in society.

Finally, like the attorney's professional obligation, the duty to obey the law is a reasonably strong prima facie duty. There will be cases in which individuals can have a high degree of certainty that obeying the law will have morally pernicious results, and in which disobedience is the morally proper course of action. But given human beings' epistemic limitations—given their limited ability to trace the systemic consequences of their actions and their known susceptibility to personal biases—it is rational to doubt individuals' ability to accurately determine the cases in which exempting themselves from the law is the morally proper course of action. Especially with regard to the rules of customary or common law, which long experience has shown to be productive of social peace, there is good reason to believe that individuals are obligated to obey the law unless they possess very strong evidence that they are facing one of the exceptional situations.

This comparison suggests that along most moral dimensions, the duty to obey the law of a customary or common law legal regime is analogous to the attorney's professional obligation. Further, we have good reason to believe that the attorney's professional obligation is morally well-grounded. Can we conclude from this that the duty to obey the law of a customary or common law legal regime is similarly morally well-grounded?

C. Step 3: Grounding the Duty to Obey the Law

The answer to this question would seem to be an obvious no. There is a clear disanalogy between the attorney's duty to abide by the Canon of Ethics and the individual's duty to obey the law. The attorney's duty is voluntarily assumed. The duty to obey the law is not.

No one is compelled to become an attorney. Those who enter the profession are fully aware of the obligations they assume by doing so. Upon their admission to the bar, they swear an oath to practice law in accordance with the Canon. Further, with the exception of cases in which attorneys are appointed by the courts to represent indigent clients, attorneys are free to decide which clients they wish to represent. Thus, they may choose not to take on clients whose representation appears likely to produce a conflict between their professional obligations and their personal moral judgment. Within certain limits, it is fair to say that attorneys choose to be bound by their professional obligations.

Such is not the case with regard to the duty to obey the law. No voluntary act of acceptance is required for the duty to obey the law to attach. The duty binds individuals regardless of their consent.

There is a long line of thinkers stretching back to Plato who argue that the duty does in fact derive from the consent of the individual, although this consent is expressed implicitly rather than explicitly—for instance, by remaining in the country, accepting the benefits provided by the legal regime, voting, etc. Because, in my judgment, this line of argument has been effectively refuted,[30] I cannot appeal to it to preserve the analogy between the attorney's professional duty and the general duty to obey the law. I accept that the duty to obey the law does not derive from any voluntary action on the part of those it binds.

The moral force behind the attorney's duty is consent. Each attorney is bound by his or her own freely given promise to comply with the Canon of Ethics and the basic ethical obligation to keep one's word. No such voluntary commitment grounds the individual's duty to obey the law. Assuming the duty to obey the law shares the morally desirable features of the attorney's professional obligation, there is still the question of where the moral force of the duty comes from. In the absence of consent, what morally binds individuals to fulfill the duty?

The only available answer appears to be that individuals have to do so to fulfill one of their natural moral duties. In the absence of consent (or any other transactional or associative grounding), individuals could be morally obligated to obey the law only if it were necessary for them to meet one of the fundamental moral obligations that they possess as human beings.

This means that two challenges remain if I am to complete the argument. First, I must identify the underlying moral obligation that is served by the existence of a duty to obey the law. Second, I must show that the duty to obey the law is necessary for individuals to fulfill that obligation.

i. Identifying the Natural Duty

Most natural duty arguments attempt to demonstrate that a duty to obey the law is directly necessary to fulfill a duty to attain a

[30] *See* Simmons, *supra* note 7, at 115–120.

fundamentally important moral end. I am not embarrassed to admit that I am not a good enough moral philosopher to make such a demonstration. I have little confidence that I can provide a creditable account of the nature of fundamental moral values such as the common good, justice, human flourishing, or respect for autonomy, or that I would be able to demonstrate that there is a natural duty to attain them even if I could. Hence, I propose to do the next best thing. I will attempt to demonstrate that a duty to obey the law is *indirectly* necessary to the attainment *any* fundamentally important moral end. I will argue that a duty to obey the law is necessary to attain an instrumental moral value, social peace, that is itself necessary to the attainment of all fundamentally important moral ends. Hence, I will claim that human beings have a natural moral duty to promote social peace.

Recall that in Chapter 4 I introduced the concept of a "primary value," a value that has universal instrumental value because whatever a moral theory's ultimate goals or requirements, that value is a means to their fulfillment. I argued there that reducing the level of interpersonal violence within a community to facilitate cooperative behavior is instrumentally valuable, regardless of the ultimate moral end one is pursuing and regardless of whether one adheres to a consequentialist, Aristotelian, or deontological ethical theory; and that, therefore, social peace is a primary value. I then used the fact that social peace is a primary value to provide the normative grounding for empirical natural rights.

I propose to make an analogous argument here. As a primary value, social peace is a prerequisite for or facilitates the realization of all fundamental moral values. This means that even if I am unable to specify what natural moral duties individuals possess, I can nevertheless know that actions that promote social peace will help individuals fulfill them. I submit that this is equivalent to the claim that human beings have a natural moral duty to promote social peace. This duty—the duty to promote social peace—is the natural duty that is served by the existence of a duty to obey the law of a customary/common law legal system.

ii. Demonstrating Necessity

If human beings have a duty to promote social peace, what can they do to meet it? If humans were omniscient, they could consider both the immediate and remote consequences of their actions on all members of their society and take only those actions that were most conducive to peaceful social relations. But human beings are not omniscient. They have a severely limited ability to track the long-term and systemic consequences of their actions. They also have a severely limited ability to escape the influence of psychological, ideological, and political factors that tend to bias their judgment and distort their evaluation of these consequences. Given the epistemic limitations inherent in the human condition, the best individuals can do to promote social peace is to conform their behavior to rules that have been shown to reduce the incentive for violence and encourage cooperation.

But stating that the duty to promote social peace requires individuals to conform to peace-enhancing rules is not very helpful. This is because it immediately leads to the question of how human beings can know what constitutes a set of peace-enhancing rules. The same epistemic limitations that prevent human beings from directly perceiving the actions that promote social peace also hamper their efforts to directly identify the rules that promote social peace.

Human beings have only one way of overcoming these epistemic limitations and learning which rules tend to promote cooperative behavior: trial-and-error experience. And this means that they must utilize the evolutionary processes inherent in customary and common law legal systems. By trying myriad solutions to the problems that bring human beings into conflict, discarding those that do not reduce conflict and retaining those that do, the customary/common law legal process slowly teaches human beings which rules are effective at promoting social peace. Because the rules of customary and common law are always in the process of evolving, they are never entirely satisfactory. There are always current problems for which adequate conflict-reducing rules have not yet been found, and old rules that need adjustment to keep up with changes in technology, social mores, and moral development. But the system's built-in self-correcting mechanism slowly but surely discovers the new or revised rules needed to replace conflict with cooperation.

The record of the customary/common law process for identifying peace-enhancing rules is quite impressive, as those of us residing in the United States or any of the British Commonwealth countries should be, but typically are not, aware. Almost all of the law that facilitates peaceful and cooperative interaction—the law that provides the infrastructure of our commercial society—is a product of the customary/common law process. Tort law, which provides compensation for wrongful personal injury; property law, which demarcates property rights; contract law, which provides the grounding for exchange; and commercial law, which facilitates complex business transactions all slowly evolved through the customary/common law's trial-and-error learning mechanism. None of this law was produced by the conscious actions of legislators.

Customary and common law legal systems speak with the voice of experience about what promotes social peace. The rules such systems produce embody decades or centuries of accumulated wisdom about what most effectively reduces violence and encourages cooperation. If individuals have a duty to promote social peace, then they have a duty to obey the rules of law that develop in a customary or common law legal system *because, given the epistemic limitations inherent in the human condition, these rules are the most reliable guide available to what actually promotes social peace.* Hence, a duty to obey the law of a customary/common law legal system is an *epistemic* necessity for fulfilling one's natural duty to promote social peace.

Notice that the argument I am advancing cannot give rise to a duty to obey the law of a state-administered legislative system. This is because the rules created by such legislative legal systems are not necessarily peace-promoting rules. In legislative systems in which the law is consciously created by human beings, the law can be designed to serve any purpose those in control of the legislative machinery find desirable on ideological or other grounds. The law can be designed to perfect human character, to paternalistically protect individuals from their own folly, to create a more equalitarian society, to enforce religious conformity, to suppress vice, to maximize individual liberty, to segregate races, to integrate races, or to favor politically powerful interests at the expense of the politically powerless. Under such legal regimes, it simply would not be true to say that the rules of law were a reliable guide to what produces social peace.

Legislative legal systems are relatively ineffective at producing peace-promoting rules because the rules are consciously created by epistemically limited individuals with diverse ends and diverse theories of justice. Customary and common law legal systems do better precisely because they function without any guiding human intelligence. Because customary and common law legal systems are conflict resolution systems that function without conscious control by any identifiable human beings, they serve no other purpose than the resolution of interpersonal human conflicts. They automatically go about their business of discovering and revising the rules that facilitate cooperative behavior among members of the relevant community.

A natural duty to promote social peace cannot give rise to a general duty to obey the law. It cannot give rise to a duty to obey the law created by a legislative legal system. But it can give rise to a duty to obey law that is created by a process designed to overcome human beings' epistemic limitations and identify the rules that most effectively channel conflict into cooperation. It can give rise to a duty to obey the law of a customary or common law legal system.

IV. Definitional Requirements

As noted in Section I(A) above, the duty to obey the law must be a prima facie, comprehensively applicable, universally borne, content-independent obligation to conform one's behavior to the law of one's community. The duty that I have argued for—the duty to obey the law of a customary or common law legal system—satisfies each of these requirements.

The duty is clearly a prima facie one. Individuals have a duty to obey the law of a customary or common law legal system because doing so is necessary for them to fulfill their natural duty to promote social peace. However, the duty to promote social peace is not their only moral duty. Although social peace is an especially important instrumental value, it is nevertheless an instrumental value. It may be overridden when it comes into conflict with more fundamental moral values.

For example, the common law does not embody any particular theory of justice and contains no guarantee that the law that evolves will not sometimes produce unjust results. In cases in which adherence to the peace-enhancing rules of law would be unjust, the duty to obey the law could be overridden by the duty to act justly. In this respect, customary and common law is no different from legislation. Under any legal system, there can be cases in which civil disobedience is the morally proper course of action.

Further, the duty is comprehensively applicable and universally borne. It is comprehensively applicable because all the rules that evolve in a customary/common law legal system evolve because they reduce interpersonal conflict. Therefore, all of them help individuals fulfill their natural duty to promote social peace. And the duty is universally borne because all members of the community are equally bound by the natural duty to promote social peace.

Finally, the duty is content independent. The duty to obey the law does not arise from the content of the rules, but from the method by which they were formed. The duty does indeed "preempt[]

the subject's individual assessment of the merits of the action required by law and is categorical in the sense that it is not contingent upon any motivating end or goal of the subject."[31] It preempts the subject's individual assessment of the merits of the action required by law because the information contained in the rules of law is more reliable than the subject's individual assessment. And it is not contingent upon any motivating end or goal of the subject because it is necessary for the subject to fulfill his or her natural duty to promote social peace.

V. Meeting the Challenges

I have offered a natural duty argument for the duty to obey the law. I believe that it can meet each of the four major challenges to such arguments.

A. The Problem of the Morally Compelling End

To succeed, natural duty arguments must identify the morally compelling end that creates an obligation for all members of the relevant society to obey the law. Many fundamentally important moral ends have been offered to fill this role, e.g., the common good, the support of just institutions, respect for individual rights, rescue from significant harm, etc. The difficulty for all such arguments lies in showing why a duty to obey the law is necessary for individuals to satisfy their natural duty to promote them.

My argument is distinct from most of those that have been previously advanced in that I do not claim that a duty to obey the law is necessary to attain a fundamental moral end or an intrinsic moral value. The morally compelling end that I offer, social peace, is an

[31] Edmundson, *supra* note 2, at 215.

instrumental, not an ultimate, value. But it is a special kind of instrumental value—a universal instrumental value that promotes all more ultimate moral values. Promoting social peace is a step toward the promotion of, for example, the common good, just institutions, individual rights, and the ability to rescue or protect individuals from harm. Thus, there is a derivative, but real, moral duty to promote it. I submit that its utility in helping human beings fulfill any and all of their natural moral duties is sufficient to qualify social peace as the type of morally compelling end that can sustain a natural duty argument for the duty to obey the law.

Other natural duty arguments founder on their inability to show how a duty to obey the law is necessary for individuals to fulfill their natural moral duties to promote the relevant morally compelling end. But this is because they are actually arguments for political obligation rather than the duty to obey the law. These arguments are efforts to show that a duty to obey the rules of law *consciously created by state legislative agencies* is necessary to fulfill one's natural duty, whether it be to promote the common good, support just institutions, respect individual rights, or rescue people from significant harm. But state legislative agencies can produce law that serves any number of purposes, many of which may be irrelevant or antithetical to the promotion of the end in question. These arguments fail because they cannot show that a duty to place oneself under the conscious authority of a state and conform one's behavior to the directives of other human beings is necessary to fulfill one's natural moral duties.

My argument does not face this difficulty. It is not an argument for political obligation. To succeed, it need only show that the duty to obey the law produced by a customary or common law legal system is necessary for individuals to fulfill their duty to promote social peace. It does this by showing that the former is *epistemically* necessary for the latter.

Customary and common law legal systems create law without a guiding human intelligence. The trial-and-error process by which the law is produced serves no purpose other than that of resolving the interpersonal conflicts that give rise to legal disputes—that is, of promoting social peace. In customary and common law legal systems, the trial-and-error process that creates the law is also the most effective practical method human beings possess for learning what promotes social peace. Without the knowledge embodied in the rules of law, human beings simply cannot know how to fulfill their duty to promote social peace. The customary/common law process *identifies* rules that promote social peace. The duty to obey them attaches because they *are* rules that promote social peace, and, given human beings' epistemic limitations, the only way for individuals to fulfill their natural duty to promote social peace is to conform their behavior to them.

B. The Problem of Particularity

A second major hurdle for natural duty arguments for the duty to obey the law is to explain how a general duty that all persons possess in their capacity as human beings can bind individuals to obey any specific code of laws. As A. John Simmons points out, "[i]t is easy to see why Socrates should promote justice. It is much harder to see why Socrates should specially support Athens or regard himself as specially bound by Athenian law if it really is after all the importance of *justice* that explains his duty."[32] Although this may be true, it is not that hard to see why Socrates should regard himself as bound by an Athenian law produced by the customary or common law process if it is the importance of *social peace* that explains his duty.

There are many paths to social peace. There typically will be many different rules that can successfully channel a particular type of conflict into cooperation. There is no telling which of these a

[32] Simmons, *supra* note 7, at 166.

particular customary/common law legal system will stumble upon first—no telling which will first give rise to the interactional expectancies that create the rules of customary law or which will be the first to be tried by a common law judge. Customary/common law legal systems do not produce optimal solutions for the problems causing conflict, just ones that are sufficient to make cooperation relatively more appealing than conflict. As a result, beyond the bare minimum of rules necessary to ensure the physical safety that all communities must have to function, the rules of customary and common law that develop in different communities will be different. The customary/common law process does not teach us what rules promote social peace in the abstract. It teaches us what rules promote social peace in particular communities *given the common history and experience of the members of that community.*

The natural duty that undergirds the duty to obey the law is the duty to promote social peace. The only way to fulfill that duty is to abide by rules that promote social peace. The rules that promote social peace differ for different communities. Therefore, the duty to promote social peace is the duty to obey the law of the particular community one finds oneself in.

The argument I offer in this chapter is indeed an argument for a general duty to obey the law. However, it is an argument for a *general* duty to obey the law of the *particular* customary or common law legal system one is functioning within. This argument is not distressed by the particularity problem because particularity is inherent in the duty being advocated.[33]

[33] Note that the duty that I advocate—the duty to obey the law of the particular community one finds oneself in—also resolves other problems that dog arguments for the duty to obey the law such as whether foreign visitors are bound to obey the local law or whether the duty can apply to nongeographical communities. Because the duty I advocate is a duty to obey the law of the particular community one is in, foreign visitors would be bound by it. Further, there is no reason why the duty cannot extend to nongeographical communities in the proper circumstances.

C. The Problem of Legitimacy

The problem of legitimacy is the problem of providing a justification for investing some human beings with the authority to restrain the autonomy of others. In the words of A. John Simmons,

> legitimating an arrangement that involves some claiming the authority to control others involves showing that a special arrangement of a morally weighty kind exists between those persons, such that those persons should have authority and those particular others should have a duty to respect that authority. . . . Only a legitimating special relationship, not a justifying virtue or benefit, can ground claims of authority and subjection. Control of some by others is personal; so must be its legitimation.[34]

My argument is not beset by the problem of legitimacy. Legitimacy is a major problem for arguments for political obligation because political obligation subjects some human beings to the control of others. But I am not offering an argument for political obligation. I am offering an argument for a duty to obey the law produced by customary/common law legal systems.

The duty to obey the law that I argue for is a duty to obey the rules that emerge from a trial-and-error learning process that functions without any guiding human intelligence. The duty does not place its bearer under anyone else's control or entail an obligation to respect anyone's else's authority. The problem of legitimacy does not apply to my argument because there is no authority to legitimate.

D. The Problem of Harmless Disobedience

Harmless disobedience is a considerable problem for arguments that are designed to show that a *comprehensively applicable* duty

[34] Simmons, *supra* note 7, at 148–149.

to obey the law is necessary for the attainment of a morally compelling end. This is because a "specific individual's failure in a particular case to obey certain traffic laws, tax laws, environmental regulations, and many other types of laws, will often have no discernable effect, or even any effect at all, on the ability of the state to provide its subjects with secure enjoyment of their basic moral rights"[35] or achieve the common good or do justice or rescue people from the dangers of the state of nature. In general, "universal obedience is as a matter of fact not necessary to achieve plausible social ends—such as order, harmony, or substantive justice."[36]

However, once again, the problem of harmless disobedience, which is a serious problem for arguments for political obligation, is not a problem for the argument I am offering. Because legislation can serve any end human imagination can devise, state-administered legal systems can include any number of rules against harmless activities. It will be very difficult to show that compliance with *all* such rules is necessary to achieve any compelling moral end. But I am not arguing for political obligation. I am arguing for the duty to obey the law created by customary or common law legal systems, which rarely if ever create rules that may be harmlessly disobeyed.

The customary/common law process does not create rules requiring one to stop at a stop sign in the desert when it is clear that no other drivers are in the area. The common law of tort requires one to drive with reasonable care. It rarely, if ever, imposes absolute duties. Running a stop sign is tortious when, and only when, it creates an unreasonable risk of harm to others.[37]

Customary and common law arises out of the settlement of actual cases. Cases arise only when there is an injured party—only

[35] Lefkowitz, *supra* note 4, at 590.

[36] Edmundson, *supra* note 2, at 235.

[37] Oliver Wendell Holmes famously attempted to create a common law duty for all drivers to stop, look, and listen at railway crossings before proceeding in 1927. *See* Balt. & Ohio R.R. v. Goodman, 275 U.S. 66 (1927). This duty lasted only seven years before being overruled in 1934. *See* Pokora v. Wabash Ry. Co., 292 U.S. 98 (1934).

when someone suffers some sort of harm. Hence, the rules that evolve are almost always rules designed to reduce harmful or threatening behavior. The mechanism that creates customary and common law affords little opportunity for the formation of rules that regulate harmless behavior.

I have argued that individuals have a natural duty to promote social peace. It follows that if all the laws that are produced by a customary/common law legal system tend to reduce conflict and promote social peace, then individuals have a duty to obey *all* the laws of that legal system. The duty to obey the law of a customary/common law legal system is comprehensively applicable because for a rule of law to evolve in such a legal system, it must be a conflict-reducing rule. In such a legal system, the problem of harmless disobedience can rarely, if ever, arise.

VII. Conclusion

Human beings regularly identify the law with the state. When we think of law, we inevitably think of legislation—the law consciously created by king or congress. We unreflectively identify law with rules by which some human beings—those invested with political authority—control the behavior of the members of society.

We should know better. We live in a society in which the vast majority of the law that allows us to cooperate without violence did not come from those with political authority. Almost all of the law that provides security—tort and criminal law—and facilitates cooperation and exchange—contract, property, and commercial law—evolved through the customary/common law process that was the heart of the Anglo-American legal system. This law, which is "the result of human action, but not the execution of any human design,"[38] is not the product of any guiding human intelligence. It

[38] FERGUSON, *supra* note 27, pt. 3, § 2.

is not a mechanism by which some human beings control the behavior of others.

It is true that much of our contemporary law is a product of legislation. And it is perfectly natural for us to focus on this portion of the law *because it is the portion of the law that gives rise to strife.* The struggle to impose one party's view of the good society or the demands of justice on others takes place through the legislative process. We notice the legislative portion of the law because it is what we fight about. We overlook the portion of the law produced by the customary/common law process because it works so well. The purpose of that portion of our law is to reduce interpersonal conflict. It does this so effectively that most of us rarely notice its existence. It fades into the background of our lives in the prosperous commercial society that it makes possible.

I have been guilty of misidentifying law with legislation myself. My longstanding belief that there cannot be a moral duty to obey the law stems from my improper association of the law with the existence of a morally binding political authority. My firm belief that one can never escape moral responsibility for one's actions on the ground that one was "just following orders," led me to believe not only that there could not be a duty to conform one's behavior to the dictates of those with political authority, but also that there could not be a duty to obey the law. But the latter implication does not follow. When we recognize that the law consists of not only legislation, but also the results of the customary/common law process, we can see that there can be a duty to obey the law without there being a duty to submit to political authority. The duty to obey the law produced by the customary/common law process does not entail a duty to obey the directives of a political authority. It does not entail the existence of political obligation. Hence, our inability to provide a cogent argument for political obligation does not imply that there is not one for the duty to obey the law.

Nevertheless, the duty to obey the law still needs justification. The duty to obey the law of a customary/common law legal system may not require one to relinquish one's moral judgment to other human beings, but it does require one to relinquish one's moral judgment. Joseph Raz has pointed out that no argument for the duty to obey the law can succeed unless there is reason to believe that the lawmakers are better able to determine how individuals should fulfill their moral duties than the individuals themselves.[39] Given human beings' epistemic limitations, this observation is the bane of all arguments that involve human lawmakers. However, it points to the strength of the argument that I am offering. For the customary/common law process is the method by which human beings simultaneously make law and discover what most effectively facilitates social peace. The social institution that is the "lawmaker" of a customary/common law legal system is not merely better at determining what behavior promotes social peace than are the individuals subject to the law it makes, it is the individuals' only reliable source of knowledge on the matter. The justification for the duty to obey the law of a customary/common law legal system is that individuals can know that they are acting in a way that promotes the primary value of social peace only by obeying the law.

An interesting implication of my argument is that there can be a duty to obey the law even under anarchy. Anarchy is the absence of the state, not the absence of law. Human beings need rules that regulate their behavior to live together in society. In the absence of a state, there must be other sources of these rules. Customary law and common law are these sources.

It is true that for several centuries the common law of England and the United States has been made in courts provided by the state. But this is not necessary for the functioning of a customary/common law system and was not true during the formative periods of English law. With the exception of property law, almost all of the common law of England evolved outside of the royal courts: contract law in the ecclesiastical courts, commercial

[39] Raz, *supra* note 16, at 151.

law in the merchant courts, and tort law in the local hundred, shire, and manorial courts. The customary/common law process is the method by which human beings bring order to their lives in the absence of centralized political authority. As such, it is the law of anarchy. And because this law teaches human beings how to live together in peace and social peace is a genuine moral value, even under anarchy, there can be a duty to obey the law.

8
The Obviousness of Anarchy

> "You see, but you do not observe."
>
> Sherlock Holmes to Dr. John Watson in
> *A Scandal in Bohemia*

In this chapter, I present an argument for anarchy that can be encapsulated in two words—look around. However, because most of us, like Dr. Watson, see without observing the significance of what we see, some commentary is required.

Anarchy refers to a society without a central political authority. But it is also used to refer to disorder or chaos. This constitutes a textbook example of Orwellian newspeak in which assigning the same name to two different concepts effectively narrows the range of thought. For if lack of government is identified with the lack of order, no one will ask whether lack of government actually results in a lack of order. And this uninquisitive mental attitude is absolutely essential to the case for the state. For if people were ever to seriously question whether government actions are really productive of order, popular support for government would almost instantly collapse.

The identification of anarchy with disorder is not a trivial matter. The power of our conceptions to blind us to the facts of the world around us cannot be gainsaid. I myself have had the experience of eating lunch just outside Temple University's law school in North Philadelphia with a brilliant law professor who was declaiming upon the absolute necessity of the state provision of police services. He did this just as one of Temple's uniformed private armed guards passed by us escorting a female student to the Metro stop

Common Law Liberalism. John Hasnas, Oxford University Press. © Oxford University Press 2024.
DOI: 10.1093/9780197784631.003.0009

in this crime-ridden neighborhood that was vastly underserved by the Philadelphia police force.

A wise man once told me that the best way to prove that something is possible is to show that it exists. That is the strategy I adopt in this chapter. I intend to show that a stable, successful society without government can exist by showing that it has and, to a large extent, still does.

I. Defining Terms and Limitations

I am presenting an argument for anarchy in the true sense of the term—that is, a society without government, not a society without governance. There is no such thing as a society without governance. A society with no mechanism for bringing order to human existence is oxymoronic; it is not "society" at all.

One way to bring order to society is to invest some people with the exclusive power to create and coercively enforce rules which all members of society must follow—that is, to create a government. Another way to bring order to society is allow people to follow rules that spontaneously evolve through human interaction with no guiding intelligence and may be enforced by diverse agencies. This chapter presents an argument for the latter approach—that is, for a spontaneously ordered rather than a centrally planned society.

In arguing for anarchy, I am arguing that a society without a central political authority is not only possible but desirable. That is all I am doing, however. I am not arguing for a society without coercion. I am not arguing for a society that abides by the libertarian nonaggression principle or any other principle of justice. I am not arguing for the morally ideal organization of society. I am not arguing for utopia. What constitutes ideal justice and the perfectly just society is a fascinating philosophical question, but it is one that is irrelevant to the current pursuit. I am arguing only that human beings can live together successfully and prosper in the absence of a centralized coercive authority. To make the case for anarchy, that is all that is required.

An additional limitation on my argument is that I do not address the question of national defense. There are two reasons for this. One is the logical one that a society without government is a society without nations. In this context, "national" defense is a meaningless concept. If you wish, you may see this as an assertion that an argument for anarchy is necessarily an argument for global anarchy. I prefer to see it merely as the recognition that human beings, not nations, need defense. The more significant reason, however, is that I regard the problem of national defense as trivial for reasons I will expand upon subsequently.[1]

II. The Question

Whether government is necessary is not an abstract metaphysical question. It is an entirely practical question concerning the delivery of goods and services. The defenders of government argue that certain goods or services that are essential to human life in society can be supplied only by a government. Anarchists deny this. The question, then, is whether there are any essential goods or services that can be supplied only through the conscious actions of human beings invested with the power to enforce rules on all members of society.

Note that the question is *not* whether the "market" can supply all necessary goods and services when market is understood as the economists' abstract realm of unregulated voluntary transactions. Some anarchists argue that competitive forces can supply all necessary goods and services. But the case for anarchy does not require that one assert this claim, and I do not. Anarchy requires, and I argue, only that no essential good or service must

[1] *See infra* Section III(E).

be supplied though the conscious actions of the agents of a coercively maintained monopoly. Properly understood, the question is whether there are some essential goods and services that must be provided politically or whether all such goods and services can be provided by nonpolitical means.

Many political theorists argue that there is a wide array of goods and services that must be provided by the state. In the present context, however, there is no need to consider whether the government must provide postal service, elementary schooling, or universal health insurance. The debate between anarchists and the supporters of a classical liberal, night watchman state concerns the core functions of government. The question thus resolves itself into whether these core functions can be supplied through nonpolitical means.

III. The Answer

A. Rules of Law

i. Creation

Supporters of government claim that government is necessary to provide the fundamental rules that bring order to human life in society. Without government to create rules of law, they contend, human beings are unable to banish violence and coordinate their actions sufficiently to produce a peaceful and prosperous society and, hence, are doomed to a Hobbesian existence that is "solitary, poor, nasty, brutish, and short."[2]

The proper response to this is: look around. Those of us residing in the United States or any of the British Commonwealth countries live under an extremely sophisticated and subtle scheme of rules, very few of which were created by government. Since almost none

[2] T. HOBBES, LEVIATHAN 107 (H. Schneider ed., 1958) (1651).

of the rules that bring peace and order to our existence were created by government, little argument should be required to establish that government is not necessary to create such rules. On the contrary, it is precisely the rules that *were* created by government that tend to undermine peace and order.

As discussed in Chapters 4, 6, and 7, English common law is case-generated law that spontaneously evolves from the settlement of actual disputes. Almost all of the law that provides the infrastructure of our contemporary society was created in this way. Tort law, which provides protection against personal injury; property law, which demarcates property rights; contract law, which provides the grounding for exchange; commercial law, which facilitates complex business transactions; and even criminal law, which punishes harmful behavior, all arose through this evolutionary process. It is true that most of our current law exists in the form of statutes. This is because much of the common law has been codified through legislation. But the fact that politicians recognized the wisdom of the common law by enacting it into statutes, hardly proves that government is necessary to create rules of law. Indeed, it proves precisely the opposite.

The historical development of the English common law was detailed in Chapter 6 and need not be rehearsed here. But it worth noting that an essential feature of the common law process is that it creates law only where it is actually needed to allow human beings to live together peacefully.

When I teach Torts, my students have difficulty understanding the tort of assault, which, as described in Chapter 2, prohibits intentionally causing another to fear he or she is about to be battered, but does not prohibit attempts at battery of which the victim is unaware or threats to batter someone in the future. They cannot see why the tort should not prohibit all attempts to batter another. After all, attempting to batter someone is morally blameworthy regardless of whether the intended victim is aware of it or the threat is not immediate.

Being products of the legislative age, the students think of the law as created by a conscious human agency to serve an intended end. Thus, they miss the simpler evolutionary explanation. The law of assault evolved from actual disputes that were litigated; the disputes that were litigated were usually those that involved violence; and conduct that threatened an immediate battery of which the target was aware were the type that usually resulted in violence. A wise, benevolent human lawgiver might prohibit all attempts to batter. The common law prohibited only immediate attempts to batter of which the target was aware because that is all that was needed to maintain a relatively peaceful social environment.

This example shows how the common law creates the rules necessary for a peaceful society with minimal infringement upon individual freedom. Law that arises from the settlement of actual conflicts, settles conflicts. It does not create a mechanism for social control. Common law is law that is created by nonpolitical forces. As such, it can give us rules that establish property rights, ground the power to make contracts, and create the duty to exercise reasonable care not to injure our fellows, but not those that impose a state religion, segregate races, prohibit consensual sexual activity, or force people to sell their homes to developers. Only government legislation, which is law that is consciously created by whatever constitutes the politically dominant interest, can give us rules that restrict the freedom of some to advance the interests or personal beliefs of others.

The unenacted common law provides us with rules that facilitate peace and cooperative activities. Government legislation provides us with rules that facilitate the exploitation of the politically powerless by the politically dominant. The former bring order to society; the latter tend to produce strife. Hence, not only is government not necessary to create the basic rules of social order; it is precisely the rules that the government does create that tend to undermine that order.

ii. Uniformity

Supporters of government claim that government is necessary to ensure that there is one law for all and that the law applies equally to all citizens. If the government did not make the law, they contend, there would be no uniform code of laws. People in different locations or with different cultural backgrounds or levels of wealth would be subject to different rules of law.

The proper response to this is probably the one Woody Allen made to Diane Keaton in *Annie Hall* when she complained that her apartment had bad plumbing and bugs, which was: "You say that like it's a negative." How persuasive is the following argument? Government is necessary to ensure that there is one style of dress for all and that all citizens are equally clothed. If the government did not provide clothes, there would be no uniform mode of dress. People in different locations or with different cultural backgrounds or levels of wealth would be clothed in garments of different styles and quality.

Why would anyone think that uniformity in law is any more desirable than uniformity in dress? The quest for uniformity leads us to treat the loving husband who kills his terminally ill wife to relieve her suffering the same way we treat Charles Manson, to apply the same rules of contracting to sophisticated business executives purchasing corporations and semi-literate consumers entering into installment contracts, and to act as though the slumlord in the Bronx and the family letting their spare room in Utica should be governed by the same rules of property law.

There are, of course, certain rules that must apply to all people—those that provide the basic conditions that make cooperative behavior possible. Thus, rules prohibiting murder, assault, theft, and other forms of coercion must be equally binding on all members of a society. But we hardly need government to ensure that this is the case. These rules always evolve first in any community; you would not even have a community if this were not the case.

The idea that we need government to ensure a uniform rule of law is especially crazy in the United States, in which the federal structure of the state and national governments is designed to permit legal diversity. To the extent that the law of the United States can claim any superiority to that produced by other nations, it is at least partially due to the fact that it was generated by the common law process in the "laboratory of the states."[3] Allowing the development of different rules in different states teaches us which rules most effectively resolve disputes. To the extent that the conditions that give rise to disputes are the same across the country, the successful rules tend to be copied by other jurisdictions and spread. This creates a fairly uniform body of law.[4] To the extent that the conditions that give rise to disputes are peculiar to a particular location or milieu, they do not spread. This creates a patchwork of rules that are useful where applied, but would be irrelevant or disruptive if applied in other settings.

One of the beauties of the common law process is that it creates a body of law that is uniform where uniformity is useful and diverse where it is not. This is the optimal outcome.

Government legislation, in contrast, creates uniformity by imposing ill-fitting, one-size-fits-all rules upon a geographically and ethnically diverse population. Once again, not only is government not necessary to the creation of a well-functioning body of law, it is a significant impediment to it. Please consider this the next time you find yourself wondering why there used to be laws requiring all businesses to be closed on Sunday in the Orthodox Jewish sections of Brooklyn.

[3] *See* New State Ice Co. v. Liebmann, 285 U.S. 262, 311 (1932) (Brandeis, J., dissenting).

[4] Fairly, but not fetishistically. The law against homicide functions quite effectively despite the fact that the definitions of first- and second-degree murder and voluntary and involuntary manslaughter differ from state to state.

iii. Accessibility

Supporters of government claim that government must make the law in order for it to be accessible to the citizens to be governed by it. The government promulgates its legislation in statute books that are available to all citizens. The unenacted rules of common law, they claim, are unintelligible to the layperson. Consisting of rules abstracted from cases over long periods of time, the common law is known only to the judges and lawyers who deal with it as part of their profession. A system of law that requires citizens to hire attorneys merely to find out what the law requires is obviously unacceptable.

The proper response to this is: Look around. Can any human being possibly be aware of the myriad of arcane government regulations to which he or she is subject? Have you ever seen the Code of Federal Regulations? When was the last time you tried to prepare your income tax return? Critics of the common law contend that laypeople would need professionals to tell them what the law is. Yet year after year, studies demonstrate that even most professional tax preparers *and IRS employees* cannot understand what the United States tax code requires. The common law rule that protects citizens against unintentional injury is the requirement to exercise the degree of care a reasonable person would employ to avoid causing harm to others. This is hardly inaccessible. Does anyone know what all the rules are that the Federal Trade Commission, the Consumer Product Safety Commission, and the National Highway Traffic Safety Administration have issued to accomplish the same end?

The common law consists of rules that have proven over time to be successful in resolving disputes. Only rules that are both intelligible to the ordinary person and correspond to the ordinary person's sense of fairness can achieve this status. Rules which are inaccessible to those to be governed by them cannot be effective. This is why, for example, the common law rules of contract and commercial law specifically incorporate references to customary business practice and the duty to act in good faith. It is also why no legal expertise is required to know that the law of self-defense permits one to use deadly force to repel a life-threatening attack, but not to shoot the aggressor after the immediate danger has passed. Understanding the traditional rules of common law requires only that one be a member of the relevant community to which the rules apply, not that one be an attorney.

Government legislation, in contrast, need have no relationship to either the understanding or the moral sensibility of the ordinary person. Legislation is law created through the political process. As such, it is inherently responsive to political considerations. Such considerations can, and frequently do, produce rules that are not intelligible to the ordinary person. This is not merely because special interests can skew the legislative process. Even if legislators were selflessly devoted to the common good, they would still need some principle of justice or moral ideal to guide their law-making. But there is no guarantee that the measures necessary to effectuate such principles or ideals will correspond to the understanding of the ordinary person. The Civil Rights Act of 1964 may have been the noblest legislative effort of our age, but the ordinary person is unlikely to understand why requiring pizza delivery men to be clean shaven constitutes illegal racial discrimination[5] or how a company with a work force consisting of almost all minorities can nevertheless be guilty of discrimination.[6]

Fraud, as it evolved at common law, consists of intentionally misrepresenting a material fact that another relies upon in parting with his or her property. It is not difficult for the ordinary person to appreciate that such action may be against the law. Fraud, as defined by federal legislation, consists of any scheme or artifice to defraud. It does not require a misrepresentation of fact. Any misleading statement or nondisclosure will do. It does not require that anyone

[5] *See* Bradley v. Pizzaco of Nebraska, Inc., 7 F.3d 795 (8th Cir. 1993).
[6] *See* Connecticut v. Teal 457 U.S. 440 (1982).

actually be misled or rely on the statement or nondisclosure. It does not require that anyone suffer any loss.[7] Martha Stewart was put on trial for securities fraud for the act of publicly declaring her innocence of insider trading.[8] It is probably fair to say that the ordinary person would not know that Stewart's comments to the media constituted a federal crime.

I understand the argument that if we had a night watchman state whose legislation was limited to simple, clear rules that are designed to secure individual rights, the law would be perfectly accessible. There are only two problems with this argument. The first is that in such a case, the legislation would merely reproduce the basic rules of common law. There is no need to create a government merely to publicize such rules. This can be, and is, done privately. The "restatements" of the common law are currently privately produced, easily accessible, and widely cited. The second is that it is impossible. The idea that there is a concise set of simple, clear rules that can preserve a peaceful, free society is a fantasy. This becomes apparent even with regard to the fundamental rules barring aggression as soon as one attempts to specify the conditions under which force may be used in self-defense or for the defense of others, or is excused by mistaken belief or insanity. And that is without considering that these fundamental rules must be supplemented by the rules of contract, property, and tort law that are necessary for people to coordinate their behavior well enough to engage in peaceful cooperation.

Legislation, even libertarian legislation, will either reproduce the common law or depart from it to gratify a political interest or realize some conception of justice. In the former case, it is precisely as accessible or inaccessible as the common law. In the latter, it will diverge from the common sense morality of the ordinary person,

[7] For a fuller account of the federal fraud statutes, see John Hasnas, *Ethics and the Problem of White Collar Crime*, 54 Am. U. L. Rev. 579 (2005).

[8] See Indictment, United States v. Stewart, 37 (S.D.N.Y. 2003) (No. 03 Cr. 717).

producing rules that are less accessible than the common law. Not only is government not necessary to ensure that the rules of law are accessible, it inevitably renders them less so.

B. Courts

Now that we have eliminated the legislature, what about the judiciary? Supporters of government claim that government is necessary to provide a system of courts for settling disputes. In the absence of the government provision of "a known and indifferent judge,"[9] human beings would have no way to peacefully resolve interpersonal disputes. For "men being partial to themselves,"[10] adverse parties would inevitably seek to employ judges who would favor their interests; and judges, who would receive their fees from the litigants, would naturally favor those who could pay the most. Hence, they would not be impartial. Because parties would be unable to agree on a neutral arbiter, they would be forced to resort to violence to resolve their disputes. Thus, without government courts, peaceful coexistence is impossible.

I know this is getting boring, but the proper response to this is: look around. This is the age of globalization. Business is contracted around the world among parties from virtually all countries. Although there is neither a world government nor world court, businesses do not go to war with each other over contract disputes. News is almost always the news of violent conflict. The very lack of reporting on international business disputes is evidence that international commercial disputes are effectively resolved without the government provision of courts. How can this be?

[9] John Locke, Second Treatise of Government (C. B. Macpherson ed., 1980) (1690), p. 66.

[10] *Id.*

The answer is simplicity itself. The parties to international transactions select, usually in advance, the dispute settlement mechanism they prefer from among the many options available to them. Few choose trial by combat. It is too expensive and unpredictable. Many elect to submit their disputes to the London Commercial Court, a British court known for the commercial expertise of its judges and its speedy resolution of cases that non-British parties may use for a fee.[11] Others subscribe to companies such as JAMS/Endispute or the American Arbitration Association that provide mediation and arbitration services. Most do whatever they can to avoid becoming enmeshed in the coils of the courts provided by the federal and state governments of the United States, which move at a glacial pace and provide relatively unpredictable results. The evidence suggests that international commercial law not only functions quite well without government courts, it functions better because of their absence.

But there is no need to focus on the international scene to observe that human beings do not need government courts to settle disputes peacefully. Labor contracts not only specify wage rates and working conditions; they create their own workplace judiciary, complete with due process guarantees and appellate procedures. Universities regularly provide their own judicial processes, as do homeowner associations. Stockbrokers agree to submit employment disputes to binding arbitration as a condition of employment.[12] Religious groups regularly settle disputes among congregants by appeal to priest or rabbi. Disfavored groups, for whom prejudice makes trial in government courts a mockery, readily devise alternative mechanisms for settling disputes without

[11] *See* Mary Heaney, *Where Business is King: London's Commercial Court Hears International Clashes*, NAT'L L. J., June 5, 1995, at C1; Campbell McLachlan, *London Court Reigns as an International Forum: Parties in Cross-Border Disputes Welcome the Commercial Court's Expertise, Neutrality, and Speed*, NAT'L L. J., June 5, 1995, at C4.

[12] Of course, this is mainly a measure designed to allow financial firms to escape from the quagmire of United States employment litigation.

violence.[13] Insurance companies provide not only compensation for personal injury and property damage, but liability insurance, by which they assume the responsibility of resolving conflicts between their clients and those of other insurance companies according to antecedently specified agreements that allow them to avoid the morass of the government judicial system. And empirical evidence demonstrates that when potential litigants in the government court system are directed into mediation, a significant portion of the lawsuits are resolved without trial.[14]

But don't just look around. Look back. Tax-supported courts of general jurisdiction are an entirely modern phenomenon. Anglo-American law evolved in the context of a richly diverse set of competing jurisdictions. The royal courts, once they developed, existed in parallel with the antecedently extant hundred, shire, manorial, urban, ecclesiastical, and mercantile courts.[15] These court systems had fluid jurisdictional boundaries, and because the courts collected their fees from the litigants, they competed with each other for business. Indeed, the law of contracts and trusts, which evolved in the ecclesiastical courts, and commercial law, which evolved in the mercantile courts, entered the common law as a result of this competition. Further, the royal courts themselves consisted of four different and competing courts: king's bench, common pleas, exchequer, and chancery. These courts, like the others, collected their fees from the litigants and, hence, competed among themselves for clients. It was only with the Judicature Act of 1873 and the Appellate Jurisdiction Act of 1876 that the British government assembled its courts into its present monolithic, hierarchical structure, with American courts following suit at varying intervals thereafter.

[13] *See* Yaffa Eliach, *Social Protest in the Synagogue: The Delaying of the Torah Reading, in* There Once Was a World 84–86.

[14] *See* Joshua D. Rosenberg & H. Jay Folberg, *Alternative Dispute Resolution: An Empirical Analysis*, 46 Stan. L. Rev. 1487 (1994).

[15] *See* Harold Berman, Law and Revolution (1983).

Further, focusing on the competition among the common law courts misleadingly underestimates the diversity of the dispute settlement mechanisms that were actually employed. Because the cost of utilizing the common law courts was too great for the typical working man, those courts were virtually irrelevant to the majority of the population. Most citizens resolved their disputes according to informal, customary procedures that varied with the location (urban or rural) and class of those employing them.[16]

Since our present relatively nonviolent, capitalistic society evolved in the context of a diverse and competitive system of courts and dispute settlement mechanisms, it cannot be the case that government provision of courts is necessary for peaceful settlement of disputes. In fact, a comparison of the amount of rancorous dissatisfaction produced by the contemporary government-supplied judiciary (consider the tort reform movement) with that associated with the more variegated traditional system of resolving disputes suggests that the government provision of courts reduces rather than augments social peace.

C. Police

Regardless of whether a state is needed to supply law and courts, supporters of government are adamant that police must be supplied exclusively by government. It may be true that the market can adequately supply most goods and services, but police services are unique in that they inherently involve the use of coercion. Obviously, no civilized society can permit competition in the use of violence. Civil society is formed precisely to escape from that situation. Unless government brings the use of violence under its monopolistic control, peaceful coexistence is

[16] *See* E. P. Thompson, Customs in Common: Studies in Traditional Popular Culture (1993).

impossible, and life is indeed as "nasty, brutish, and short"[17] as Hobbes contended.

Before I respond to this by suggesting that you look around, reflect for a moment on the silliness of this argument. For if civil society cannot exist without a government monopoly over the use of coercion, then civil society does not exist. Societies do not spring into existence complete with government police forces. Once a group of people has figured out how to reduce the level of interpersonal violence sufficiently to allow them to live together, entities that are recognizable as governments often develop and take over the policing function. Even a marauding band that imposes government on others through conquest must have first reduced internal strife sufficiently to allow it to organize itself for effective military operations. Both historically and logically, it is always peaceful coexistence first, government services second. If civil society is impossible without government police, then there are no civil societies.

In the 1960s Broadway musical *Oliver*, there is a song called "Be Back Soon" in which Fagan's boys sing the line "We know the Bow Street Runners." The Bow Street Runners were famous because they were London's first government-sponsored police force, organized in the latter half of the eighteenth century by the magistrates of the Bow Street court, Henry and John Fielding. I think it is fair to say that the formation of the Bow Street Runners does not represent the moment that London was transformed from a Hobbesian state of nature to a civil society.

Note also the conflation of police services with coercion. Coercion may be employed aggressively for purposes of predation or defensively to repel attempts at predation. Police services involve the use of coercion for defensive purposes only. Competition among aggressors is, indeed, a bad thing that is antithetical to the existence of civil society. But it is not competition for the provision

[17] T. Hobbes, Leviathan 107 (H. Schneider ed., 1958) (1651).

of police services. If competition among those offering the defensive use of coercion inevitably resulted in the equivalent of aggressive gang warfare, then we would want to eschew such competition. But whether this occurs is the very question under consideration. Identifying competition among providers of police services with competition among aggressors is entirely question-begging. It is avoiding, rather than making, an argument.

But I digress. The proper response to the claim that government must provide police services is: look around. I work at a university that supplies its own campus police force. On my drive in, I pass a privately operated armored car that transports currency and other valuable items for banks and businesses. When I go downtown, I enter buildings that are serviced by private security companies that require me to sign in before entering. I shop at malls and department stores patrolled by their own private guards. While in the mall, I occasionally browse in the Security Zone store that sells personal and home protection equipment. I converse with attorneys and, once in a while, with a disgruntled spouse or worried parent who employ private detective agencies to perform investigations for them. I write books about how the United States federal government coerces private corporations into performing criminal investigations for it.[18] When I was younger, I frequented nightclubs and bars that employed "bouncers." Although it has never happened to me personally, I know people who have been contacted by private debt collection agencies or have been visited by repo men. Once in a while, I meet people who are almost as important as rock stars and travel with their own bodyguards. At the end of the day, I return home to my community that has its own neighborhood watch. I may be missing something, but I haven't noticed any of these agencies engaging in acts of violent aggression to eliminate their competitors.

[18] *See* John Hasnas, Trapped: When Acting Ethically Is Against the Law (2006).

Ah, but that is because the government police force is in the background making sure that none of these private agencies step out of line, the supporters of government contend. Really? How does that explain London before the Bow Street Runners? The New York City police force was not created until 1845. The Boston Police Department, which describes itself as "the first paid, professional public safety department in the country,"[19] traces its history back only to 1838. What kept the nonpolitical police services in line before these dates?

Regardless of Hobbes's and Locke's philosophical musings, for most of English history, there was little government provision of police services.[20] It is true that as the kings of England learned how to collect revenue by declaring all violence and sinful activity a breach of the King's peace for which they were owed payment, they began to develop an administrative machinery to facilitate the collection of fines for "criminal" activity. Thus, the local representative of the Crown, the shire reeve (later sheriff), became tasked with reporting and eventually apprehending offenders. But since the sheriffs were only interested in pursuing offenders with the means to pay the amercement, this never represented a significant portion of the police activity within the realm. The customary, nonpolitical methods of policing provided security for most of the population of England until quite recently.

My father's oldest brother, who was born in 1902, often told me about the tontine insurance arrangement my grandfather participated in through his fraternal organization that provided both term life insurance and an old-age annuity. Since the advent of the federal social security program, you don't hear much about tontine insurance. Most residents of New York, who assume that only the government can provide and maintain the city's subway system, are

[19] *See* Boston Police Department website at http://www.cityofboston.gov/police/glance.asp.
[20] *See* Bruce Benson, The Enterprise of Law, 73–74 (1990).

puzzled as to why part of the system is named the BMT and part the IRT. They have no idea that in 1940, the City of New York purchased the privately built and operated Brooklyn-Manhattan Transit Corporation and the Interborough Rapid Transit Company to create the city-run Metropolitan Transportation Authority. When government begins providing services formerly provided nonpolitically, people soon forget that the services were ever provided nonpolitically and assume that only government can provide them. But just as this is not true for old-age annuities and subway service, it is not true for police services. Traditionally, police services were not provided by government, and, to a large extent, they still are not. Therefore, government is not necessary to provide police services.

Advocates of government can still argue that because of the special nature of police services, a government monopoly can provide such services more efficiently than nonpolitical entities can. I must concede that there is nothing *a priori* wrong with this argument. It is certainly possible that when it comes to police services, a miracle occurs and investing a single politically directed agency with the power to supply the desired services by exacting involuntary payment from all members of society actually produces a better result than allowing the services to be supplied by nonpolitical means. I can, however, find no evidence for this in the real world. To all outward appearances, when police services are supplied by a politically controlled monopoly, the public receives police services driven by political, rather than efficiency, considerations. Thus, disfavored, politically powerless groups are typically underserved, police resources are frequently directed toward politically favored ends (e.g., suppression of victimless crimes) rather than their most productive use (e.g., suppression of violence), and the nature of the service is determined by political budgetary concerns rather than actual need (e.g., SWAT teams in Wisconsin). Further, because government police are not dependent on voluntary contributions for their revenue, they are less likely to be responsive to the concerns of the public (e.g., police brutality) and more susceptible to corruption (see, e.g., the Knapp Commission Report[21] or just watch the movie *Serpico*).

Supporters of government often point to the high inner-city crime rate, the profusion of violent gangs, and the persistence of organized crime and drug cartels to argue that we dare not abandon the government monopoly on police services. I confess to being perplexed by this argument. How can highlighting the utter failure of the government system of policing possibly be an argument for its necessity?

It is worth noting that the contemporary crime problem is most severe where nonpolitical methods of policing have been most completely displaced by government. The inner cities are the areas most dependent on government policing. Arguing that the high rate of inner-city crime and the presence of gangs implies that we must maintain a government monopoly on police services is a bit like arguing that the abysmal quality of inner-city public schools implies that we should not permit parents to use their tax money to send their children to private schools. And it can hardly be surprising that it is difficult to suppress the violent organizations that exist to exploit the black markets created by government prohibitions on the legal marketing of drugs, prostitution, gambling, and other "vices." But how any of this demonstrates the necessity of government provision of police is beyond me.

If a visitor from Mars were asked to identify the least effective method for securing individuals' persons and property, he might well respond that it would be to select one group of people, give them guns, require all members of society to pay them regardless of the quality of service they render, and invest them with the discretion to employ resources and determine law enforcement priorities however they see fit subject only to the whims of their political paymasters. If asked why he thought that, he might simply point to the Los Angeles or New Orleans or any other big-city

[21] *See* Knapp Commission, The Knapp Commission Report on Police Corruption.

police department. Are government police really necessary for a peaceful, secure society? Look around. Could a nonpolitical, nonmonopolistic system of supplying police services really do worse than its government-supplied counterpart?

D. Internalizing Externalities

Supporters of government often argue that government is essential to provide needed regulation of market activities. Individuals contracting with each other in a market often act in ways that impose harm or unconsented-to costs on others. Manufacturers make and consumers purchase products whose use imposes an unacceptable risk of injury on third parties. For example, automobile companies can produce and drivers will purchase cars that can move at speeds or have handling properties that create an unreasonable risk of injury to pedestrians. Oil companies can ship oil to consumers in ways that create an unreasonable risk of spills that would pollute the land or body of water over which the oil is transported. More generally, because people do not bear the costs their activities impose on others, they will often act in ways that impose greater costs on society than are justified by the personal benefits they realize. These unconsidered costs to others are the social costs of market activity—what economists call negative externalities. Supporters of government contend that only government can regulate market activity to ensure that private contractors consider the social costs of their transaction. Thus, even if rules of law, courts, and police services could be supplied nonpolitically, government would nevertheless be essential to internalize externalities.

In response I could refer you to Chapter 2, in which the substance of this argument is addressed in detail, but, for present purposes, "look around" is probably sufficient. That this argument has any plausibility at all is a testament to how completely oblivious people can be to what is going on around them. In a world in which one of the dominant political issues is tort reform, in which businesses are continually complaining to Congress that they are overregulated by the common law of tort and begging government to protect them from this nonpolitical method of internalizing externalities, how can anyone seriously assert that government regulation is needed to deal with the problem of social costs?

Tort law is precisely that portion of the law that evolved to protect individuals' persons and property from the ill-considered actions of their fellows, which means, to internalize externalities. It is only by ignoring the existence of this form of nonpolitical regulation that one could possibly believe that government is necessary to address the problem of social costs. Of course, one should never underestimate the power of a conceptual model to blind intellectuals to what is going on in the real world.

But, supporters of government claim, common law can never be an adequate regulatory mechanism because it is necessarily retroactive in operation. Lawsuits arise only after harm is done. Therefore, civil liability could never provide the type of proactive regulation necessary to prevent serious harm from occurring. Really? The basic rules of tort law prohibit individuals from intentionally harming others and require them to act with reasonable care to avoid causing harm inadvertently. There is nothing retroactive about this. It is true that precisely what constitutes reasonable care may have to be determined on a case-by-case basis, but in this respect, the common law is no different than government legislation that announces a general rule and then leaves it up to the courts to determine how it applies in particular cases. Furthermore, the common law can act prospectively in appropriate cases. The injunction, an order not to engage in a specified activity, evolved precisely to handle those cases in which one party's conduct poses a high risk of irreparable harm to others.[22] And by the

[22] Note that to obtain an injunction at common law and thereby curtail another citizen's freedom, one must meet a very high evidentiary threshold by establishing a

way, government legislation is almost always retroactive as well. Limitations on human knowledge (not to mention public choice considerations) mean that legislators are rarely able to accurately anticipate future harm. If I remember correctly, Dodd-Frank was passed after the Great Recession. And when was the USA Patriot Act passed? Oh, yes, after 9/11.

Recall the McDonald's coffee-spill case discussed in Chapter 2. Prior to that decision, fast food restaurants across the country served coffee at between 180°F and 190°F, a temperature that could cause third-degree burns in two to seven seconds. I did not notice any proactive legislative regulation designed to internalize this dangerous externality. The day after the verdict in the McDonald's lawsuit, fast food restaurants across the United States reduced the temperature at which it served its coffee by at least 10 degrees. There may be many things wrong with contemporary tort law, but being ineffective at internalizing externalities is most assuredly not among them. The only way to believe that government is necessary to resolve the problem of social costs is to be studiously blind to the nature of both common law and government legislation.

E. Public Goods

Supporters of government claim that government is necessary to produce "public goods"—goods that are important for human well-being but either cannot be produced or will be underproduced by the market. Public goods are goods that are both nonrivalrous in consumption—that is, their use by one person does not interfere with their use by others—and nonexclusive—that is, if the good is

high likelihood of *irreparable* harm. This is in contrast to government legislation that can curtail citizens' freedom whenever the politically dominant faction of the legislature deems it necessary, even if only to effectuate the "precautionary principle." I leave it to the reader to decide which is the superior standard for addressing potential future harm.

available to one person, it is available to all whether they help produce it or not. Supporters of government argue that such goods cannot be produced without government because, due to the free-rider and assurance problems, individuals will not voluntarily contribute the capital necessary for their production. The free-rider problem refers to the fact that because people can enjoy public goods without paying for them, many will withhold their contribution to the goods' production and attempt to free ride on the contribution of others. The assurance problem refers to the fact that in the absence of some assurance that others will contribute enough to produce the good, people are more likely to regard their own contribution as a waste of money and withhold it. Therefore, government is necessary to ensure the production of important public goods.

The proper response to the argument that government is necessary to produce public goods is: Like what? Like lighthouses? The light they provide is available to all ships, and its use by one does not impair its value to others. But wait, lighthouses can be and have been supplied privately.[23] Like radio and television? A wag I know likes to say that he does something impossible every night by watching commercial television. After all, television signals are nonrivalrous in consumption and nonexclusive. Therefore, they cannot be produced by the market. Like the internet? But wait, that is privately funded also.

Perhaps like police and courts? Theorists frequently argue that police services and courts are public goods that must be supplied by government. With regard to police services, for example, the argument is made that

> [s]ecurity of person is to a large degree a collective good. . . . [A]n important part of the service provided by public police and systems of criminal justice generally is to *deter* potential violators from harming people. And this deterrence is an indivisible

[23] *See* Ronald H. Coase, *The Lighthouse in Economics*, 17 J. L. Econ. 357 (1974).

> nonexcludable good to neighbors and visitors. . . . In addition to deterrence, there may be the benefits that follow from incarceration of the thief—namely, incapacitation—benefits that are also indivisible and nonexcludable.
>
> Social order, at least security of persons and possessions, then, is to a considerable degree a collective good. Accordingly, to the degree that this is the case, social order may not be efficiently provided in the absence of a state.[24]

Similarly, with regard to courts, it is argued that because the existence of definite and widely known rules of behavior provides a nonexcludable benefit to all, private courts lack an incentive to establish the clear precedents that give rise to rules. Indeed, because clear precedents "would confer an external, an uncompensated benefit, not only on future parties, but also on competing judges, . . . judges might deliberately avoid explaining their results because the demand for their services would be reduced by rules that, by clarifying the meaning of the law, reduce the incidence of disputes."[25] Hence, government courts are necessary for the development of rules of law.

These are perfectly logical theoretical arguments belied only by the facts of reality. The evidence that police services and courts are not public goods is that, like lighthouses, television, and the internet, they have been supplied nonpolitically for most of human history. It is true, of course, that if government exists and creates areas of unowned, politically controlled property that no private party has an interest in maintaining, police services are likely to be underproduced in these locations. Policing of this "public" property may indeed have to be supplied by the government. However, this is not because police services are a public good that cannot

[24] Christopher W. Morris, An Essay on the Modern State 60–61 (1998).

[25] *See* William M. Landes & Richard A. Posner, *Adjudication as a Private Good*, 6 Journal of Legal Studies 235 (1979).

be supplied by the market, but because police services will not be supplied when the market has been suppressed by the government. And although it is certainly true that private police services produce an uncompensated positive externality in that their deterrent effects make even those who have not paid for them more secure, this can hardly be a reason for believing that such services will not be produced. It is actually quite difficult to think of any useful activity that does not produce some uncompensated positive externality. My using deodorant and going about clothed certainly do, but government is not required to pay me to induce me to bathe and dress. Further, it is at least odd to argue that a system of competitive courts will not produce rules of law in a common law legal system in which the rules on which our civilization rests actually arose out of just such a system.[26]

Like national defense? National defense is perhaps the archetypical public good. The security it provides is both nonrivalrous in consumption and benefits all members of society whether they pay for it or not. Can national defense be adequately supplied without government?

If "national defense" refers to the type of military expenditures associated with contemporary national governments, the answer is an obvious "no." Once a state becomes invested with the power to expropriate the wealth of its citizenry to provide for national defense, almost any desired expenditure begins to look like a requirement for national defense. Before long propping up Southeast Asian dictators and overthrowing Middle Eastern ones are being characterized as urgent national defense concerns. The fact that there is no nongovernmental way to raise sufficient capital to

[26] For the true intellectuals among my readers who simply cannot accept that facts should be allowed to undermine a perfectly good theoretical model, I refer you to DAVID SCHMIDTZ, THE LIMITS OF GOVERNMENT: AN ESSAY ON THE PUBLIC GOODS ARGUMENT (1991). Schmidtz explains how the assurance problem can be handled by the assurance contract or money-back guarantee and how the free-rider problem can be cabined to a relatively small number of cases in which using coercion to produce the public good is ethically questionable.

realize this conception of national defense proves nothing about the viability of anarchy, and, in fact, serves as one more argument in favor of markets.

However, if "national defense" refers to only what is strictly necessary to protect the citizens of a nation against outside aggression, I am willing to admit that I do not know the answer to this question. I am not discomforted by this admission, however, because as I said at the outset, the question of national defense is, as a practical matter, a trivial one. No one believes that we can transition from a world of states to anarchy instantaneously. No reasonable anarchist advocates the total dissolution of government tomorrow. Once we turn our attention to the question of how to move incrementally from government to anarchy, it becomes apparent that national defense would be one of the last governmental functions to be de-politicized. If my argument for anarchy is flawed and anarchy is not a viable method of social organization, this will undoubtedly be revealed long before doing away with national defense becomes an issue. On the other hand, to the extent that the gradual transition from government to anarchy is successful, the need for national defense continually lessens.

Consider what it would mean for a nation to seriously undertake a process of de-politicization. Every reduction in the size and scope of government releases more of the creative energy of the population. The economic effects of this are well-known and have recently been demonstrated in China. As economists point out, revolutionary change can be wrought by marginal effects. Even a slow process of liberalization *that is sustained over time* will produce massively accelerated economic and technological growth. And the increase in freedom and prosperity in this nation would have profound external effects as well. Many of the bravest and most industrious residents of more repressive nations would attempt to immigrate to the liberalizing one, and some other nations would learn by the liberalizing nation's example and begin to copy its policies.

As the economic and technological gap between the liberalizing nation and the rest of world widens, as the rest of the world becomes more dependent upon the goods and services manufactured and supplied by that nation, and as a greater number of other nations are moved to adopt liberalizing policies themselves, the threat the rest of the world poses to the liberalizing nation decreases. Evidence of this is supplied by the demise of the Soviet Union. Radical regimes and terrorist organizations may constitute a serious and continuing threat, but consider it in historical context. Such a threat is considerably less serious and less expensive to address than the threat of thermonuclear war.

Recall that we are considering the cost only of protecting citizens against aggression, not the cost of foreign adventures or "preemptive" warfare. How significant a threat of foreign invasion does the United States currently face? How much of its "national defense" spending is actually devoted to preventing such invasion? After years or decades of continual and sustained reduction in the size of government, how much wider will the economic and technological gap between the prenatal anarchy and the more repressive nations be? How much more sophisticated its defensive technology? How much more dependent will the repressive nations be on its goods and services? Let a nation begin to tread the path toward anarchy, and by the time the question of whether national defense is a public good that must be supplied by government becomes relevant, it is very likely to be moot.

IV. Conclusion

Aristotle called man the rational animal, identifying human beings' ability to reason as their essential defining characteristic. I think this is a mistake. I think man is the imaginative animal. Human beings undoubtedly have the ability to reason, but they also have the ability to imagine that the world is different than it is, and the latter is a far more powerful force. People root for the New York Jets because they can imagine the Jets returning to the Super Bowl, despite all evidence to the contrary. People regularly get married because they can imagine that they will change their obviously incompatible partner into the ideal husband or wife. People devote their time, effort, and money to political campaigns because they can imagine that if only Barack Obama or Mitt Romney or Hillary Clinton or Donald Trump or Joe Biden were elected, Washington, DC, would be transformed into Camelot. And more significantly, people volunteer to fight wars because they can imagine themselves running through a field of machine gun fire unscathed. Only the ability to imagine an afterlife for which they have absolutely no evidence can explain why human beings would strap explosives to themselves and blow themselves up in an effort to kill as many innocent people as possible.

Do you ever wonder why people believed in the divine right of kings, despite the fact that the monarchs of their time were patently not the type of individuals an all-knowing, all-good god would choose to reign over them? They believed in it because they were taught to believe in it and because they could imagine that it was so, regardless of all evidence to the contrary. We no longer believe in such silly things as the divine right of kings. We believe that government is necessary for an orderly peaceful society and that it can be made to function according to the rule of law. We believe this because we have been taught to believe it from infancy and because we can imagine that it is so, regardless of all contrary evidence.

One should never underestimate the power of abstract concepts to shape how human beings see the world. Once one accepts the idea that government is necessary for peace and order and that it can function objectively, one's imagination will allow one to see the hand of government wherever there are law, police, and courts and render the nonpolitical provision of these services invisible. But if you lay aside this conceptual framework long enough to ask where these services originated and where, to a large extent, they still come from, the world assumes a different aspect. If you want the strongest argument for anarchy, simply remove your self-imposed blinders and look around.

APPENDIX

Guide to Legal Terminology

Distinctions

Common law = Law that arises from the decisions in particular cases over time (emergent law). Law created without a guiding human intelligence.

Statutory law (legislation) = Law that is consciously created by the political representatives of the community/state/nation.

Administrative law = Law (regulations) that is consciously created by the executive branch of the community/state/nation and its agencies.

Public law = Law that regulates the relationship between the state and individuals. Public law is the law that creates and limits state power to restrict the liberty of individual citizens (criminal law, administrative law, and constitutional law).

Private law = Law that regulates relationships among the individual members of society (tort (personal injury) law, contract law, property law, commercial law).

Criminal law = Law that determines when the state is permitted to punish—to coercively impose harm on—those subject to its jurisdiction. Criminal law is public law. Criminal liability is liability to be punished by the state.

Tort law = Law that determines when one who has caused harm to another is required to compensate that person for the injury he or she has suffered. Tort law is private law. Tort law gives rise to civil liability—the liability to make compensatory (and sometimes exemplary) payments to an injured party.

Federal law = Legislation enacted by the Congress of the United States. There is no federal common law.

State law = Legislation enacted by the state legislatures + state common law.

Disambiguations

The term "common law" has at least three different meanings depending on context.

1) Generic usage = Law that arises from the decisions in particular cases over time (emergent law). Law created without a guiding human intelligence.
2) Parochial usage = The law that evolved in the royal courts of England.
3) Systemic usage = The legal systems of the British Commonwealth of countries: the "common law countries."

The term "civil law" has at least two different meanings depending on context.

1) Parochial usage = In a common law context, civil law = The law that concerns private parties; a synonym for private law.
2) Systemic usage = In a global context, civil law = A legal system originating in continental Europe and derived from Roman law. Civil law systems do not recognize the binding force of precedent.

Bibliography

Abrams v. United States, 250 U.S. 616 (1919).

Adler, Jonathan H. "Money or Nothing: The Adverse Environmental Consequences of Uncompensated Land Use Controls." *Boston College Law Review* 49, no. 2 (2008): 301–366.

Aharoni, Eyal, and Alan J. Fridlund. "Punishment without Reason: Isolating Retribution in Lay Punishment of Criminal Offenders." *Psychology Public Policy and Law* 18, no. 4 (2011): 1–27.

Alberts v. California, 354 U.S. 476 (1957).

All Things Considered. "An Exit Interview with George Mitchel." NPR radio broadcast (October 17, 1994).

Anderson, Debra R. "The Cost of Frivolous Lawsuits Is No Joke." *Minneapolis Business Journal*. August 10, 1997. https://perma.cc/RLT5-UP9H.

Ashcroft v. Free Speech Coalition, 535 U.S. 234 (2002).

"Boston Police Department." *Boston Police Department*. Last accessed October 22, 2023. http://www.cityofboston.gov/police/glance.asp.

Baker, J. H. *An Introduction to English Legal History*, 4th ed. London: Butterworth-Heinemann (2002).

Baltimore & Ohio Railroad Company v. Goodman, 275 U.S. 66 (1927).

Barman, Harold. *Law and Revolution*. Cambridge, MA: Harvard University Press (1983).

Beito, David T. *From Mutual Aid to the Welfare State: Fraternal Societies and Social Services 1890–1967*. Chapel Hill: University of North Carolina Press (2000).

Benson L., Bruce. *The Enterprise of Law: Justice without the State*. California: Independent Institute (1990).

Benson, Bruce. "The Spontaneous Evolution of Cyber Law: Norms, Property Rights, Contracting, Dispute Resolution and Enforcement without the State." *Journal of Economics and Policy* 1, no. 2 (2005): 269–348.

Berman, Harold J. "The Origins of Historical Jurisprudence: Coke, Selden, Hale." *Yale Law Journal* 103 no. 7 (1994): 1651–1738.

Berman, Harold J., and Charles J. Reid, Jr. "The Transformation of English Legal Science: From Hale to Blackstone." *Emory Law Review* 45, no. 2 (1996): 437–522.

Berman, Harold. *Law and Revolution*. Cambridge, MA: Harvard University Press (1983).

Blackstone, William. *Commentaries on the Laws of England*, 9th ed. Chicago: Callaghan and Cockcroft (1871).

Blinder, Alan S. "Individual Choice Is a Bad Fit for Covid Safety." *Wall Street Journal*. August 13, 2020.

BMW of North America, Incorporated v. Gore, 517 U.S. 5591 (1996).

Boomer v. Atlantic Cement Company, 257 N.E.2d 870 (N.Y. 1970).

Bourne, Rochard. "Medical Monitoring without Physical Injury; The Least Justice Can Do for Those Industry Has Terrorized with Poisonous Products." *Southern Methodist University Law Review* 58, no. 2 (2005): 251–296.

Bradley v. Pizzaco of Nebraska, Incorporated, 7 F.3d 795 (8th Cir. 1993).

Bratspies, Rebecca M. "A Regulatory Wake-Up Call: Lessons from BP's Deepwater Horizon Disaster." *Golden Gate University Environmental Law Journal* 5, no. 1 (2011): 7–60.

Brown v. Entertainment Merchants Association, 564 U.S. 786 (2011).

Buckley v. Valeo, 424 U.S. 1 (1976).

Cain, Kevin G. "And Now the Rest of the Story... The McDonald's Coffee Lawsuit." *Journal of Consumer and Commercial Law* 11 (2007).

California State Constitution, Article I, § 2 (1879).

Caplan, Bryan, and Ed Stringham. "Networks, Law, and the Paradox of Cooperation." *Review of Austrian Economics* 16, no. 4 (2003): 309–326.

Central Hudson Gas and Electric Corporation v. Public Service Commission, 447 U.S. 557 (1980).

Chaplinsky v. New Hampshire, 315 U.S. 568 (1942).

Cid. J. "Is Imprisonment Criminogenic? A Comparative Study of Recidivism Rates Between Prison and Suspended Prison Sanctions." *European Journal of Criminology* 6, no. 6 (2009): 459–480.

Coase, Ronald H. "The Lighthouse in Economics." *Journal of Law and Economics* 17, no. 2 (1974): 357–376.

"Code of Federal Regulations Total Pages 1938–1949, and Total Volumes and Pages 1950–2021." *Office of the Federal Register*. 2002. https://www.federalregister.gov/uploads/2015/05/Code-of-Federal-Regulations-Total-Pages-and-Volumes-1938-2014.pdf.

Cohen, Felix. "Transcendental Nonsense and the Functional Approach." *Columbia Law Review* 35, no. 6 (1935): 809–849.

Collin v. Smith, 578 F.2d 1197 (7th Cir. 1978).

Connecticut v. Teal, 457 U.S. 440 (1982).

Connolly, Ceci. "Democrats Have No Argument with Trial Lawyers." *Washington Post*. April 9, 2000.

Constitution of the United States, Amendment I (1791).

Coster, Helen. "More People Are Avoiding the News, and Trusting It Less, Report Says." *Reuters*. June 14, 2022. https://www.reuters.com/business/media-telecom/more-people-are-avoiding-news-trusting-it-less-report-says-2022-06-14/.

Cowen, Tyler. "Law as a Public Good: The Economics of Anarchy." *Economics and Philosophy* 8, no. 2 (1992): 249–267.

Cowen, Tyler. "Public Goods and Externalities: Old and New Perspectives." In *The Theory of Market Failure: A Critical Examination*, edited by Tyler Cowen. Fairfax, VA: George Mason University Press (1988).

Cowen, Tyler. *The Theory of Market Failure: A Critical Examination*. Fairfax, VA: George Mason University Press (1988).

Cox, Jane B. "No Tragedy of the Commons." *Environmental Ethics* 7, no. 1 (1985): 49–61.

Curtis Publishing Company v. Butts, 388 U.S. 130 (1967).

"Deepwater Horizon—BP Gulf of Mexico Oil Spill." *Environmental Protection Agency*. Last updated December 4, 2020. https://www.epa.gov/enforcement/deepwater-horizon-bp-gulf-mexico-oil-spill [https://perma.cc/2RNZ-Q6XL]

De Jonge v. Oregon, 299 U.S. 353 (1937).

Definition of Waters of the United States, 40 C.F.R. § 230.3 (2006).

Delgado, M. R., C. D. Labouliere, and E. A. Phelps. "Fear of Losing Money? Aversive Condition with Secondary Reinforcers." *Social Cognitive and Affective Neuroscience* 1, no. 3 (2006): 250–259.

Demsetz, Harold. "Toward a Theory of Property Rights." *American Economic Law Review* 57, no. 2 (1967): 347–359.

Dennis v. United States, 341 U.S. 494 (1951).

Dodd-Frank Wall Street Reform and Consumer Protection Act, Pub. L. No. 111-203, 124 Stat. 1376 (2010).

Edmundson, William A. "State of the Art: The Duty to Obey the Law." *Legal Theory* 10, no. 4 (2004): 215–259.

Eliach, Yaffa. "Social Protest in the Synagogue: The Delaying of the Torah Reading." In *There Once Was a World: A 900-Year Chronicle of the Shtetl of Eishyshok*, edited by Yaffa Eliach. New York: Back Bay Books (1999).

Ellickson, Robert C. "Property in Land." *Yale Law Journal* 102, no. 6 (1993): 1315–1400.

Endangered and Threatened Wildlife and Plants—Introduction and General Provisions, 50 C.F.R. § 17.3 (1994).

Endangered Species—Definitions, 16 U.S.C. §1532(19) (2018).

"Final and Proposed Rules." *United States Consumer Product Safety Commission*. Last accessed July 31, 2021. https://www.cpsc.gov/Regulations-Laws--Standards/Rulemaking/Final-and-Proposed-Rules [https://perma.cc/Q5HR-AQ2R]

Farnham, Alan. "Woman Sues Dunkin' Donuts Over Hot Cider; A Look Behind Beverage Suit Tsunami." *ABC News*. February 24, 2014. https://abcnews.go.com/Business/dunkin-donuts-sued-hot-apple-cider-burns/story?id=22556060- -[--https://perma.cc/H4J9-QQ4A-]-.-

Federal Oil and Gas Royalty Management Act of 1982, 30 U.S.C.A. § 1701. (1983).

Federal Water Pollution Control Act of 1948, 33 U.S.C. § 466 (1948).

Ferguson, Adam, *An Essay on the History of Civil Society*. Ontario: Batoche (2001).

Finnis, John. "Law as Co-ordination." *Ratio Juris* 2, no. 1 (1989): 97–104.

Finnis, John. "The Authority of Law in the Predicament of Contemporary Social Theory." *Notre Dame Journal of Legal Ethics and Public Policy* 1, no. 1 (1984): 115–138.

Fisher v. Carrousel Motor Hotel, Incorporated, 424 S.W.2d 627 (Tex. 1967).

Florida State Constitution, Article I, § 4 (1838).

Freidman, Milton. *Capitalism and Freedom*. Chicago: University of Chicago Press (1962).

Friedman, David. "Private Creation and Enforcement of Law: A Historical Case." *Journal of Legal Studies* 8, no. 2 (1979): 399–416.

Frishberg, David. *I'm Just a Bill (School House Rock Song)*. ABC Publishing (1973).

Fuller, Lon L. "Human Interaction and the Law." In *The Principles of Social Order: Selected Essays of Lon Fuller*, edited by Kenneth I. Winston. Durham, NC: Duke University Press (1981).

Fuller, Lon L. "Positivism and Fidelity to Law—A Reply to Professor Hart." *Harvard Law Review* 71, no. 4 (1958): 630–672.

Gerlin, Andrea. "A Matter of Degree: How a Jury Decided That a Coffee Spill Is Worth $2.9 Million." *Wall Street Journal*. September 1, 1994.

Gitlow v. New York, 268 U.S. 652 (1925).

Goebel Jr., Julius. *Felony and Misdemeanor: A Study in the History of English Criminal Procedure*. London: Oxford University Press (1937).

Green, Marlow H. "Common Law, Property Rights and the Environment: A Comparative Analysis of Historical Developments in the United States and England and a Model for the Future." *Cornell International Law Review* 30, no. 2 (1997): 541–586.

Griswold v. Connecticut, 381 U.S. 479. (1965).

Grogger, J. "Certainty vs. Severity of Punishment." *Economic Inquiry* 29, no. 2 (1991): 297–309.

Haines, Richard F. "A Breakdown in Simultaneous Information Processing." *Presbyopia Research* (1991): 171–175.

Hardin, Garrett. "The Tragedy of the Commons." *Science* 162, no. 3859 (1968): 1342–1348.

Hasnas, John. "Back and the Future: From Critical Legal Studies Forward to Legal Realism, of How Not to Miss the Point of the Indeterminacy Argument." *Duke Law Journal* 45, no. 1 (1995): 84–107.

Hasnas, John. "Ethics and the Problem of White Collar Crime." *American University Law Review* 54 (2005): 579–660.

Hasnas, John. *Trapped: When Acting Ethically Is Against the Law*. Washington, DC: Cato Institute (2006).

Hayek, Friedrich A. *Individualism and Economic Order*. Chicago: University of Chicago Press (1948).

Hayek, Friedrich A. *Law, Legislation and Liberty*. Chicago: University of Chicago Press (1978).

Heaney, Mary. "Where Business Is King: London's Commercial Court Hears International Clashes." *National Law Journal* (June 5, 1995): C1–C3.

Henkin, Louis. "Morals and the Constitution: The Sin of Obscenity." *Columbia Law Review* 63, no. 3 (1963): 391–414.

Hobbes, Thomas. *Leviathan*, edited by Herbert Schneider. Indianapolis: Bobbs-Merrill (1958).

Hogue, Arthur R. *Origins of Common Law*. Carmel, IN: Liberty Fund (1986).

Holmes, Oliver W. "The Path of the Law." *Harvard Law Review* 10, no. 8 (1897): 457–478.

Hudson, John. *The Formation of the English Common Law: Law and Society in England from the Norman Conquest to Magna Carta*. New York: Longman World (1996).

In re: Subway Footlong Sandwich Marketing and Sales Practices Litigation, 316 F.R.D. 240 (E.D. Wis. 2016).

Indiana Harbor Belt Railroad Company v. American Cyanamid Company, 916 F.2d 1174 (7th Cir.1990).

Indictment, No. 03 Cr. 717. *United States v. Stewart*, 44 F.3d 273 (S.D.N.Y. 2003).

Jarvis, Judith T. "Some Ruminations of Rights." In *Reading Nozick: Essays on Anarchy, State and Utopia*, edited by Jeffery Paul. Lanham, MD: Rowan & Littlefield (1981).

Jones, Keith J. "Drill Baby . . . Spill Baby: How the Oil Pollution Act's Economic-Damage Liability Cap Contributed to the Deepwater Horizon Disaster." *Environmental Law Reporter News & Analysis* 40, no. 11 (2010): 11132–11136.

Joseph Burstyn, Incorporated v. Wilson, 343 U.S. 495 (1952).

Kalman, Laura. "Legal Realism at Yale, 1927–1960." *Michigan Law Review* 85, no. 5 (1987): 1105–1109.

Kant, Immanuel. *The Foundations of the Metaphysics of Morals*. Translated by Lewis White Beck. Indianapolis: Bobbs-Merrill (1959).

Katz, Eric D. "Defensive Medicine: A Case and Review of Its Status and Possible Solutions." *Clinical Practice & Cases Emergency Medicine* 3, no. 4 (2019): 329–332.

Kaufman, Marc. "Increased Demand for Ivory Threatens Elephant Survival." *Washington Post*. February 27, 2007.

Keeton, W. Page and William L. Prosser. *Prosser and Keeton on Torts*, 5th ed. St. Paul, MN: West Group (1984).

Kerkvliet, Joe and Christian Langpap. "Learning from Endangered and Threatened Species Recovery Programs: A Case Study Using U.S. Endangered Species Act Recovery Scores." *Ecological Economics* 63, no. 2 (2007): 499–510.

Khamsi, Roxanne. "Proof That Losing Money Really Is Scary." *New Scientist Daily*. October 18, 2006.

Klerman, Daniel. "Settlement and the Decline of Private Prosecution in Thirteenth-Century England." *Law and History Review* 19, no. 1 (2002): 5–8.

Koyama, Mark. "The Law and Economics of Private Prosecutions in Industrial Revolution England." *Public Choice* 159, no. 1 (2014): 277–298.

Kramer, Matthew H. "Moral and Legal Obligation." In *The Blackwell Guide to the Philosophy of Law and Legal Theory*, edited by Martin P. Golding and William A. Edmunson. Oxford: Blackwell Publishing (2005).

Kravitz, Derek and Mary Pat Flaherty. "Report Says Oil Agency Ran Amok." *Washington Post*. September 11, 2008. https://www.washingtonpost.com/wp-dyn/content/article/2008/09/10/AR2008091001829_pf.html [https://perma.cc/6KUL-GMPC].

"Lawsuits Take School's Swing Sets Away from Kids." *Faces of Lawsuit Abuse*. June 15, 2018. https://www.facesoflawsuitabuse.org/2018/06/lawsuits-take-schools-swing-sets-away-from-kids/ [https://perma.cc/WGH3-P5XS].

Ladenson, Robert. "Legitimate Authority." *American Philosophy Quarterly* 9, no. 4 (1972): 335–341.

Landres, William M., and Richard A. Posner. "Adjudication as a Private Good." *Journal of Legal Studies* 8, no. 2 (1979): 235–284.

Laster, Richard E. "Criminal Restitution: A Survey of Its Past History and an Analysis of Its Present Usefulness." *University of Richmond Law Review* 5, no. 1 (1970): 71–98.

Lease of Oil and Gas Lands, 30 U.S.C. § 226 (2006).

Lefkowitz, David. "A Contractualist Defense of Democratic Authority." *Ratio Juris* 18, no. 3 (2005): 346–364.
Lefkowitz, David. "The Duty to Obey the Law." *Philosophy Compass* 1, no. 6 (2006): 571–598.
Leichtman v. WLW Jacor Communications, Incorporated, 634 N.E.2d 697 (Ohio Ct. App. 1994).
Leonhardt, David. "Spillonomics: Underestimating Risk." *New York Times*. June 6, 2010. https://www.nytimes.com/2010/06/06/magazine/06fob-wwln-t.html [https://perma.cc/YH55-YXUU].
Lincoln, Abraham. *Gettysburg Address*, delivered November 19, 1863.
Llewellyn, Karl. "Some Realism About Realism—Responding to Dean Pound." *Harvard Law Review* 44, no. 8 (1931): 1222–1264.
Locke, John. *Essays of the Law of Nature*, W. Von Leyden ed. London: Oxford University Press (1988).
Locke, John. *Second Treatise of Government*, edited by C. B. MacPherson. Indianapolis: Hackett Publishing (1980).
Lomasky, Loren E. *Persons, Rights, and the Moral Community*. New York: Oxford University Press (1990).
Long Forgotten Videos. "Saiontz & Kirk - Free Injury Hotline - 1995 Commercial." *YouTube*. August 23, 2019. https://www.youtube.com/watch?v=8ez_Hu5SkOU [https://perma.cc/QBF4-RYAG].
Lueck, Dean, and Jeffrey A. Michael. "Preemptive Habitat Destruction Under the Endangered Species Act." *Journal of Law and Economics* 46, no. 1 (2003): 27–60.
Lyon, Bruce. *Constitutional and Legal History of Medieval England*. New York: Norton (1980).
MacDonald, Margaret. "Natural Rights." In *Theories of Rights*, edited by Jeremy Waldron. Oxford: Oxford University Press (1984).
Marbury v. Madison, 5 U.S. 137 (1803).
McCormack, Michael T. "The Need for Private Prosecutors: An Analysis of Massachusetts and New Hampshire Law." *Suffolk University Law Review* 37 (2004): 497–511.
McLachlan, Campbell. "London Court Reigns as an International Forum." *National Law Journal* (June 5, 1995): C4–C8.
McLean, Iain. *Public Choice: An Introduction*. Oxford: Basil Blackwell (1987).
McQuaid, John. "Anatomy of the BP Oil Spill: An Accident Waiting to Happen." *Yale Environment 360*. May 10, 2010. https://e360.yale.edu/features/the_gulf_of_mexico_oil_spill_an_accident_waiting_to_happen [https://perma.cc/P4UV-B5ZM].
Megan's Law. Pub. L. No. 104-145. 110 Stat. 1345 (1996).
Miller, William I. *Bloodtaking and Peacemaking: Feud, Law, and Society in Saga Iceland*. Chicago: University of Chicago Press (1997).
Moore, George E. *The Encyclopedia of Philosophy*, edited by Paul Edwards. New York: Macmillan (1967).
Morris, Christopher W. *An Essay on the Modern State*. Cambridge: Cambridge University Press (1998).
Morse v. Frederick, 551 U.S. 393 (2007).

Mufson, Steven. "Siphoning Off Corn to Fuel Our Cars." *Washington Post*. April 30, 2008.
Muller v. Oregon, 208 U.S. 412 (1908).
Murray, Charles. *In Pursuit: Of Happiness and Good Government*. Washington, DC: ICS Press (1994).
Nagel, Thomas. "Libertarianism without Foundations." In *Reading Nozick: Essays on Anarchy, State and Utopia*, edited by Jeffery Paul. Lanham, MD: Rowan & Littlefield (1981).
New State Ice Company v. Liebmann, 285 U.S. 262 (1932).
New York City Commission to Investigate Allegations of Police Corruption. *The Knapp Commission Report on Police Corruption*. 1973. https://www.ojp.gov/ncjrs/virtual-library/abstracts/knapp-commission-report-police-corruption.
New York State Constitution, Article I, § 8 (1777).
New York Times v. Sullivan, 376 U.S. 254 (1964).
New York v. Ferber, 458 U.S. 747 (1982).
Niskanen Jr., William A. *Bureaucracy and Representative Government*. New York: Routledge (1971).
Nova: The Kingdom of the Seahorse. PBS Television. April 15, 1997.
Nozick, Robert. *Anarchy, State, and Utopia*. London: Blackwell (1974).
Olson, Trisha. "The Medieval Blood Sanction and the Divine Beneficence of Pain: 1100–1450." *Journal of Law and Religion* 22, no. 1 (2006): 63–129.
Orwell, George. *1984*. New York: Everyman's Library (1992).
"Our Common Future, From One Earth to One World." *World Commission in Environment and Development*. August 4, 1987. https://sustainabledevelopment.un.org/content/documents/5987our-common-future.pdf.
Outer Continental Shelf Lands Act, 43 U.S.C. § 1332(3) (2006).
Pennsylvania State Constitution, Article I, § 7 (1776).
Peterson, Hayley. "Three Reasons Why You Should Order Your Starbucks Drink 'Extra Hot.'" *Business Insider*. December 16, 2023.https://www.businessinsider.com/starbucks-drink-extra-hot-2013-12 [https://perma.cc/3S9U-N7AE].
Plucknett, Theodore F. T. *A Concise History of the Common Law*, 5th ed. Boston, MA: Little, Brown, and Co. (1956).
Pokora v. Wabash Railway Company, 292 U.S. 98 (1934).
Polasky, Stephen, and Holly Doremus. "When the Truth Hurts: Endangered Species Policy on Private Land with Imperfect Information." *Journal of Environmental Economics & Management* 35, no. 1 (1998): 22–47.
Pollock, Frederick and Frederic W. Maitland. *The History of English Law Before the Time of Edward I*, 2nd ed. Cambridge, MA: Cambridge University Press (1989).
Pollock, Frederick. *First Book of Jurisprudence*, 6th ed. London: Macmillan (1929).
Popper, Andrew F. "Capping Incentives, Capping Innovation, Courting Disaster: The Gulf Oil Spill and Arbitrary Limits on Civil Liability." *DePaul University Law Review* 60, no. 4 (2011): 975–1006.
"Preamble." *American Bar Association Model Rules of Professional Conduct*. (1983).
Pallardy, Richard. "Deepwater Horizon Oil Spill." *Encyclopedia Britannica*. November 2, 2020. https://www.britannica.com/event/Deepwater-Horizon-oil-spill [https://perma.cc/4LZZ-PFBJ].

Purcell Jr., Edward A. *The Crisis of Democratic Theory*. Lexington: University of Kentucky Press (1973).

R.A.V. v. City of St. Paul, 505 U.S. 377 (1992).

Rabin, Edward H. et al. *Fundamentals of Modern Property Law*, 4th ed. Westbury, NY: Foundation Press (2000).

Radio Act of 1927, 47 U.S.C.A. § 83 (1927).

Rawls, John. *A Theory of Justice*. Cambridge, MA: Harvard University Press (1971).

Raz, Joseph. "The Obligation to Obey: Revision and Tradition." *Notre Dame Journal of Legal Ethics and Public Policy* 1, no. 1 (1984): 139–155.

Restatement (Second) of Torts: Harmful Contact § 13. *American Law Institute* (1965).

Restatement (Second) of Torts: Invasions of Interests in Land Other Than by Trespass § 821D. *American Law Institute* (2000).

Restatement (Second) of Torts: Liability for Intentional Intrusions on Land § 158. *American Law Institute* (2000).

Restatement (Third) of Property: Servitudes § 2.15. *American Law Institute* (2000).

Restatement (Third) of Torts: Physical and Emotional Harm § 20. *American Law Institute* (2010).

Rose, Carol. "Energy and Efficiency in the Realignment of Common Law." In *Property and Persuasion: Essays on the History, Theory, and Rhetoric of Ownership*, edited by Carol Rose. Boulder, CO: Westview Press (1994).

Rose, Carol. "Possession as the Origin of Property." *University of Chicago Law Review* 52, no. 1 (1985): 73–88.

Rose, Carol. "The Comedy of the Commons." In *Property and Persuasion: Essays on the History, Theory, and Rhetoric of Ownership*, edited by Carol Rose. Boulder, CO: Westview Press (1994).

Rose, Carol. "The Comedy of the Commons: Custom, Commerce, and Inherently Public Property." *University of Chicago Law Review* 53, no. 3 (1986): 711–781.

Rosenberg, Joshua D., and H. Jay Folberg. "Alternative Dispute Resolution: An Empirical Analysis." *Stanford Law Review* 46 (1994): 1487–1551.

Roth v. United States, 354 U.S. 476 (1957).

"Rule 1.6: Confidentiality of Information." *American Bar Association Model Rules of Professional Conduct* (1983).

Saiontz & Kirk, P.A. "Saiontz & Kirk: You Have a Lawyer." *YouTube*. June 10, 2019. https://www.youtube.com/watch?v=QGE4mPJzRDU [https://perma.cc/UJG6-XCJ3].

Sammons v. City of Gloversville, 67 N.E. 622 (N.Y. 1903).

Scales v. United States, 367 U.S. 203 (1961).

Schenck v. United States, 249 U.S. 47 (1919).

Schmadtke, Alan. "Helmet Companies Facing Tough Times." *Chicago Tribune*. October 16, 1988. https://www.chicagotribune.com/news/ct-xpm-1988-10-16-8802080430-story.html [https://perma.cc/S2XU-2SQN].

Schmidtz, David. *The Limits of Government: An Essay on the Public Goods Argument*. Boulder, CO: Westview Press (1991).

Sedition Act of 1798, Chapter 74 § 2. 1 Stat. 596 (1798).

Seipp, David J. "The Distinction Between Crime and Tort in the Early Common Law." *Boston University Law Review* 76 (1996): 59–87.

Seitz, Amanda. "Disinformation Board to Tackle Russia, Migrant Smugglers." *Associated Press.* April 28, 2022. https://apnews.com/article/russia-ukraine-immigration-media-europe-misinformation-4e873389889bb1d9e2ad8659d9975e9d.

Seymour, Ben et al. "Differential Encoding of Losses and Gains in the Human Striatum." *Journal of Neuroscience* 27, no. 18 (2007): 4826–4831.

Simmons, John A. "Locke's State of Nature." *Political Theory* 17, no. 3 (1989): 449–470.

Simmons, John A. "The Duty to Obey and Our Natural Moral Duties." In *Is There a Duty to Obey the Law?* Cambridge: Cambridge University Press (2005).

Simmons, John A. *Justification and Legitimacy: Essays on Rights and Obligations.* Cambridge: Cambridge University Press (2001).

Simmons, John A. *The Lockean Theory of Rights.* Princeton, NJ: Princeton University Press (1992).

Simons, Daniel J. "Inattentional Blindness." *Scholarpedia.* April 30, 2007. http://www.scholarpedia.org/article/inattentional_blindness [https://perma.cc/4UKS-RNZY].

Simons, Daniel J., and Christopher F. Chabris. "Gorillas in Our Midst: Sustained Inattentional Blindness for Dynamic Events." *Perception* 28, no. 9 (1999): 1059–1074.

Sindell v. Abbott Laboratories, 607 P.2d 924 (Cal. 1980).

Singh, Kanishka. "U.S. Advisers Say No Need for Disinformation Governance Board." *Reuters.* July 18, 2022. https://www.reuters.com/world/us/us-advisers-say-no-need-disinformation-governance-board-2022-07-19/.

Smith, Adam. *An Inquiry into the Nature and Causes of the Wealth of Nations*, edited by R. H. Campbell and A. S. Skinner. London: Oxford University Press (1976).

Social Security and Medicare Board of Trustees. "A Summary of the 2023 Annual Reports." *Social Security Administration.* Last accessed September 8, 2023. https://www.ssa.gov/OACT/TRSUM/2023/index.html/.

Solum, Lawrence B. "On the Indeterminacy Crisis: Critiquing Critical Dogma." *University of Chicago Law Review* 54, no. 2 (1987): 462–503.

Stigler, George. "The Theory of Economic Regulation." *Bell Journal Economics and Management Science* 2, no. 1 (1971): 3–21.

Stout, Hillary. "Not Just a Hot Cup Anymore." *New York Times.* October 21, 2013. https://www.nytimes.com/2013/10/21/booming/not-just-a-hot-cup-anymore.html [https://perma.cc/36EX-FR9G].

Stromberg v. California, 283 U.S. 359 (1931).

Submerged Lands Act of 1953, 43 U.S.C.A. §§ 1301-1315 (2007).

Sugg, Ike C. "Caught in the Act: Evaluating the Endangered Species Act, Its Effects on Man and Prospects for Reform." *Cumberland Law Review* 24, no. 1 (1993): 1–78.

Surowiecki, James. *The Wisdom of Crowds.* New York: Doubleday (2004).

Taylor, Charles. "Atomism." In *Powers, Possessions and Freedom*, edited by Alkis Kantos. Toronto: University of Toronto Press (1979).

Terminiello v. Chicago, 337 U.S. 1 (1949).

Terry Anderson and P. J. Hill. "The Evolution of Property Rights: A Study of the American West." *Journal of Law and Economics* 18, no. 1 (1975): 169–173.

Thompson, E. P. *Customs in Commons: Studies in Traditional Popular Culture.* New York: The New Press (1993).
Tinker v. Des Moines Independent Community School District, 393 U.S. 503 (1969).
Trakman, Leon E. *The Law Merchant: The Evolution of Commercial Law.* Littleton, CO: Rothman & Co. (1983).
Uniform Commercial Code § 1-303. *American Law Institute & Uniform Law Commission* (2012).
Uniform Commercial Code §§ 1-205, 2-202, 2-208. *American Law Institute & Uniform Law Commission* (2012).
United States v. Callender, 25 F. Cas. 239 (C.C.D. Va. 1800).
United States v. Knott, 106 F. Supp. 2d 174 (D. Mass. 2000).
United States v. O'Brien, 391 U.S. 367 (1968).
United States v. United Auto Workers, 352 U.S. 567 (1957).
Uniting and Strengthening America by Providing Appropriate Tools Required to Intercept and Obstruct Terrorism (USA PATRIOT Act) Act of 2001, Pub. L. No. 107-56, 115 Stat. 272 (2001).
Valentine v. Chrestensen, 316 U.S. 52 (1942).
Virginia State Board of Pharmacy v. Virginia Citizens Consumer Council, Incorporated, 425 U.S. 748 (1976).
Virginia State Constitution, Article I, § 12 (1776).
Virginia v. Black, 538 U.S. 343 (2003).
Waldron, Jeremy. "Introduction." In *Theories of Rights*, edited by Jeremy Waldron. London: Oxford University Press (1984).
Waldron, Jeremy. "Special Ties and Natural Duties." *Philosophy and Public Affairs* 22, no. 1 (1993): 3–30.
Washington v. Glucksberg, 521 U.S. 702. (1997).
Wellman, Christopher H. "Samaritanism and the Duty to Obey the Law." In *Is There A Duty to Obey the Law?*, edited by Christopher H. Wellman and John Simmons. Cambridge: Cambridge University Press (2005).
Wellman, Christopher H. "Toward a Liberal Theory of Political Obligation." *Ethics* 111, no. 4 (2001): 735–759.
West, Robin. "Jurisprudence and Gender." *University of Chicago Law Review* 55, no. 1 (1988): 1–72.
Western Union Telegraph Company v. Hill, 150 So. 709 (Ala. Ct. App. 1933).
Whalen v. Union Bag & Paper Company, 101 N.E. 805 (N.Y. 1913).
White, Edward G. *Tort Law in America.* New York: Oxford University Press (1980).
Whitney v. California, 274 U.S. 357 (1927).
"Why Losing Money May Be More Painful than You Think." *Wellcome Trust.* May, 2007. https://www.eurekalert.org/news-releases/580607.
Wickard v. Filburn, 317 U.S. 111. (1942).
Wilcove, David S. et al. "Quantifying Threats to Imperiled Species in the United States." *Bioscience* 48, no. 8 (1998): 607–615.
"WPS Starbucks FY16 Beverage Resource Manual 031516." *Starbucks Corporation.* 2013. https://studylib.net/doc/25255636/wps-starbucks-fy16-beverage-resource-manual-031516 [https://perma.cc/L5H6-QUEU].
Zywicki, Todd. "The Rise and Fall of Efficiency in the Common Law: A Supply-Side Analysis." *Northwestern University Law Review* 97, no. 4 (2002): 1551–1634.

Index

For the benefit of digital users, indexed terms that span two pages (e.g., 52–53) may, on occasion, appear on only one of those pages.

Note: Page numbers in bold indicate overarching discussions.

Figures are indicated by an italic *f*, following the page/paragraph number